Leadership Selection and Patron–Client Relations in the USSR and Yugoslavia

SELECTED PAPERS FROM THE SECOND WORLD CONGRESS FOR SOVIET AND EAST EUROPEAN STUDIES

Sponsored by

INTERNATIONAL COMMITTEE FOR SOVIET AND EAST EUROPEAN STUDIES
and
DEUTSCHE GESELLSCHAFT FÜR OSTEUROPAKUNDE

General Editor

Roger E. Kanet, *University of Illinois at Urbana-Champaign*

Leadership Selection and Patron–Client Relations in the USSR and Yugoslavia

Edited by

T. H. Rigby
The Australian National University

and

Bohdan Harasymiw
The University of Calgary

London
GEORGE ALLEN & UNWIN
Boston   Sydney

George Allen & Unwin (Publishers) Ltd,
40 Museum Street, London WC1A 1LU, UK

George Allen & Unwin (Publishers) Ltd,
Park Lane, Hemel Hempstead, Herts HP2 4TE, UK

Allen & Unwin, Inc.,
9 Winchester Terrace, Winchester, Mass. 01890, USA

George Allen & Unwin Australia Pty Ltd,
8 Napier Street, North Sydney, NSW 2060, Australia

First published in 1983

British Library Cataloguing in Publication Data

Leadership selection and patron-client relations in the USSR and
Yugoslavia.
1. Elite (Social sciences) – Soviet Union
2. Elite (Social sciences) – Yugoslavia
3. Soviet Union – Politics and government – 1953–
4. Yugoslavia – Politics and government
I. Rigby, T. H.   II. Harasymiw, Bohdan
322.4'3'0947   JN6569.E/
ISBN 0-04-322010-X

Library of Congress Cataloging in Publication Data

World Congress for Soviet and East European Studies
(2nd: 1980: Garmisch-Partenkirchen, Germany)
Leadership selection and patron-client relations in the USSR and
Yugoslavia.
"Selected papers from the second World Congress for Soviet and East
European Studies [Garmisch-Partenkirchen, 1980] sponsored by
International Committee for Soviet and East European Studies and
Deutsche Gesellschaft für Osteuropakunde."
Includes index.
1. Patronage, Political – Soviet Union – Congresses.
2. Patronage, Political – Yugoslavia – Congresses.
3. Elite (Social sciences) – Soviet Union – Congresses.
4. Elite (Social sciences) – Yugoslavia – Congresses.
5. Soviet Union – Politics and government – 1953– – Congresses.
6. Yugoslavia – Politics and government 1945– – Congresses
I. Rigby, T. H. (Thomas Henry), 1925–   .   II. Harasymiw, Bohdan.
III. International Committee for Soviet and East European Studies.
IV. Deutsche Gesellschaft für Osteuropakunde.   V. Title.
JN6549.E9W67   1980   306'.2'09457   83-7131
ISBN 0-04-322010-X

Set in 11 on 12 point Times by Computape (Pickering) Ltd
and printed in Great Britain by
Mackays of Chatham

85005891

Contents

Scheduled Publications from the Second World Congress for Soviet and East European Studies, Garmisch-Partenkirchen, 1980

English-language publications: published for the International Committee for Soviet and East European Studies by a number of different publishers; general editor, Roger E. Kanet, University of Illinois at Urbana-Champaign, USA.

I   **Humanities and History** Berkeley Slavic Specialities, PO Box 4605, Berkeley, CA 94704, USA
  1 *East European Literature: Selected Papers from the Second World Congress for Soviet and East European Studies*, edited by Evelyn Bristol, University of Illinois at Urbana-Champaign (Spring 1982, paper, *ca*120 pp., $8·50).
  2 *Russian and Eastern European History: Selected Papers from the Second World Congress for Soviet and East European Studies*, edited by R. C. Elwood, Carleton University (1982, paper).
  3 *Religion and Communist Society: Selected Papers from the Second World Congress for Soviet and East European Studies*, edited by Dennis J. Dunn, Southwest Texas State University (1982, paper).
  4 *Russian Literature and Criticism: Selected Papers from the Second World Congress for Soviet and East European Studies*, edited by Evelyn Bristol (1982, paper).
  5 *Soviet Investment for Planned Industrialization, 1929–1937: Policy and Practice. Selected Papers from the Second World Congress for Soviet and East European Studies*, edited by R. W. Davies, University of Birmingham (1982, paper).
II **International Relations** Pergamon Press, Inc., Maxwell House, Fairview Park, Elmsford, NY 10523, USA
  6 *Soviet Foreign Policy and East-West Relations*, edited by Roger E. Kanet, University of Illinois at Urbana-Champaign (Summer 1982, *ca*200 pp.).
III **Politics** Praeger Publishers, 521 Fifth Ave, New York, NY 10175, USA

7   *Politics and Participation under Communist Rule*, edited by Peter J. Potichnyj, McMaster University, and Jane Shapiro Zacek, New York State Governor's Office of Employee Relations (1982).

IV   **Politics**   George Allen & Unwin, PO Box 18, Park Lane, Hemel Hempstead, Herts HP2 4TE, England; 9 Winchester Terrace, Winchester, Mass. 01890, USA; 8 Napier Street, North Sydney, NSW 2060, Australia

8   *Leadership Selection and Patron–Client Relations in the USSR and Yugoslavia*, edited by T. H. Rigby, Australian National University, and Bohdan Harasymiw, University of Calgary (1983).

V   **Information Science**   Russica Publishers, Inc., 799 Broadway, New York, NY 10003, USA

9   *Access to Resources in the '80s: Proceedings of the First International Conference of Slavic Librarians and Information Specialists*, edited by Marianna Tax Choldin, University of Illinois at Urbana-Champaign (1982, 110 pp., $7·50).

VI   **Economics**

10   *Planning, Efficiency and Development in the Soviet-Type Economies: Selected Topics*, edited by Zbigniew M. Fallenbuchl, University of Windsor, and Gertrude Schroeder Greenslade, University of Virginia.

VII   **Law**   Martinus Nijhoff Publishers, PO Box 566, 2501 CN The Hague, The Netherlands

11   *Perspectives on Soviet Law for the 1980s*, no. 24 in the series *Law in Eastern Europe*, edited by F. J. M. Feldbrugge and William B. Simons, Rijksuniversiteit te Leiden (1982).

VIII   **Education**   Published as a special issue of *Slavic and European Education Review International*, c/o Editor, Office of East/West Education, Bowling Green State University, Bowling Green, OH 43403, USA

12   *Soviet Education Policy: Perspectives and Problems*, edited by Patrick L. Alston, Bowling Green State University.

IX   **Philosophy**   D. Reidel Publishing Co., PO Box 17, Dordrecht, The Netherlands

13   *East European and Western Developments in the Philosophies of Science, Technology, Society and Human Values: Selected Papers from the Second World Congress for Soviet and East European Studies*, edited by Peter P. Kirschenmann, Vrije Universiteit Amsterdam, and Andreis Sarlemijn, Technische Hogeschool Eindhoven.

German-language publications: published for the Deutsche Gesellschaft für Osteuropakunde in the series *Osteuropaforschung*: general editor, Wolfgang Kasack, Universität zu Köln. All volumes published by Berlin Verlag, Pacelliallee 5, 1000 Berlin 33, Germany

1 *Sicherheitspolitik und internationale Beziehungen der Sowjetunion. Ausgewählte Beiträge zum Zweiten Weltkongress für Sowjet- und Osteuropastudien*, edited by Georg Brunner and Horst Herlemann, Universität Würzburg.

2 *Bildung und Erziehung in Osteuropa im 20. Jahrhundert. Ausgewählte Beiträge zum Zweiten Weltkongress für Sowjet- und Osteuropastudien*, edited by Oskar Anweiler, Ruhr-Universität Bochum.

3 *Politische Kultur, Nationalitäten und Dissidenten in der Sowjetunion. Ausgewählte Beiträge zum Zweiten Weltkongress für Sowjet- und Osteuropastudien*, edited by Georg Brunner and Horst Herlemann, Universität Würzburg.

4 *Literatur und Sprachentwicklung in Osteuropa im 20. Jahrhundert. Ausgewählte Beiträge zum Zweiten Weltkongress für Sowjet- und Osteuropastudien*, edited by Eberhard Reissner, Universität Mainz.

5 *Grundrechte und Rechtssicherheit im sowjetischen Machtbereich. Ausgewählte Beiträge zum Zweiten Weltkongress für Sowjet- und Osteuropastudien*, edited by Georg Brunner, Universität Würzburg.

6 *Wirtschaftsrecht, internationaler Handel und friedliche Koexistenz aus osteuropäischer Sicht. Ausgewählte Beiträge zum Zweiten Weltkongress für Sowjet- und Osteuropastudien*, edited by Georg Brunner, Universität Würzburg.

7 *Wirtschaftsprobleme Osteuropas in der Analyse. Ausgewählte Beiträge zum Zweiten Weltkongress für Sowjet- und Osteuropastudien*, edited by Heinrich Vogel, Bundesinstitut für ostwissenschaftliche und internationale Studien.

8 *Kunst, Architektur und Musik in Osteuropa im 20. Jahrhundert. Ausgewählte Beiträge zum Zweiten Weltkongress für Sowjet- und Osteuropastudien*, edited by Hans-Jürgen Drengenberg, Freie Universität Berlin, with the cooperation of Milka Bliznakov, Virginia Polytechnic Institute and State University, John E. Bowlt, University of Texas at Austin, Joachim Braun, Bar-Ilan University, and Peter Spielmann, Museum der Stadt Bochu.

9 *Modernisierungsprobleme in der Sowjetunion. Ausgewählte Beiträge zum Zweiten Weltkongress für Sowjet- und Osteuropastudien*, edited by Georg Brunner and Horst Herlemann, Universität Würzburg.

French-Language Publication: special issue of the journal *Revue d'Etudes comparatives Est–Ouest*

'Europe de l'Est: Economie officielle et économies parallèles', *Revue d'Etudes Comparatives Est–Ouest*, vol. XII, no. 2 (June 1981).

Foreword by the General Editor

The articles published in this volume have been selected from among those presented at the Second World Congress for Soviet and East European Studies, held in Garmisch-Partenkirchen, Federal Republic of Germany, 30 September–4 October 1980. The Congress was sponsored by the International Committee for Soviet and East European Studies in conjunction with the Deutsche Gesellschaft für Osteuropakunde and was attended by well over 1,400 scholars from around the world.

Among the approximately 500 formal papers and additional papers presented at the Congress, more than 150 were submitted for consideration to the editorial committee for the official English-language Congress publications. From among these, a substantial number have been accepted for publication in the series of volumes to be published by Berkeley Slavic Specialties (Berkeley, California, USA), Pergamon Press (New York, USA), Russica (New York, USA), Praeger (New York, USA), George Allen & Unwin (London, Boston and Sydney) and Martinus Nijhoff (The Hague, The Netherlands). In addition, several other volumes are scheduled for publication in Germany.

As general editor of the series of English-language Garmisch Congress publications I wish to express my sincere appreciation to all of the individuals and organizations that made the conference and the resulting publications possible. This includes the numerous organizations that provided financial support for the Congress itself, the Executive Committee of the International Committee for Soviet and East European Studies (including the past president, Adam Bromke) and, in particular, the members of the German Planning Committee, who organized the Congress (including the chairman and current president of the International Committee, Oskar Anweiler). Finally, I wish to thank the Congress participants who submitted their papers for consideration, the members of the editorial committee that selected the essays to be included in the various volumes and the editors of those volumes. Their contributions and cooperation have made possible the publication of this volume and the other volumes in the series.

Roger E. Kanet
*University of Illinois
at Urbana-Champaign*

Preface

Students of politics from Aristotle on have perceived that familiarity with the character and mode of recruitment of those actively engaged in politics and government is of central importance for understanding political systems. Serious study of the personnel aspects of Soviet politics, following some earlier pioneering efforts, began in the 1950s. While it has grown much over the years in scale and in theoretical and methodological sophistication, it has embraced from the beginning both the analysis of processes, and the analysis of quantitative data; investigating both how the political leadership in these centralized bureaucratic systems seeks to manage elite recruitment and careermaking, and how individuals and groups seek to work the system of 'cadre' management to their advantage.

These two basic aspects of the question form the twin foci of the present book. It is based on papers presented in two complementary panels at the Second International Congress on Soviet and East European studies, the one dealing with the operation of the *nomenklatura* system of personnel selection and the other with political clientelism in Soviet politics. The papers have been extensively revised in the light of discussion at the Congress and their findings related to more general aspects of the politics of Soviet-type systems in introductory and concluding chapters.

The editors and authors wish to express their deep appreciation to the many distinguished scholars whose observations contributed so much to improving the quality of this volume, and especially to those who participated as discussants in the relevant Congress panels, namely, Professors Zygmunt Bauman, James H. Seroka, Philip D. Stewart and Michael Voslensky.

There are many others without whose efforts and encouragement this book would not have seen the light of day and we wish, in particular, to mention the organizers of the Garmisch Congress, the chairman of its Politics Section, Professor Georg Brunner, and the general editor of this series, Professor Roger Kanet. Finally, we should like to express our thanks to Mr Russell McCaskie for his assistance in translating the chapter by Dr Józsa, and to Maureen Novak for retyping the manuscript.

T. H. Rigby
Bohdan Harasymiw

Introduction

T. H. RIGBY

'Cadres', to quote Stalin's now neglected but still valid aphorism, 'decide everything'.[1] On the face of it a rather vacuous assertion about the importance of proper personnel selection, these words acquire particular force from two basic features of the Soviet sociopolitical system.

The first is that it is a centrally managed or 'monoorganizational' system, one in which all social entities are incorporated into various hierarchical chains of command integrated by the apparatus of the Communist Party. Every segment of social activity in such a system is thus peculiarly dependent on the officials in charge of it, whose tasks, powers and resources, moreover, are predominantly determined at higher organizational levels. This situation contrasts sharply with that prevailing in modern 'Western' societies, where although the element of management and direction by agencies of the state is now substantial, most social entities retain a high level of decision-making autonomy and are generally responsible for setting their own tasks and marshaling their own resources, overall integration being achieved largely through the processes of various economic, political and other markets.[2]

The second pertinent feature of the Soviet system is that the choice of officials is itself a purely administrative matter, operating according to formal rules that prescribe which subordinate posts are to be filled by which superior bodies and the criteria to be used. It is true that many party, government and other posts are formally elective, but the officially 'recommended' candidates are never opposed and the processes governing their selection differ in no significant way from those whereby formally appointive officials are chosen.[3]

It is clear, then, why Stalin assigned such central importance to official programs of personnel selection, and why his successors continue to do so. It will also be apparent why the word 'cadres' (*kadry*), a term originally denoting complements or establishments of military officers, has become synonymous in the Soviet Union and other communist countries for occupants of positions of responsibility generally. The military analogy, already embodied in the 'advance guard' concept of the party, was frequently invoked by Lenin both in relation to the pre-revolutionary Bolshevik organization and the early phases of the Soviet regime, and later by Stalin in reference to the developed Soviet system, most graphically in a speech he delivered to the Central Committee in 1937, where he described the party's 3,000–4,000 higher leaders as its generals (*generalitet*), its 30,000–40,000 middle-level leaders as its officer corps (*partiinoe ofitserstvo*) and its 100,000–150,000 'lower-command staff' as its non-commissioned officers (*partiinoe unter-ofitserstvo*).[4] In fact, the progressive application of the term to virtually all segments of the workforce, thus treating them as essentially bodies of personnel available to be deployed on various 'fronts' at the behest of the party 'high command' necessitated the invention of the somewhat tautological expression 'leading cadres' (*rukovodiashchie kadry*) to denote those actually giving or transmitting the orders. Such language, moreover, is not applied only to party officialdom: one constantly reads of 'industrial cadres', 'judicial cadres', 'scientific cadres', and so on. As we have seen, such statements are not merely a matter of style and rhetoric, they accurately epitomize the action-systems of Soviet-type monoorganizational societies. The main constituent units of such action-systems are the 'tasks' (*zadaniia*) assigned from above in a chain of command, and although Soviet cadres, like military officers in the field, are expected to exercise initiative in the performance of their tasks or missions, success or failure in the achievement of these is the essential criterion whereby their actions are judged.[5]

Given the crucial importance necessarily acquired by personnel programs in such a monoorganizational system, it is not surprising that they are an object of constant attention by the political leadership and that the Communist Party, the 'leading and directing force in Soviet society', plays a dominant part in administering them. The major programmatic congress and conference 'reports' delivered by the chief party secretary at each hierarchical level from the general secretary down invariably include a substantial passage on the cadre question, criticizing shortcomings and abuses and prescribing the current policy position on the role of such selection criteria as education, career experience and political qualifications, on turnover levels, geographical mobility, advancing underrepresented groups such as women and local nationalities, and so on.[6] Such broad guidelines are then spelt out in greater detail and their application to particular regions and fields of activity prescribed in Central Committee decisions, authoritative articles in party journals, statements by subordinate leaders, and so on.[7] And behind these generalities, of course, there lie the thousands upon thousands of particular decisions authorizing the appointment, dismissal, transfer, promotion, demotion and retirement of individual officials not only within the party machine itself, but in all spheres of social activity.

Such a vast system of personnel administration naturally calls for a well-thought-out and consistently applied division of labor, and the basic instrument of this is the *nomenklatura*, the schedule of posts, changes in the tenure of which require the nomination or approval of a particular unit in the party hierarchy. The fundamental significance of this document is such that the whole complex of personnel procedures in Soviet-type societies is sometimes referred to as 'the *nomenklatura* system'. Studying the operation of this system in detail is not at all easy, since it is surrounded with considerable secrecy, a fact that reflects the extreme official coyness regarding anything related to the actual exercise of power in these societies, aggravated in this case, as Bohdan Harasymiw has pointed out, by the fact that so many of the personnel decisions made through these behind-the-scenes administrative processes apply to posts which are in form elective.[8] Too much frankness about such matters would call in question the democratic fictions through which communist regimes seek to legitimate their rule.[9] Nevertheless, books and articles intended to guide party officials in their 'work with cadres' inevitably cite many specific facts which the assiduous scholar can put together to reveal at least the main outlines of the *nomenklatura* system. At this point the more general policy statements mentioned earlier can be employed to yield more pieces for the jigsaw puzzle, as can the comparative study of individual careers and of the occupants of particular categories of posts.

Such researches have already told us a good deal. There appear to be something over 2 million 'nomenclatured workers' at present (or some 1·5–2 percent of the laborforce)[10] and we have a good idea of the number of posts on the *nomenklatury* of different levels in the party hierarchy, and of how the main categories of posts are distributed between them. We know that while governmental, trade union, Komsomol (Communist Youth League) and other organizations also have personnel departments with their own *nomenklatury*, their key officials are chosen by the party machine, whose approval is also required for many of the personnel decisions which they are empowered to initiate themselves. We have learned much about the distribution of personnel powers and responsibilities within the party apparatus at different levels. We are familiar with the main problems besetting the operation of the *nomenklatura* system and the kinds of conflicts it engenders.[11] We have discerned certain characteristic political and administrative career patterns and established some of the major criteria employed in filling different categories of posts. Finally, we have some idea of how all these things have changed over the years.[12] That said, it must immediately be added that the gaps in our knowledge remain daunting, and the wider implications of the *nomenklatura* system are only now beginning to be seriously discussed.

To grasp how broad these implications may be we have only to recall that with a handful of exceptions (mainly scientists and artists) an individual's material rewards, power and status in monoorganizational societies of the Soviet type are overwhelmingly a function of the official position to which he or she has been appointed under the *nomenklatura* system. This fact obviously bears upon the views of those analysts and critics of Soviet-type societies that see them as dominated by a new kind of privileged ruling 'class' or 'stratum', variously identified as the 'bureaucracy' (Trotsky), the 'managers' (James Burnham), or simply the 'new class' (Milovan Djilas). In fact, a number of writers have suggested in recent years that this 'new class' can be identified with the totality of those occupying posts on the *nomenklatury* of party bodies.[13]

The proposition has considerable plausibility. Certainly, the 'nomenclatured workers' (*nomenklaturnye rabotniki*) are referred to by party spokesmen as a distinct and 'leading' category of the employed population which cuts across differences of occupation, age, sex, nationality, location, and so on,[14] and this category is commonly identified by informed Soviet citizens (who often speak simply of 'the *nomenklatura*') as the new or ruling class.[15] No less certainly, enormous value is placed on being 'in the *nomenklatura*' both by those who have achieved it and those who aspire to it. While it is hard to get in, moreover, once in you are likely to stay there, for even if you are demoted, it will almost certainly be to another 'nomenclatured post'. Writing of the Nikolaev *oblast* in 1952 one journalist reported that the common saying there was 'once you've entered the *nomenklatura* of the *obkom* [regional party committee], even the devil can't hurt you';[16] and if this could be so even in the purge-prone conditions of the late Stalin period, how much more true must it be in the present era of 'stability of cadres', to use the official euphemism. Nor is it difficult to see *why* being a 'nomenclatured worker' is so valued, for there is ample evidence that it confers not only the coveted status and the power formally embodied in the position concerned, but also important 'incidental' personal privileges, not so much through the medium of higher salaries as through the *administrative* allocation of all kinds of material and other benefits not available on the market.[17] Of course, the status varies vastly according to the *level* of the *nomenklatura* concerned, the crucial steps from a *raikom* or *gorkom nomenklatura* to that of an *obkom* or republic Central Committee, and thence the CPSU Central Committee *nomenklatura* itself being comparable in status terms to the steps from the lower gentry in Britain to the baronetcy and thence to the peerage.[18] And finally, while the *nomenklatura* is not a closed caste, and like the prerevolutionary Russian gentry or the bourgeoisie in capitalist countries constantly absorbs into its ranks able and ambitious individuals from the 'lower classes', it now appears to enjoy a high level of intergenerational continuity, in the sense that it is unusual for the children of 'nomenclatured workers' not to eventually acquire some level of nomenclature status themselves. Andrei Sakharov sums it up as follows:

> This stratum has its own life-style, its own sharply defined position in society, that of 'the boss' or 'the head', and its own language and way of thinking. The *nomenklatura* is virtually inalienable and is now becoming hereditary. Thanks to the complex system of secret and open official privileges and also to connections, acquaintances, reciprocal 'favours' and to high salaries these people enjoy the opportunity of living in far better housing and of eating and dressing better – often for less money in special 'closed' shops, or for foreign currency tokens, or again by virtue of journeys abroad (in our circumstances a special and supreme form of reward for loyalty).[19]

Nevertheless, a number of serious theoretical and empirical problems would need to be dealt with before we could confidently identify 'the *nomenklatura*' with 'the ruling class'. In particular, what are our criteria of 'class', and of 'ruling' and how do we justify them in terms of general sociological theory? Do the boundaries of 'the *nomenklatura*' really correspond with those of 'the ruling class'? Does it manifest the essential homogeneity (both vertically and horizontally) to constitute a 'class'? Such questions are not merely semantic: they do not disappear if we simply replace the term 'class' by 'elite', 'stratum', 'partocracy', or what have you.[20] We cannot claim to solve these problems in this book. Indeed, we would argue that much more knowledge will need to be accumulated before the wide differences of opinion over them can be seriously narrowed. It is rather to the task of filling some of the existing gaps in our knowledge that our efforts here are devoted.

Parts 1 and 2 of the book are concerned respectively with the formal and informal dimensions of the operation of the *nomenklatura* system, that is to say, with on the one hand official cadre policies and procedures and the patterns of careermaking and officeholding that result from them, and on the other with the identification and evaluation of patron–client links within Soviet officialdom. The latter call for a few words at this point. As already suggested in the words of Andrei Sakharov quoted above, if the 'nomenclatured workers' are to be understood as a distinct *social* category of the Soviet population, attention must be given to the nexus between official position and personal advantage, and a key element in this nexus is provided by informal interpersonal networks of reciprocal 'favors'. The objective basis of these is obvious: in a system where the disposal of resources depends almost entirely on chains of *administrative* decision, those responsible for making such decisions, large and small, are uniquely placed to benefit themselves, their families and friends, *and* those who are in a position to offer reciprocal benefits in matters subject to their decision. As I have tried to demonstrate elsewhere, such networks of reciprocal favor not only emerged very early in the history of Soviet officialdom, but they quickly came to dominate the power structure at least at provincial and local levels.[21]

Because of the *nomenklatura* system, one of the resources – and surely the most valuable one – subject to administrative decision and, therefore, forming part of the 'stock' of reciprocal favor is position itself. Those senior officials – and for reasons we have seen this applies particularly to senior *party* officials who have most say over the filling of appointments – are consequently much courted as 'patrons' and are in a position to exact from their 'clients' loyal service and reciprocal favors both on the official and personal levels: nor should one underestimate the power resources of subordinate officials in the USSR (as in any hierarchical organization) *vis-à-vis* their superiors, especially by virtue of their control over the flow of information to the latter and over the implementation of his decisions.[22] Historically it can be shown that such patron–client groupings assumed salience within the world (or underworld) of interpersonal networks only as the centralized procedures of personnel administration which later evolved into the mature *nomenklatura* system became established.[23] To grasp the continued vitality of the forces making for clientelism in the USSR we have only to recall the progressive packing of top party and government posts by long-term associates of Khrushchev and Brezhnev as these two party leaders consolidated their power. Of course, bureaucratic patronage is not unique to the USSR, but it is peculiarly pervasive and salient there, along with other communist countries.[24] I have outlined above what I believe to be the main reason for this, though doubtless there are subsidiary reasons.[25] What gives it its exceptional political importance in Soviet-type systems is virtually universal scope of administrative direction of social activities, the integration of the multifarious specialized hierarchies of officials into a single mono-organizational system and the prohibition (in the interests of this integration) of openly interest-based or policy-based factions or pressure groups.

We would thus be naïve to view political clientelism in Soviet-type systems simply as a form of corruption, as a perversion of some ideally 'rational' or 'Leninist' principles of personnel management. For just as the 'second economy' of black, gray and otherwise-hued markets can be seen as an essential and indispensable complement to the official or 'first' economy,[26] so the interpersonal network and patronage clique is 'functional' to the politicoadministrative system, in the sense that without it the latter would not only operate less effectively, but would arguably not operate at all. While, therefore, for purposes of analysis it is sometimes convenient to discuss separately the 'formal' and 'informal' dimensions of the *nomenklatura* system, as we do in Parts 1 and 2 respectively of this book, we must always keep in mind that they are just dimensions of the *one* system.[27] Like any organized system of human action, it can only be understood as the product of on the one hand how the system uses people, and on the other how people use the system.

The chief focus of this book is the USSR, and its object is to illuminate one particular aspect of the sociopolitical system of which the USSR is the type case, in the hope that this will contribute to a fuller understanding of the fundamentals of this system. As hinted earlier, however, one prerequisite to such fuller understanding is to compare it with other systems and ultimately to develop a mutually consistent set of explanations for the similarities and differences we detect. For this reason, we have set out to include here some substantial comparative material. Thus in Part 1, while the chapters by Joel Moses and John Miller deal with Soviet personnel policies focusing on the regional level, that by Lenard Cohen looks at a similar level of 'cadres management' in Yugoslavia, a Communist-ruled country which has sought to move away from the Soviet monoorganizational model of socialism. And in Part 2, along-side Gyula Józsa's chapter which seeks to trace the present contours of political clientelism at the apex of the Soviet power structure, we have two others offering alternative bases of comparison, with prerevolutionary Russia in the case of Daniel Orlovsky's, and with Japan – a *non-communist* industrialized country in which political clientelism is salient – in the case of Shugo Minagawa's. While it is the view of the authors that a great deal more research will be necessary before confident answers can be offered to some of the major questions raised here, we trust that this volume will bring us a step closer to properly understanding the sense in which 'cadres decide every-thing' in Soviet-type societies.

Notes: Introduction

1   The only recent example the author has seen of Stalin's phrase being given prominence was, significantly enough, in his native Georgia: see *Zaria Vostoka*, 28 January 1981. Although its source was not cited, politically literate readers would be aware that it stemmed from the 'greatest son of the Georgian people'.

2   I discuss this point in greater detail in T. H. Rigby, Archie Brown and Peter Reddaway (eds), *Authority, Power and Policy in the USSR* (London: Macmillan, 1980), ch. 2.

3   One class of officials whose 'election' is sometimes more than a mere formality are the secretaries of basic-level (mainly workplace) party organizations; cases still occur where the 'recommended' candidates for these positions are rejected, giving the elections something of a 'plebiscit-ary' character. Another area in which elections retain real force and do not simply give force to party 'recommendations' is the process of selection (in effect co-option) of members of the Academy of Sciences.

4   See I. V. Stalin, *Works. Vol. 1 (XIV), 1934–1940*, ed. Robert H. McNeal (Stanford, Calif.: Hoover Institution, 1967), pp. 220–1.

5   Further on the significance of the use of this military language, see Rigby *et al.*, *Authority, Power and Policy*, op. cit., p. 20.

6   See, for instance, Brezhnev's reports at recent party congresses, *XXIVs''ezd Kommunisticheskoi partii Sovetskogo Soiuza, 30 marta–9 aprelia 1971 goda: Stenograficheskii otchët* (Moscow: Politizdat, 1971), Vol. 1, pp. 124–6; *XXV s''ezd Kommunisticheskoi partii Sovetskogo*

Soiuza, 24 fevralia–5 marta 1976 goda. Stenograficheskii otchët (Moscow: Politizdat, 1976), Vol. 1, pp. 96–7; and *Pravda*, 24 February 1981, p. 8.

7 See, for instance, the Central Committee decisions, 'On the work of the Vladimir *obkom* of the CPSU on the selection and training of cadres in trade and personal services', *Spravochnik partiinogo rabotnika. Vypusk deviatyi 1969* (Moscow: Politizdat, 1969), pp. 343–6; 'On the work of the Ministry for Construction of the USSR with leading and engineering-technical cadres', *Spravochnik partiinogo rabotnika. Vypusk deviatnadtsatyi 1979* (Moscow: Politizdat, 1979), pp. 378–81; 'On the work of the Central Committee of the Communist Party of Estonia with leading party cadres', *Partiinaia zhizn*, no. 6 (1967), pp. 8–12; 'On the work of the Udmurt *obkom* of the CPSU on the selection, assignment and training of leading cadres', *Partiinaia zhizn*, no. 23 (1979), pp. 17–20; and *Pravda* articles by republic and regional party secretaries dealing with cadre questions, on 12 December 1966 (Tatar *obkom*), 25 October 1968 (Volgograd *obkom*), 6 January 1969 (Estonia), 20 August 1971 and 31 August 1973 (Ukraine), 24 March 1976 (Georgia), 23 July 1976 (Krasnoyarsk *kraikom*). Plenary meetings of party committees at republic, regional and local levels can serve as authoritative occasions for detailing the application of cadres policies under local conditions; see, for instance, *Zaria Vostoka*, 31 October 1979; and *Sovetskaia Litva*, 31 October 1979.

8 See Bohdan Harasymiw, '*Nomenklatura*: the Soviet Communist Party's leadership recruitment system', *Canadian Journal of Political Science*, vol. 2, no. 4 (1969), p. 493.

9 See Georg Brunner, 'Legitimacy doctrines and legitimation procedures in East European systems', in T. H. Rigby and Ferenc Fehér (eds), *Political Legitimation in Communist States* (London: Macmillan, forthcoming).

10 This estimate is arrived at on the basis of figures appearing in Soviet sources for particular republics and regions and different levels in the hierarchy. For instance, it was stated in 1978 that there were altogether 23,000 officials on the *nomenklatury* of the Bashkir *obkom* and of all the *gorkomy* (city committees) and *raikomy* (district committees) in the Bashkir Autonomous Republic; see *Partiinaia zhizn*, no. 20 (1978), p. 42. This number would account for most (though not all) of the 'nomenclatured workers' in the republic. In 1979 it was stated in Georgia that the 42,000 'nomenclatured workers' with higher education equalled 93 percent of all persons on the *nomenklatury* of all party committees in the republic, that is, the total was about 45,000 (see *Zaria Vostoka*, 31 October 1979). These figures represent 0·6 and 0·9 percent of the populations of the respective republics. Although these two areas together contain only some 3 percent of the USSR's population, the high level of consistency in personnel practices throughout the country allows us to employ them as a basis for arriving at a USSR estimate, even though as in all such calculations one must make allowances for the effects of differences in hierarchical level, economic structure, party membership levels, ethnicity, and so on. The figure of 2 million plus is of the same order of magnitude as that arrived at by Bohdan Harasymiw on the basis of both employment data and a more systematic analysis of local *nomenklatura* figures, in his forthcoming book, *Political Elite Recruitment in the Soviet Union*, ch. 7. Michael S.

Voslensky, in his *Nomenklatura: Die Herrschende Klasse der Sowjetunion* (Vienna: Molden, 1980), pp. 184–8, working from employment data only, arrives at an estimate of about three-quarters of a million, a figure which clearly omits several categories of cadres known to be on the *nomenklatury* of party committees (mainly at district and city levels) and which cannot be reconciled with any reasonable computation from actual figures for various regional, city and district committee *nomenklatury*.

11   An obvious potential source of conflict is that many posts are on the *nomenklatury* of more than one body, for example, a senior party official at regional level may be on the *nomenklatury* both of the Central Committee and the *obkom*, or a senior regional government official on those of both the *obkom* and a central government ministry. In such cases formal rules as to which body takes the initiative on an appointment and which has the right simply to approve or reject it scarcely catch the realities of the political relationships involved.

12   For the operation of the *nomenklatura* system up to the late 1930s, see Merle Fainsod, *Smolensk under Soviet Rule* (London: Macmillan, 1958), chs 2–4. This is based on documents contained in the archive of the Smolensk *obkom*, which owing to the fortunes of war found their way to Germany and later to the USA. The archive contains the only known copies of actual *nomenklatury*. Cadre practices in the postwar years up to 1954 are described in T. H. Rigby, 'The selection of leading personnel in the Soviet state and Communist Party', PhD thesis, University of London, 1954, pt 3. For the post-Stalin period, see Bohdan Harasymiw, '*Nomenklatura*: the Soviet Communist Party's leadership recruitment system', *Canadian Journal of Political Science*, vol. 2, no. 4 (1969), pp. 493–512; and Bohdan Harasymiw, 'Die Sowjetische Nomenklatur', *Osteuropa*, vol. 27, no. 7 (1977), pp. 583–98, and no. 8 (1977), pp. 665–81. The last-named contains the fullest and most up-to-date source-list on the subject. See also Borys Lewytzkyj, 'Die Nomenklatur: ein wichtiges Instrument sowjetischer Kaderpolitik', *Osteuropa*, vol. 11, no. 6 (1961), pp. 408–12. Literature on the operation of the *nomenklatura* system in other Soviet-type societies is scanty, but of particular value is Gert-Joachim Glaessner's *Herrschaft durch Kader. Leitung der Gesellschaft und Kaderpolitik in der DDR* (Opladen: Westdeutscher Verlag, 1977).

13   So far as I am aware this identification was first explicitly made by A. Ivanov in his short article, 'Nomenklaturnyi klass', *Posev* (March 1973), pp. 34–6. Two years later Alec Nove presented an interesting case for the same point (though he limited the 'class' to those on the Central Committee *nomenklatura*) in his 'Is there a ruling class in the USSR?', *Soviet Studies*, vol. XXVII, no. 4 (1975), pp. 615–38. Then in 1980 there appeared the first book-length development of this view, Michael Voslensky's *Nomenklatura: Die herrschende Klasse der Sowjetunion* (Vienna: Molden, 1980).

14   For a very revealing example, see Shevardnadze's speech to the Georgian Central Committee, *Zaria Vostoka*, 31 October 1979.

15   See, for instance, Andrei Sakharov, *O strane i mire* (New York: Khronika Press, 1976), p. 33.

16   *Pravda Ukrainy*, 7 September 1952.

17   See Mervyn Matthews, *Privilege in the Soviet Union. A Study of Elite Life-Styles under Communism* (London: Allen & Unwin, 1978), pp. 34–5 and ch. 2; and Voslensky, op. cit., ch. 6.

18   A weakness of this analogy is that in the Soviet case the conferment of

successive degrees of *nomenklatura* status is not published to all and
sundry as in the case of a UK Honours List, but becomes known only to
those '*in* the know'. In this respect it is comparable, as Zygmunt Bauman
has suggested (personal communication), to having one's name printed in
the *Social Register* of Boston or Philadelphia.

19 Sakharov, *op. cit.*, pp. 33–4.

20 Maria Hirszowicz offers an interesting discussion of a number of such
points in her article, 'Is there a ruling class in the USSR – a comment',
Soviet Studies, vol. 28, no. 2 (1976), pp. 262–73; see also Vladimir V.
Kusin, 'A propos Alec Nove's search for a class label', in ibid., pp. 274–5.

21 T. H. Rigby, 'Early provincial cliques and the rise of Stalin', *Soviet
Studies*, vol. 32, no. 1 (1981), pp. 3–28.

22 Melville Dalton, in his analysis of what he labels 'vertical symbiotic
cliques', describes a pattern of reciprocal favor between patron and client
in American industrial undertakings in terms which capture much of the
reality of such relationships in the Soviet bureaucracy as well; see his *Men
who Manage: Fusions of Feeling and Theory in Administration* (New
York: Wiley, 1959), pp. 58–9.

23 Rigby, '*Early provincial cliques*', op. cit., pp. 23–7.

24 See the symposium entitled 'Clientelism', in *Studies in Comparative
Communism*, vol. 12, no. 2–3 (1979), pp. 159–211. Other relevant
literature touching on the role of personal clienteles and networks in
Soviet politics includes: Philip D. Stewart, *et al.*, 'Political mobility and
the Soviet political process: a partial test of two models', *American
Political Science Review*, vol. 66, no. 4 (1972), pp. 1269–90; Joel C.
Moses, 'Regional cohorts and political mobility in the USSR: the case of
Dnepropetrovsk', *Soviet Union*, vol. 3, pt 1 (1966), pp. 63–89; T. H.
Rigby, 'Crypto-politics', *Survey*, no. 50 (1964), pp. 183–94; and John
McDonnell, 'The Soviet defense industry as a pressure group', in Michael
McCGwire, Ken Booth and John McDonnell (eds), *Soviet Naval Policy:
Objectives and Constraints* (New York: Praeger, 1975), pp. 87–122. Much
case material may be found in more general accounts of Soviet politics;
see especially R. Conquest, *Power and policy in the USSR: The Study of
Soviet Dynastics* (London: Macmillan, 1961), and Michel Tatu, *Power in
the Kremlin: From Khrushchev's Decline to Collective Leadership*
(London: Collins, 1969).

25 See Zygmunt Bauman, 'Clientelism: Eastern Europe', *Studies in Comparative Communism*, vol. 12, no. 2–3 (1979), pp. 184–9.

26 See Gregory Grossman, 'The second economy of the USSR', *Problems of
Communism*, vol. 26, no. 5 (1977), pp. 25–40.

27 Zygmunt Bauman argued this point persuasively in discussing the papers
on which the chapters of Part 2 are based when they were presented at the
Second International Congress on Soviet and East European Studies in
Garmisch-Partenkirchen, FRG, in October 1980.

PART ONE

Recruiting Regional Political Elites

1

Functional Career Specialization in Soviet Regional Elite Recruitment

JOEL C. MOSES

If any consensus can be found among the many Western scholars who have analyzed Soviet elites and the underlying determinants of Soviet cadre policy, it has been the common recognition of diversity in the backgrounds, capabilities and even likely attitudes of those selected to full-time leadership roles in the party, state and mass bureaucracies. For some Western scholars, the extent of non-political specialist careers among Soviet cadres has been singled out as an important characteristic in their backgrounds and the source of a major cleavage within the Soviet political bureaucracy.[1] Soviet cadres with lengthy non-political careers prior to becoming full-time officials in the bureaucracy have been alternatively termed 'dual executives', 'co-opted officials', or 'political managers' by Western analysts and assumed to be more pragmatic in policymaking than cadres whose entire adult lives have been spent in leadership positions in the bureaucracy.[2] Other Western scholars have isolated allegedly important differences among Soviet cadres in their ages, party-entry periods, gender, ethnic nationality and geographical origin; and Western analysts have hypothesized that differences in these career-demographic factors affect not only opportunities for advancement among Soviet cadres, but the varying attitudes and values which they continue to project in later leadership positions throughout their careers.[3] From these differences, Western analysts have argued that the Soviet political bureaucracy is rent with internal subgroup conflict corresponding to the generational gaps, party-entry periods, sex, ethnic nationalities and geographical locales by which Soviet cadres can be differentiated. A few analysts of Soviet cadres (including Soviet dissidents and émigrés like Roy Medvedev and Alexander Yanov) have contended that Soviet officials differ so markedly and consistently in their policy orientations that they should be grouped by their position along a Soviet political-ideological spectrum. These policy subgroups, dependent on how the analyst views the Soviet political-ideological spectrum, include an array of 'centralizers', 'decentralizers', 'reformers', 'conservatives', 'liberals', 'neo-Leninists', 'dogmatists', 'Russophiles', 'aristocrats' and 'right-wingers'. So different are the policy subgroups that Soviet cadres consciously identify themselves by these labels and engage in conflict with those in other subgroups.[4]

Differing in what they consider the principal lines of cleavage among all Soviet cadres, analysts at least have provided a major challenge to those who still contend that all cadres advanced to leadership positions in the Soviet Union under the *nomenklatura* system exhibit the same narrow and opportunistic range of personalities, motivations and outlooks characteristic of the stereotypical Soviet *apparatchik*. Jerry Hough, perhaps the most eminent Western analyst of Soviet elites, has gone so far as to refute the merits of using the term *apparatchik* in referring to Soviet cadres. As Hough has argued, not only has the term not been used in the Soviet Union for several decades to describe cadres, but its continued use by some Western analysts connotes a bureaucratic mind-set and homogeneity of backgrounds that our knowledge of internal bureaucratic conflict and the dissimilar origins of Soviet cadres directly contradicts. An appreciation of the differences among Soviet cadres is absolutely essential to understand the political fragmentation and internal policy conflict (what Hough would term 'institutional pluralism') that have become ever more the dominant features of Soviet political life.[5] Underlying and patterned diversity rather than homogeneity among Soviet cadres has been a byproduct of the leadership recruitment process in the Soviet Union, even with all positions directly or indirectly controlled by central cadre organs under *nomenklatura* to ensure relatively similar background characteristics and criteria in cadre promotion.

Indeed, as Hough and Grey Hodnett, among other Western analysts, have pointed out, one of the most obvious differences can be found even at a superficial level in the widely varying career or task specializations associated with distinct subgroups of Soviet cadres. In what suggests a deliberate and planned course of leadership development many Soviet cadres are early in their political careers locked into distinct functional specializations and far from randomly reassigned to comparable policy responsibilities and roles in the party, state and mass bureaucracies during their careers.[6] Hough and Hodnett have provided detailed evidence of these distinct career subgroups among those selected to leadership positions at the All-Union and union republic levels of the political bureaucracy over recent decades, but career specialization appears to be an even more prevalent factor at an earlier stage in the careers of Soviet cadres prior to their advancement into union republic and All-Union positions, particularly by the time Soviet cadres at the lower regional level have been selected to one of the thirteen to fifteen leadership positions in the *obkom* (regional party committee) bureau. As previous research has indicated, the composition of the approximately 150 *obkom* bureaux in the Soviet Union over recent decades has been made up of those holding one of these thirteen to fifteen positions in all regions. Paralleling what Robert Daniels contends are 'job slots' by which individuals become All-Union Central Committee members by their promotion to positions equated as Central Committee in political status,[7] the composition of full and candidate members on Soviet *obkom* bureaux can be approximately equated with those simultaneously selected to one of these several thirteen to fifteen leadership positions in the party, state and mass bureaucracies of the 150 regions.[8] It is important to note that, if one traces the careers of several *obkom* bureau members, their positions both prior and subsequent to *obkom* tenure in many instances follow narrow functional specializations consistent with the particular leadership positions and functional responsibilities which they held as bureau members. In essence, *nomenklatura* and the criteria by which regional leaders are selected actually contribute to creating differences among Soviet cadres by assigning them primarily to distinct functional specializations.

So prevalent is the overlapping nature of career assignments among *obkom* bureau members in the party, state and mass bureaucracies that five quite different functional subgroups can be distinguished and classified on the basis of internal consistency in positions held during their careers: agricultural specialists, industrial specialists, ideological specialists, cadre specialists and mixed generalists. As bureau members, agricultural specialists typically are those elected during their bureau tenure as the *obkom* agriculture secretary, the chairman or first deputy chairman of the *oblispolkom* (regional soviet or state executive committee) (positions in most rural regions with primary responsibilities for the agricultural sector), and *obkom* first secretary in predominantly rural regions; it is not unusual to find the same agricultural specialists holding more than one of these positions during their bureau tenure. As career preparation for their bureau positions the overlapping early assignments of agricultural specialists often find them as first party secretary and state deputy chairman of a rural district, director of a regional agricultural department or deputy chairman for agriculture in the *oblispolkom*, and head of the *obkom* agricultural department.[9] Over time in certain regions agricultural specialists in the same bureau positions have originated from those in identical lower-level positions: the head of the *obkom* agricultural department or the first secretary of a particular rural district have over decades of electing bureau members been the automatic stepping-stones for agricultural specialists elected *obkom* agriculture secretary or *oblispolkom* chairman.[10] When they are reassigned outside their regions, these same agricultural specialists more likely will become a regional official in a predominantly agricultural region, sector head in the agricultural department of the All-Union Central Committee, or deputy minister in an All-Union Agricultural Ministry.[11]

Another subgroup of functional specialists distinct by their specific administrative expertise and closed pattern of overlapping career assignments at the regional level are the industrial specialists. On the *obkom* bureau industrial specialists serve interchangeably as the *obkom* industry secretary, first secretary of the regional capital (in which most regional industries are concentrated), regional trade union council chairman, first secretary of a large industrialized city or borough with ascribed bureau membership in certain regions, and *obkom* first secretary in a highly industrialized region. Early in their careers they are identifiable by their apprenticeship in positions logically related to their eventual bureau positions. Industrial specialists can be found as party secretary or even manager in an industrial enterprise, party secretary of an industrial district and, probably, later head of some industrial-construction department in the *obkom* or state chairman (mayor) of the regional capital.[12] As is evident for agricultural specialists, almost the same lower-level positions in certain regions have been common training-grounds for industrial specialists later elected to identical bureau positions.[13] Typical industrial specialists transferred from their regions will become either an official in a predominantly industrial region, industry secretary of a union republic, or deputy minister in an industrial ministry on the All-Union state level.[14]

Closed and patterned careers are even the more predictable lot of ideological specialists. On *obkom* bureaux the ideological specialists can be defined by those interchangeably assigned to be *obkom* ideology secretary, editor of the regional newspaper, or first secretary of the regional Komsomol. Prior to their bureau election, the careers of ideological specialists are already set by their prominence in positions normally associated with implementing various facets of ideological policy: director of regional publishing, movies, cultural departments or deputy chairman for education-culture in the *oblispolkom*; head of the *obkom* propaganda-agitation or science-educational institutions departments; urban or regional Komsomol secretary; or party secretary for a borough in which strategic scientific-cultural institutes and many cultural intelligentsia reside.[15] Reassigned from a region, ideological specialists reasonably can expect to find themselves only in positions for which their career specialization allegedly prepares them: secretary in the union-republic Komsomol, minister of publishing affairs, deputy editor of an All-Union newspaper, or department head of propaganda in the All-Union Central Committee.[16]

The fourth evident subgroup represented on *obkom* bureaux are the cadre specialists, so termed because of their consistent and logical assignments to a narrow range of positions associated with the supervision or selection of cadres on the regional level. On the *obkom* bureaux cadre specialists interchangeably serve as regional Komsomol first secretary, head of the *obkom* organizational-party work department, chairman of the regional trade union council or control committee, and *obkom* cadres secretary (a position frequently but not always equivalent to the *obkom* second secretary). Other career specialists are elected at times to any one of these positions (industrial specialists as chairman of the trade union council, ideological specialists as regional Komsomol first secretary), but cadre specialists are unique in holding two or three of them during their bureau tenure. Prior to their bureau election, the cadre specialist has been prepared as a lower-ranking Komsomol secretary, cadres secretary or head of an organizational-party work department in an urban party committee, secretary or head of the organizational-instruction department in the *oblispolkom*, or secretary of a regional trade union committee.[17] For some, their cadre responsibilities have even included postings as head of the regional MVD and KGB.[18] The pure cadre specialist, once reassigned from a region, will become a cadres secretary for a union republic, sector head in the organizational-party work

Table 1.1 614 Officials in 25 Obkom Bureaux by Other Positions in Same Bureaux during Tenure, 1953–79

Bureau positions	Other bureau positions held during tenure															Total
	(1)	(2)	(3)	(4)	(5)	(6)	(7)	(8)	(9)	(10)	(11)	(12)	(13)	(14)	(15)	
1 Obkom 1st secretary	—	22	18	8	1	2	19	2	12	2	2	1	1		3	125
2 Obkom cadres/2nd secretary*	22	—	16	17	4	5	25	6	11	3	3	7	2	1	—	97
3 Obkom industry secretary†	18	16	—	1	3	4	13	6	26	7	3	3	7	1	—	102
4 Obkom agriculture secretary	8	17	1	—	1	1	19	8				1	1	1	4	65
5 Obkom ideology secretary	1	4	3	1	—	2	3	1	1		5	1	3	6	—	65
6 Head of organizational-party work department	2	5	4	1	2	—	3	1	2		2	4	1			29
7 Oblispolkom chairman	19	25	13	19	3	3	—	12						1	1	108
8 Oblispolkom 1st deputy chairman	2	6	6	8	1	1	12	—						3		49
9 1st secretary regional capital	12	11	26		1	2			—	1	5					88
10 1st secretary urban‡ city or district	2	3	7						1	—			1	1	1	18
11 Regional Komsomol 1st secretary	2	3	3		5	2			5		—	1	1	1		49
12 Chairman regional trade union council	1	7	3	1	1	4					1	—	1	1		41
13 Chairman regional§ control committee	1	2	7	1	3	1				1	1	1	—			20
14 Editor regional newspaper		1	1	1	6		1	3		1	1	1		—		28
15 Chairman regional Sovnarkhoz (1957–65)	3			4			1			1					—	27
Total in bureau positions	125	97	102	65	65	29	108	49	88	18	49	41	20	28	27	614

* Included are: (a) obkom secretaries officially designated second secretary of a region at a time when responsibilities of second secretary primarily concerned cadre policy; or (b) obkom secretaries not officially second secretary of a region but primarily responsible for cadre policy.

† At times in some regions the obkom industry secretary has been the official obkom second secretary; in such instances the official has been coded for this bureau position as the industry secretary, not the second secretary.

‡ Positions with ascribed bureau membership unique to certain regions; included are the 1st secretary of the Krivoi Rog gorkom and 1st secretary of the Dneproderzhinsk gorkom in Dnepropetrovsk, 1st secretary of the Lenin raikom in Zaporozhe, 1st secretary of the Sevastopol gorkom in the Crimea, 1st secretary of the Rybinsk gorkom in Iaroslavl and 1st secretary of the Cherepovets gorkom in Vologda.

§ Termed Party–State Control Committee through 1965, People's Control Committee since 1965.

Source: Compiled by author; all subsequent tables in this chapter cover the same span of time, 1953–79.

department of the All-Union Central Committee, or a major official in the central leadership of the Komsomol, trade union council and control committees.[19]

How accurately these four career types can be identified by their bureau positions alone can be seen in Table 1.1, in which are cross-listed the bureau positions held by 614 officials in twenty-five representative regions of the Russian and Ukrainian republics in 1953–79. Table 1.1 essentially is a matrix in which the rows are the fifteen positions presumed to have conferred full or candidate bureau membership; the columns are the additional positions held at some time during bureau tenure by the officials elected to any of these fifteen positions. Collectively the 614 officials held 911 different bureau positions during the period of twenty-seven years. The most apparent finding is the highly selective patterning of their positions on the bureaux.

Among predominantly agricultural roles, consider the close overlap among those who have been elected *obkom* agriculture secretary, *oblispolkom* chairman and *oblispolkom* first deputy chairman. Nineteen of the sixty-five agriculture secretaries also have been elected *oblispolkom* chairman, and eight first deputy chairman, during their tenure. Twelve of the forty-nine *oblispolkom* first deputy chairmen in turn have been elected *oblispolkom* chairman – the only position besides *obkom* agriculture secretary identified with first deputy chairman on the bureaux. Although nineteen were elected *obkom* first secretary and twenty-five cadres/second secretary, the 108 *oblispolkom* chairmen have also followed a fairly closed career pattern on the regional bureaux: during their tenure very few have ever been elected to ideological or cadre positions as head of the organizational-party work department, *obkom* ideology secretary, regional Komsomol first secretary, or chairman of the regional trade union council or control committee.

Predominantly industrial roles form a similar interlocking subset of bureau positions. Twenty-six of the 102 *obkom* industry secretaries also were elected first secretary of the capital *gorkom*, and sixteen *obkom* second secretary, in regional bureaux where this position had major industrial responsibilities. A clear indication of industrial specialization is that only one of the 102 industry secretaries was also elected the *obkom* agriculture secretary during his tenure. Similarly to those in agricultural positions, few *obkom* industry secretaries had a bureau career association with the ideological or cadre positions.

The overlap of ideological positions on bureaux can be noted by the infrequency of *obkom* ideology secretary, editor of the regional newspaper, or first secretary of the regional Komsomol holding any position other than his own or one of the other two during his tenure. Cadre positions have been as selectively assigned as the others. Among heads of the *obkom* organizational-party work department, eleven of the twenty-seven other positions held on bureaux were cadres/second secretary, regional Komsomol first secretary and trade union council chairman. Twelve of the additional twenty-six positions held by trade union council chairmen in turn were *obkom* cadres/second secretary, head of the organizational-party work department and chairman of the control committee. Nor have control committee chairmen proven to be exceptional. The seven elections to *obkom* industry secretary occurred during the bifurcation of regions in 1963–4, when some chairmen of the party–state control committee were simultaneously designated industry secretary in the industrial *obkom*.

We would probably have found an even higher direct association among positions by career types in Table 1.1, except for the presence of a fifth career type on bureaux – mixed generalists. If the four other subgroups imply something of a bureaucratic rationality in assigning officials to particular bureau positions, mixed generalists are exceptional by the lack of any logical consistency in the positions which they have held over their careers. They appear to be the administrative 'troubleshooters', designated by the party to alleviate any major problem areas of leadership on the regional level or to fill leadership positions with a variety of responsibilities unsuited to a narrow functional specialist. Although mixed generalists most frequently hold cadre positions during their careers, they differ from the pure cadre specialists on bureaux by the lapses in their careers during which they have been assigned positions associated with ideological, industrial and agricultural responsibilities. Alternatively, during their bureau tenure, mixed generalists can be found as the cadres secretary, first secretary, ideology secretary, trade union council chairman and *oblispolkom* chairman. Before their bureau election, mixed generalists are likely to have been in a wide range of functional roles, from first secretary of either an urban or rural party committee to head of either *obkom* propaganda-agitation or industrial department.[20] Subsequent to their bureau membership, mixed generalists are reassigned

to various functional roles in other locales or to diverse departments and ministries in the central party and state organs.[21]

Frequently transferred among regional bureaux, mixed
generalists fit the stereotypical notion of the *apparatchik* in
Western scholarship of Soviet cadres. They appear to be admin-
istrators-enforcers without any particular policy specialization
designated to preserve uniformity in local leadership. Their role
in regional bureaux may be decisive in countering divisions
which might otherwise emerge among the distinct functional
specialists; some Western analysts have argued that local policy
conflict in the Soviet Union arises in part from the divergent
concerns of these functional specialists. By the commonality of
their careers and concerns agricultural specialists in the local
party and state bureaucracies may align along a similar position
and emphasize the 'agricultural' dimension of a problem against
an alignment of industrial specialists in the local party–state
bureaucracies who, in turn, may find their 'industrial' percep-
tion of the problem and priorities opposed by the ideological
specialists in leadership positions of the local Komsomol, state
and party bureaucracies.[22]

Even if one does not accept the thesis of functional conflict
among local officials, the relative importance of these distinct
career types in understanding the *nomenklatura* process in the
Soviet Union cannot be underestimated. Not only are certain
bureau positions so closely associated that they almost form
distinct career subsets, but it seems that the very opportunities
for advancement among Soviet cadres at the regional level
depend on the particular functional specialization with which
their entire careers have become identified. In this regard I have
previously found that since 1954 *obkom* bureau members in
these same twenty-five locales had a better opportunity for
advancement beyond their regions if they were functional
specialists from regions in which their particular responsibilities
conferred a heightened political status and visibility on them.
This status and visibility logically derived from the greater
demands associated with their particular positions and functional roles in their regions. Quasi-bureaucratic routines appear
to have been adopted by which, in the course of several years,
identical bureau functional specialists from the same regions
among the twenty-five were elevated to identical functional
positions in other locales or to higher organs in Kiev and
Moscow. Agricultural specialists originating from bureaux of
certain agricultural regions, industrial specialists from bureaux
of certain industrial regions and ideological specialists from

bureaux of regions with prestigious scientific-cultural centres have consistently better prospects for eventual reassignment beyond their locales than do their counterparts in less agri-cultural, less industrial, or less cultural regions.[23]

Even opportunities for promotion within a region may hinge on functional specialization of careers. Based on analysis of approximately 2,000 regional and territorial officials simul-taneously holding offices in the Russian Republic during 1973 wide variation was found in their ages relative to the specific functional specialization of their positions in that year. On the average in 1973 agricultural specialists were younger and pro-moted sooner in their careers to bureau positions than were industrial, cadre and ideological specialists in the Russian locales. This age contrast between agricultural and other specialists was even more noticeable among officials in the predominantly rural regions and territories of the Russian Republic in 1973.[24]

Further support that cadres differ by functional specialization has been inadvertently provided by Soviet officials in published analyses of cadre policy. In attempting to rationalize cadre policy since 1965 and the reduction in leadership turnover throughout the Soviet Union, officials and party theoreticians have defended this 'stabilization' of cadre ranks as a deliberately enacted change. By retaining cadres for longer periods in their positions, so it is reasoned, cadres have a better opportunity to become administrative experts in their particular roles, 'Politi-cal maturity' and practical 'worldly wisdom' have been the euphemisms to depict the enhanced leadership capabilities of cadres retained in their positions. During recent years, to further their mastery of a particular administrative policy area, cadres have more consistently been screened and have been designated to higher positions only after demonstrating a suf-ficient level of functional competence in subordinate positions.[25] Local party secretaries are among those more apt since 1965 to be policy specialists with career backgrounds matched to the positions in which they have been assigned.[26]

Leadership competence has also allegedly been enhanced by the lateral rotation across party, state and mass bureaucracies of cadres with functional skills equally suited to leadership posi-tions in these different bureaucracies. Several articles illustrat-ing this trend within local party organs have appeared in such party periodicals as *Partiinaia zhizn'*. These have cited specially trained agitprop professionals being appointed regional ideo-logical officials, local instructors in party agricultural and industrial state administrators, and regional state department heads recruited from among party instructors with long practical experience matched to their specific responsibilities in the state bureaucracy.[27]

Most Western analysts would not accept them at their face-value, but such discussions of cadre policy written in the Soviet Union at least give recognition to functional career differences among lower cadres as being the norm. Proof that the careers of Soviet cadres actually differ by functional specialization could be independently determined with detailed biographical data for a large random sample of local cadres like *obkom* bureau members. Unfortunately, data on most local officials have been unavailable to Western analysts. In most instances Western analysts probing career variance among Soviet cadres have been forced to limit their studies to All-Union Central Committee members or other officials in central positions. Often these are the same officials for whom detailed biographies have regularly appeared since 1958 in the published directories of Supreme Soviet deputies and the biographical appendices of Soviet encyclopaedic yearbooks in the years following party congresses. In truth, the only local officials whom Western analysts have been able to examine for career variance have been *obkom* first secretaries, and then only because several first secretaries are elected to the Central Committee or otherwise merit published biographies as *ex officio* deputies from their regions in the Supreme Soviet.[28] Without detailed and extensive biographical data on most local cadres, our knowledge of career patterns for typical cadres has been extrapolated from information on the exceptional but known universe of those who made it to the top – central officials and *obkom* first secretaries. Until now it has remained unclear whether the diverse functional specialization among these officials who have made it to the top represent more generally patterned diversity as a rule among all local cadres in the Soviet Union.

Yet the lack of sufficient data for local officials like those in *obkom* bureaux need not be an insurmountable obstacle. First, given the isolated career examples cited at the beginning of this chapter, the extensive studies of functional specialization among All-Union and union republic officials by Hough and Hodnett, and indirect allusions to the significance of career specialization by Soviet officials in published analyses, we can assume that the careers of those who comprise *obkom* bureaux over time may fall into distinct functional types. Secondly, if we further assume that the kinds of positions held by bureau members over their careers indicate their particular functional specialization, we can derive some important generalizations about the 'structure of political opportunities',[29] leading to bureau membership which may be directly linked to their distinct functional specializations prior and subsequent to bureau tenure. Thirdly, many bureau members can be classified into one of our five distinct functional specialists from scattered but revealing indicators of their specific functional type published over time in the Soviet press. The numerous personnel changes and other career references for an individual at some time elected a bureau member which form a distinct functional pattern; indirect determinants of their functional specialization in the political bureaucracy like patterned consistency in the kinds of topics which they address at party–state forums, the kinds of legislative commissions to which they have been assigned in All-Union and union republic soviets, and the kinds of policies particularly emphasized in their published articles when bureau members; and other even more subtle signs of their functional specializations like designated responsibility to respond for the regional leadership to criticism leveled at the region by accounts of policy failures published in *Izvestiia* and *Pravda*. Together these diverse indicators form distinct career profiles by functional type for bureau members. In addition, even if we lack information on certain bureau members, other than their position and the number of years which they held it as bureau member, those retained in the same position or parallel functional role on their bureaux for several years could be logically classified as a particular functional specialist based solely on their lengthy tenure.

Comparing several bureau members over time we should expect to find consistent variance in their careers paralleling differences in their long-term functional career specialization. Agricultural specialists may not be recruited in equivalent proportion to membership on *obkom* bureaux as would cadre specialists; industrial specialists may be advanced earlier in their careers to bureau membership than would ideological specialists; and mixed generalists may be elected bureau members more frequently as *obkom* secretaries than agricultural specialists. The consistent variance supports the thesis of Hough and Hodnett that Soviet cadres differ significantly in terms of their functional specialization within the Soviet political bureaucracy. From an aggregate level of analysis, consistent variance in the origins of *obkom* bureau members by functional career type would verify that the 'structure of political opportunities' for

Soviet cadres under the *nomenklatura* system follows relatively prescribed bureaucratic routines of advancement even if the promotion of any one particular official may be directly dependent on his personal connections with an influential patron at a higher political level.

Career Patterns of *Obkom* Bureau Members

In order to determine that the careers of Soviet cadres differ by functional specialization I have classified each of the 614 *obkom* bureau members previously cited in Table 1.1 into one of the five distinct functional types. These 614 bureau members constitute my elite sample not because they are all the known bureau members elected in these twenty-five regions since 1953 (nor because they are necessarily representative of all bureau members in these two union republics since 1953), but because they were those over the last ten years of my research on these regions for whom I felt sufficient minimal information was available to classify them by functional type. Career profiles for some of the 614 bureau members were derived from published biographies in all volumes of the Supreme Soviet directories since 1958, the biographical appendices in the Soviet encyclopaedic yearbooks, obituaries and the various Western biographical directories of Soviet officials. For the vast majority of the 614 bureau members, however, career profiles were reconstructed from information on them in my personal files: the formal titles and functional roles of their positions over time; indirect determinants of their functional type like speeches before party–state forums, legislative commissions assigned to in soviets and policies emphasized in their published articles; and other subtle signs of their patterned functional career specialization. Bureau members were only included in the sample if they served a minimum of ten years in known positions on the *obkom* bureaux and/or if they could be identified in a functional type by three consecutive positions which they held prior, during and subsequent to bureau tenure. The criteria of a minimum ten-year bureau tenure or three known positions were set somewhat arbitrarily only because they allowed me with some confidence to include the largest number of bureau members for comparative analysis. In cross-checking bureau members for whom I had only partial information with those on whom I had detailed published biographies it was found that either criterion had some face-validity in establishing the functional type of a bureau member. Three known positions or a minimum ten-year bureau tenure for those with published biographies were fairly predictable indicators of the functional specialization into which they were tracked throughout their careers.[30]

If Soviet cadres differ by functional specialization, I hypothesize that my analysis should over the twenty-seven years reveal consistent and significant variance in the career patterns of these 614 bureau members directly corresponding to their distinct functional types. As the dependent variables and measure of any such variance, career patterns were defined to include career-demographic data which I found for the largest number of the 614 in the elite sample: the specific bureau positions held; the geographic locales from which they were recruited onto the bureaux; their party tenure at the time they were first elected bureau members; the total number of years which they served on the bureaux through 1979; and the specific positions to which some were transferred from their original regions.

Furthermore, I have differentiated bureau members by the particular nature of the region in which they were elected. My assumption, supported by previous research on local Soviet officials, is that career patterns should vary depending on the locale in which officials originate.[31] In defining the nature of a region I grouped bureau members by Russian and Ukrainian regions, rural and urban, and the eleven historic-economic regional areas encompassing the twenty-five regions. My reason for distinguishing bureau members by union republic is that Russian bureau members, without an intermediate republic party organization, fall directly under the selection powers of the All-Union central organs in Moscow. To some extent I would assume that the guidelines for cadre policy followed in these Russian regions differ from those in the Ukrainian regions, where union-republic party leaders can exercise some intervening influence on cadre policy. Cadre policy and career patterns may also subtly vary between urban and rural regions. Logically the burdens and career opportunities of agricultural and industrial specialists, as two examples, should differ if they are elected to positions on *obkom* bureaux in urban or rural regions; these differences should be evident in their career patterns relative to the urban or rural economic context of their regions. Similarly, the careers of functional types may evolve from patterns more strictly adhered to in certain historic-economic areas than in others. Even within the same union republic and comparable urban environments, functional specialists in the central industrial regional area may differ in their career patterns from specialists in the Western Siberian regional area either because of the complex of economic-cultural-societal factors unique to each of these two geographically distinct areas, or because within departments of the Central Committee Secretariat in Moscow personnel selection is overseen by different sections for each of the historic-economic areas of the country.[32] Thus, the presumed relationship between functional career types and career-demographic variables will be controlled in my analysis by the nature of the region – defined in turn by union republic, urban-rural context and historic-economic regional area.

In the following tables I have assumed that the career-demographic variables are characteristics of a true sample of all bureau members in these twenty-five regions since 1953. From this assumption, I have calculated chi-square values, levels of statistical significance and a standardized nominal-level measure of association for each table and subtable (controlling for regional characteristics). The nominal level measure of association employed in the tables is Cramer's V. Based on the chi-square values and number of cases in each table and sub-table Cramer's V corrects for differences in rows and columns in each table and subtable and provides an exactly comparable measure of the interdependency between the independent variable (functional type) and dependent variables. Cramer's V ranges in value from 0 to 1, with 1 expressing a perfect association between the values of the independent and dependent variables. In essence, Cramer's V allows us to conclude how related are differences in career patterns to differences in functional types. In the tables and subtables I have assumed that values of 0·30 or higher on Cramer's V indicate a strong measured association between my independent variable of functional type and my dependent variables, values between 0·15 and 0·29 indicate a moderate association and values below 0·15 indicate a weak or non-existent association.[33]

Regional Origins and Bureau Positions

Are there significant differences among *obkom* bureau members by functional specialization? And are those differences more pronounced or evident in certain kinds of regions than in others?

In Table 1.2 the 614 bureau members are differentiated by functional types and regional origins. The percentage differences in the table indicate that access to bureau membership for many cadres has depended in part on their particular functional specialization. At one extreme are industrial and agricultural specialists, whose 29 and 24 percent representation among all

Table 1.2 *Bureau Functional Specialists by Regional Characteristics*

| Region | Functional specialists (%) | | | | | N |
	Agricul-tural	Indus-trial	Ideo-logical	Cadre	Mixed general-ist	
Union republic						
Russian*	24	28	13	11	24	407
Ukrainian†	23	30	14	16	17	207
Urbanization						
rural‡	30	19	15	13	23	233
urban§	20	34	12	13	21	381
Historic-economic‖						
regional areas						
Southwest Ukraine	24	14	18	18	26	50
South Ukraine	29	25	13	11	23	56
Southeast Ukraine	20	40	13	18	10	101
Northwest	20	25	10	13	33	40
Central Industrial	25	29	12	14	20	100
Central Black Earth	39	14	19	6	22	64
Volga	22	28	13	10	27	60
Volga-Viatka	35	25	20	15	5	20
North Caucasus	13	38	6	6	38	32
Urals	24	36	12	8	20	25
Western Siberia	17	35	11	15	23	66
Total bureau members	24	29	13	13	21	614

	Union republic	Urbanization	Regional area
Chi-square (χ^2)	5·08	18·19	56·73
Significance (*P*)	0·28	0·001	0·04
Cramer's *V*	0·09	0·17	0·15

* Belgorod, Briansk, Iaroslavl, Kaliningrad, Kaluga, Kemerovo, Kirov, Kursk, Novosibirsk, Orel, Perm, Saratov, Smolensk, Tambov, Tomsk, Volgograd, Vologda.

† Crimea, Dnepropetrovsk, Kharkov, Lvov, Odessa, Transcarpathia, Zaporozhe.

‡ Belgorod, Briansk, Kaluga, Kirov, Kursk, Orel, Smolensk, Tambov, Transcarpathia, Vologda.

§ Crimea, Dnepropetrovsk, Iaroslavl, Kaliningrad, Kemerovo, Kharkov, Novosibirsk, Odessa, Lvov, Perm, Rostov, Saratov, Tomsk, Volgograd, Zaporozhe.

‖ Southwest Ukraine (Lvov, Transcarpathia), South Ukraine (Crimea, Odessa), Southeast Ukraine (Dnepropetrovsk, Kharkov, Zaporozhe), Northwest (Kaliningrad, Vologda), Central Industrial (Briansk, Kaluga, Iaroslavl, Orel, Smolensk), Central Black Earth (Belgorod, Kursk, Tambov), Volga (Volgograd, Saratov), Volga-Viatka (Kirov), North Caucasus (Rostov), Urals (Perm), Western Siberia (Kemerovo, Novosibirsk, Tomsk).

Source: Compiled by author.

bureau members since 1953 clearly demonstrates the advantage of these functional types as pathways to eventual bureau membership. At the opposite extreme are the 13 percent of ideological and cadre specialists elected bureau members since 1953. The logical conclusion would be that lower-level Soviet cadres reduce their opportunities for eventual bureau membership to the extent that they become too closely identified with either one of these specializations early in their careers. Falling somewhere between these two extremes are the 21 percent of all bureau members since 1953 who would be classified mixed generalists. More preferred for bureau membership than ideological and cadre specialists, mixed generalists still are overshadowed as a presence on most *obkom* bureaux by the industrial and agricultural specialists, who together made up over half of all bureau members. The percentages in the table also discount any importance to the union republic in which bureau members have been recruited. Almost the same percentage of bureau members by functional type has been recruited in both union republics since 1953, and the clear implication is that cadre policy – at least in the criteria for selecting functional types to bureaux – has been uniformly implemented in both republics over the twenty-seven-year period. A precise measure of this uniformity is the weak 0·09 magnitude for Cramer's V, the statistical measure of association between union republic and functional type.

On the other hand, the extent of urbanization in a region and the location of a region in a particular historic-economic area do provide advantages to different functional types in gaining bureau positions. By level of urbanization 10 percent more agricultural specialists have been elected bureau members in the rural regions of the sample, and 15 percent more industrial specialists have been elected bureau members in the urban regions of the sample. Urban-rural differences are statistically significant: the probability that the same observed distribution could have occurred by chance is less than one in 1,000 ($P = 0·001$); and the statistical measure of association is 0·17.

The same selectivity of bureau members also can be seen by comparing the mix of functional types recruited in different historic-economic areas. Industrial specialists have been singled out for bureau membership in much higher percentages in predominantly industrial areas: 35–40 percent of all bureau members since 1953 in the coal–steel centers of the Southeast Ukraine, Urals and Western Siberia have been industrial specialists. Conversely, agricultural specialists have dominated bureau membership in the regional areas which constitute the farmbelt economies of the Russian and Ukrainian republics: 29–35 percent of all bureau members since 1953 in the Central Black Earth, Volga-Viatka and South Ukraine regions have been agricultural specialists. In the Volga and central industrial regions the equivalent importance of agriculture and industry as economic sectors in these areas may be reflected in the almost identical percentage of agricultural and industrial specialists since 1953 in these regional bureaux. Policy considerations other than economic may also weigh in selecting functional types to bureau membership. For example, the combination of cadre specialists and mixed generalists is comparatively much higher only in the mixed ethnic border areas of the Soviet Union or those where ethnic conflict has periodically represented a major concern: 44–46 percent of all bureau members in South-west Ukraine, Northwest and North Caucasus regions. Overall the percentage variance among functional types by historic-economic areas is statistically significant ($P = 0.04$); and the level of association between functional types and areas is of a high enough magnitude ($V = 0.15$) to confirm the conclusion that different functional types have more consistently been sought as bureau members in certain areas.

The functional specializations of cadres also determine the specific bureau positions which they will likely hold during their tenure, as we can see in the distribution of positions by functional types in Tables 1.3 and 1.4. In Table 1.3, among bureau positions with the most clearly defined roles, individuals typically elected to those positions have long-term career specializations carefully matched to their roles. Thus since 1953, among *obkom* agriculture secretaries, *oblispolkom* chairmen and *oblispolkom* first deputy chairmen, 63–94 percent have been agricultural career specialists. Among *obkom* industry secretaries, first secretaries of the regional capital and first secretaries of major urban centers, industrial specialists have made up 72–79 percent of the 206 times these positions have been filled. Among *obkom* ideology secretaries and editors of regional newspapers, 79 and 93 percent have been recruited from ideological career specialists.

Even for positions with cadre role responsibilities, we find a tendency to select specialists in cadre affairs as the regional Komsomol first secretary, regional chairman of the trade union council, regional chairman of the control committee, head of the organizational-party work department and *obkom* cadres/second secretary. True, the correlation between positions and

Table 1.3 *Bureau Functional Specialists by Bureau Positions*

Bureau positions	Functional specialists (%)					N
	Agricultural	Industrial	Ideological	Cadre	Mixed Generalist	
Obkom 1st secretary	26	28	2	6	38	125
Obkom cadres/ 2nd secretary*	30	19	4	23	25	97
Obkom industry secretary*	1	79		6	14	102
Obkom agriculture secretary	94	2			5	65
Obkom ideology secretary			79		21	63
Head of organizational- party work department	3	3		48	45	29
Oblispolkom chairman	64	17	2		18	108
Oblispolkom 1st deputy chairman	63	22		2	12	49
1st secretary regional capital	1	74		1	24	88
1st secretary urban* city or district		72			28	18
Regional Komsomol 1st secretary		6	22	57	14	49
Chairman regional trade union council	2	20		49	29	41
Chairman regional* control committee	5	5		30	60	20
Editor regional newspaper	4		93	4		28
Chairman regional Sovnarkhoz (1957–65)		93			4	27

* For designations, see Table 1.1.
Source: Compiled by author.

functional type varies more for these positions than for identifiable agricultural, industrial and ideological bureau positions.
Actually, 49 percent of all cadres/second secretaries have been
agricultural or industrial career specialists, origins which attest
to the diverse career preparation considered appropriate to this
position on the regional level. Yet the tendency to recruit cadre
specialists as heads of regional mass organizations contradicts a
belief that officials in these organizations have little career
association or identity with the groups they oversee. On the
contrary, it is not unusual to find the regional Komsomol first
secretary selected from cadres in lower posts of the Komsomol

bureaucracy and transferred to the central Komsomol bureaucracy subsequent to tenure as regional first secretary. This pattern has been particularly the rule in regions with large student populations like Kharkov and Novosibirsk.[34]

If career specialists have been preferred for the most specific bureau roles, the diversity of role responsibilities thrust upon an *obkom* first secretary as the leader of the region may be mirrored in the opposite tendency to select mixed generalists for this position; 38 percent of the 125 first secretaries since 1953 would fall into this functional type. A more narrow career specialization, however, has not disqualified cadres from being elected first secretary, as witnessed by the 54 percent with explicit agricultural and industrial career specializations.

Functional types selected for different bureau positions have also varied significantly, dependent on the union republic and urban-rural context of the region. Examples of this variance are *obkom* cadres/second secretary, *obkom* first secretary, *oblispolkom* first deputy chairman and regional Komsomol first secretary. Thirty-five percent of all cadres/second secretaries in the Russian Republic have been mixed generalists compared to only 9 percent in the Ukrainian Republic, where a much higher 20 percent have been agricultural or industrial specialists. While an equivalent 38 percent of first secretaries in both rural and urban regions have been mixed generalists, we find not surprisingly a higher proportion of agricultural specialists as first secretaries in rural regions (by 22 percent) and a higher proportion of industrial specialists as first secretaries in urban regions (by 13 percent). Functional types selected as *oblispolkom* first deputy chairmen have differed between Russian and Ukrainian bureaux, with agricultural specialists preferred by 26 percent in Ukrainian bureaux and industrial specialists preferred by 24 percent in Russian bureaux. Among all Komsomol first secretaries, 20 percent more cadre specialists have been recruited in urban regions.

This association between functional type and bureau position by regional characteristics can be precisely specified by the comparative measures in Table 1.4. If magnitudes of 0·30 or higher indicate a strong association, we would conclude that cadres are most likely to differ either by union republic or urbanization among those selected *obkom* first secretary, cadres/second secretary, industry secretary, first secretary of a major urban center other than the regional capital, Komsomol first secretary and chairman of the trade union council or control committee. Where our measure of association falls below 0·20,

Table 1.4 *Regional Association of Functional Specialists by Bureau Position*

Bureau positions	*Cramer's V*	
	Union republic	*Urbani- zation*
Obkom 1st secretary	0·28*	0·30*
Obkom cadres/2nd secretary	0·40†	0·21
Obkom industry secretary	0·18	0·30*
Obkom agriculture secretary	0·15	0·15
Obkom ideology secretary	0·06‡	0·16‡
Head of organizational-party work department	0·17	0·27
Oblispolkom chairman	0·25	0·18
Oblispolkom 1st deputy chairman	0·37	0·23
1st secretary regional capital	0·24	0·19
1st secretary urban city or district	0·35‡	0·27‡
Regional Komsomol 1st secretary	0·21	0·48*
Chairman regional trade union council	0·26	0·35
Chairman regional control committee	0·25	0·47
Editor regional newspaper	0·16	0·27
Chairman regional *Sovnarkhoz* (1957–65)	0·18‡	0·13‡

* Derived from a chi-square value for this subtable statistically significant ($P < 0.05$).
† Derived from a chi-square value for this subtable statistically significant ($P < 0.01$).
‡ Measured association for this position is phi, the same nominal level measure of association as Cramer's V in a two-by-two contingency table.
Source: Compiled by author.

uniform cadre policy prevails in recruiting the identical functional type to this position regardless of the regional context. An example is the position of *obkom* agriculture secretary. Almost an equivalent proportion have been agricultural specialists in Russian and Ukrainian bureaux (92 and 100 percent) and in rural and urban bureaux (92 and 95 percent).

Time Periods of Bureau Election

Up to now we have assumed that the proportion of functional types among bureau members remained unchanged over the twenty-seven-year period. Yet these twenty-seven years coincided with immense changes in leadership at the central level of the Soviet Union which should have affected the kinds of officials preferred at the regional level. Consider that the period of analysis encompasses a time through 1953 when Stalin's priorities unquestionably shaped cadre policy at the regional level, the interregnum of 1954–7 with the succession struggle and Khrushchev's ascendancy, the 1958–64 period with Khrushchev's dominance, the six years 1965–70 following Khrushchev's ouster with Brezhnev's increasing prominence at the center and the most recent 1971–9 period with Brezhnev's apparent ability to dictate the outlines of both domestic and foreign policy. Logically we would anticipate changes in the proportion of functional types first elected to positions on the *obkom* bureaux coincidental with these time periods and reflective of shifting regime priorities in cadre policy.

Table 1.5 *Bureau Functional Specialists by Time Periods First Elected to Obkom Bureau*

| Time periods | Functional specialists (%) | | | | | N |
	Agricul- tural	Indus- trial	Ideo- logical	Cadre	Mixed Genera- list	
1939–53*	27	20	4	10	39	51
1954–7	29	26	12	10	23	145
1958–64	21	3	16	11	19	210
1965–70	23	26	15	15	22	128
1971	23	33	11	20	14	80

$\chi^2 = 27 \cdot 15$　　　$P = 0 \cdot 04$　　　$V = 0 \cdot 11$
* Included are the 51 bureau members in 1953 first elected in 1939–53.
Source: Compiled by author.

Table 1.6　*Regional Association of Functional Specialists by Time Periods First Elected to Obkom Bureau*

	Cramer's V	N
Union republic		
Russian	0·12	407
Ukrainian	0·14	207
Urbanization		
Rural	0·15	233
Urban	0·11	381
Historic-economic regional areas		
Southwest Ukraine	0·33	50
South Ukraine	0·23	56
Southeast Ukraine	0·17	101
Northwest	0·30	40
Central Industrial	0·19	100
Central Black Earth	0·29	64
Volga	0·26	60
Volga-Viatka	0·49	20
North Caucasus	0·40	32
Urals	0·38	25
Western Siberia	0·31	66

Source: Compiled by author.

The actual impact of these regime changes on regional leadership can be assessed in Tables 1.5 and 1.6 by the time periods in which the 614 were first elected to positions equivalent in status to *obkom* bureau membership. In Table 1.5 the proportion of functional types first elected in each time period varies only slightly, with the statistical measure of association between time periods and functional types only 0·11. Typical are ideological and cadre specialists, elected in roughly equivalent percentages in each of the five time periods, and agricultural specialists, the proportion elected for the first time to positions on the bureaux ranging from 21 to 27 percent. Among industrial specialists, the 32 percent first elected in 1958–64 perhaps reflected Khrushchev's attempts to redirect the role of local party organs more to industrial decisionmaking and to reduce their preoccupation with agriculture alone. If this were the reason, it is interesting that a similar concern of the central leadership prompted bureaux once again to recruit 33 percent industrial specialists among their newly elected members after 1971.

If the proportion of narrow functional specialists first elected to positions on the bureaux has fluctuated only slightly over the five time periods, the percentages in Table 1.5 also clearly indicate a consistent trend since 1939–53 away from recruiting mixed generalists to positions on the bureaux. By 1971–9 mixed generalists made up only 14 percent of all newly elected bureau members compared to the zenith of 39 percent of all newly elected bureau members in 1939–53. The actual significance of this downward trend is less clear.

On the one hand, the percentage of mixed generalists for comparison in the 1939–53 period is derived from a total number of only fifty-one bureau members for whom we had sufficient information to classify them into different functional types. Some would question the low 14 percent of mixed generalists among those first elected to positions in the most recent 1971–9 period, contending that this actually understates the real proportion of mixed generalists classified as industrial, agricultural, ideological, or cadre specialists on the basis of their early postings through 1979 whose later reassignments in the bureaux would more clearly justify their reclassification as mixed generalists. On the other hand, Soviet officials since 1965 have persistently defended the reduced turnover of officials as a means to provide those officials such as regional leaders with extensive on-the-job learning for their specific functional specializations in the political bureaucracy. Those first elected to the bureaux since 1971 as *obkom* industrial or ideological secretary or head of the *obkom* organizational-party work department have more typically been retained in these same positions throughout the 1970s and will very likely be reassigned to other bureau-status positions in the 1980s directly related to their specific administrative-functional roles in the regional leadership.[35] Furthermore, the decline of mixed generalists at the regional leadership level supports the contention of Seweryn Bialer that the emergence of more narrow functional specialists and the disappearance of party generalists within the Soviet political bureaucracy constitute a major underlying change in cadre policy.[36]

Insignificant as the independent variable of time period by itself is to the proportion of functional types first elected bureau members, there is a consistent variation within certain historic-economic regional areas. In Table 1.6 particular time periods are more closely associated with recruitment of different functional types. The functional specialization of cadres is strongly associated with the time periods in which they most likely would have been first elected bureau members in the Southwest Ukraine, the Northwest, the Urals, Western Siberia, Volga-Viatka and the North Caucasus. At the same time bureau membership controlled for union republic and urbanization differs little, with the four comparative measures of association moderate or weak between 0·11 and 0·15. Nor do all regional areas exhibit any difference in the periods when functional types were first elected. The Southeast Ukraine stands out in the table as a particularly deviant case. The moderate 0·17 measure of association for Southeast Ukraine means that an almost equivalent percentage of functional types has been first elected in each time period; predictably 40 percent of all newly elected bureau members in each time period in Southeast Ukraine are industrial specialists.

Geographical Origins

Tables 1.7 and 1.8 disclose the importance of functional specialization in explaining where bureau members have been recruited for their positions. Among the 391 bureau members for whom I was able to determine their positions immediately prior to their first bureau election, 59 percent originated from lower-level positions within the same region, 11 percent either from regions in the same area or from bordering regions (including those adjacent across union republic boundaries like Belgorod and Kharkov), and 30 percent from positions completely outside

Table 1.7 Bureau Functional Specialists by Geographical Origin prior to First Election on Obkom Bureau

| Functional specialists | Geographical origin (%) | | | N |
	Inside region	Inside reg-ional area*	Outside	
Agricultural	55	16	29	113
Industrial	74	5	21	114
Ideological	68	5	27	37
Cadre	58	3	40	38
Mixed generalist	42	19	39	89
Total bureau members	59	11	30	391

$\chi^2 = 30 \cdot 81$, $P = 0 \cdot 0002$, $V = 0 \cdot 20$.
* Officials either in regional area encompassing this region or in bordering region.
Source: Compiled by author.

Table 1.8 Regional Association of Functional Specialists by Geographical Origin prior to First Election on Obkom Bureau

	Cramer's V	N
Union republic		
Russian	0·23*	248
Ukrainian	0·18	143
Urbanization		
rural	0·13	140
urban	0·24*	251
Historic-economic regional areas		
Southwest Ukraine	0·27	33
South Ukraine	0·22	38
Southeast Ukraine	0·22	72
Northwest	0·41	22
Central Industrial	0·33	55
Central Black Earth	0·26	39
Volga	0·32	45
Volga-Viatka	0·51	11
North Caucasus	0·42	21
Urals	0·60	18
Western Siberia	0·40	37

* Derived from a chi-square value for this subtable statistically significant ($P < 0 \cdot 001$).
Source: Compiled by author.

their region and area (including those in positions at the union republic and All-Union levels, even if their regions formed part of the same area encompassing the Kiev and Moscow regions).

While positions inside a region have been the favored career paths for a majority of bureau members, they have varied significantly relative to particular functional type. The most evident contrast in Table 1.7 is that between industrial and agricultural functional specialists, with 74 percent of the former and only 55 percent of the latter recruited inside their regions. At the same time an additional 16 percent of agricultural specialists originated from regions within the same area or those bordering. In selecting bureau members central cadre officials may reason that the agricultural sectors of large regional areas are so comparable that agricultural specialists like this 16 percent can be laterally transferred to bureaux in any region of the area and still have sufficient background to oversee agricultural policy. The same reasoning may not apply in selecting industrial specialists, where 74 percent are insiders. Central cadre officials may perceive that the differences of industrial branches even within a contiguous regional area require industrial specialists in bureau positions to have practical experience in coping with the unique industrial problems of each region. They can only have gained that practical experience as former lower-level cadres in the region.

An interesting contrast in Table 1.7 is also the much smaller 42 percent of mixed generalists recruited inside the region, although an additional 19 percent were transferred from positions in intermediate regions. Together with cadre specialists, mixed generalists stand out by the comparatively high 40 percent of both functional types originating outside the region and regional area. Overall the nominal level measure of association between functional type and geographical origin is moderately strong $(V = 0.20)$, a magnitude which suggests that functional specialization by itself influences where cadres originate prior to their first bureau election.

Controlling for regional characteristics in Table 1.8 we find an even higher direct association between functional type and geographical origin in certain regions. Seven of the eleven historic-economic areas have magnitudes above 0.30 in the degree to which different functional types correspond to different geographical origins. Indicative are the forty-five functional bureau members included from the Volga regional area. Since 1953 71 percent (33) of the bureau members have been recruited from lower-level cadres inside their regions, but that percentage varies from 92 (12 of 13) for agricultural specialists to only 42 (5 of 12) for mixed generalists. In regional areas falling below 0.30 in the table the trend has been to recruit bureau members primarily from inside or outside the region regardless of their functional specialization. In one such regional area, Southeast Ukraine, 79 percent of bureau members (57 of 72) have been insiders, and the proportion of insiders among all functional types forms a narrow range from 71 percent of mixed generalists (5 of 7) to 84 percent of industrial specialists (27 of 32). Thus while functional types vary in origin by region, the effect comparatively is more pronounced within certain regional clusters than in others.

Regions in Table 1.8 also vary by union republic and urbanization, with higher levels of variance among functional types in Russian and urban than in Ukrainian and rural regions. In urban regions a much higher percentage of industrial and even agricultural specialists originate inside the region: 79 percent of industrial specialists and 61 percent of agricultural specialists, compared to 50 and 48 percent of the same functional types in rural regions. By differences of 19 and 13 percent rural regions have recruited more of their industrial and agricultural specialists outside the region and regional area than has been true of urban regions. In delegating more officials to these bureau positions from outside, central cadre officials may have revealed their bias in discounting the projected competency of lower-level industrial and agricultural cadres in rural regions. In contrast central cadre officials may have greater confidence in the leadership potential of the same functionaries in urban regions to promote them onto their regional bureaux. Central cadre officials may reason that the same functionaries have undergone more demanding political apprenticeships as lower-level cadres in the complex industrialized economy of an urban region. Thus, it may not be coincidental that 19 percent more industrial specialists in urban than in rural regions were urban-district party secretaries within their regions at the time they were first elected to offices equivalent in status to bureau membership.

Party and Bureau Tenure

Dependent on functional specialization, the careers of bureau members have varied according to their party tenure when first elected and to the total number of years they have held offices in the same regional bureaux. These two career dimensions are presented in Tables 1.9 and 1.10. Typical bureau members (Table 1.9) entered the party eleven to twenty years before their first bureau election, but the percentage is much higher for industrial specialists. Almost two-thirds of all industrial specialists fall in this median category of party tenure, exceeding by 15–22 points the comparable percentages for the other functional types. In contrast mixed generalists make up the most

Table 1.9 *Bureau Functional Specialists by Party Tenure when First Elected to Obkom Bureaux*

Functional specialists	Party tenure (years as party member) (%) 1–10 years	11–20 years	21 + years	N
Agricultural	9	49	42	122
Industrial	9	64	27	133
Ideological	9	46	46	46
Cadre	26	43	32	47
Mixed generalist	5	42	53	104
Total bureau members	10	51	39	452

$\chi^2 = 32\cdot97$, $P = 0\cdot0001$, $V = 0\cdot19$.
Source: Compiled by author.

Table 1.10 *Bureau Functional Specialists by Bureau Tenure*

Functional specialists	Bureau Tenure (years as bureau member)* (%) 1–5 years	6–10 years	11–15 years	16+ years	N
Agricultural	31	35	16	18	147
Industrial	39	31	22	8	175
Ideological	38	25	27	10	81
Cadre	52	13	25	10	79
Mixed generalist	42	30	16	13	132
Total bureau members	39	29	20	12	614

$\chi^2 = 28\cdot96$, $P = 0\cdot004$, $V = 0\cdot13$.
* The length of time counted is that separating the date of election to the bureau for the first time and the last year through 1979 in which the official served on the bureau. Officials may not have served continuously on the bureau for all years in the time span; and the date of first election for some officials was prior to 1953.
Source: Compiled by author.

politically experienced members of the bureau, 53 percent having entered the party at least twenty-one years before; cadre specialists the least, with 26 percent less than eleven years in the party when first elected. The 452 bureau members whose party entry dates could be determined do vary relative to their particular functional type, as evidenced by the moderately strong magnitude of association ($V = 0\cdot19$) and the high statistical level of significance ($P = 0\cdot0001$).

If cadre specialists have been party members only a few years when first elected bureau members, many can also anticipate remaining on the bureaux fewer years than any of the other functional types. In Table 1.10, which compares bureau tenure by functional specialization, 52 percent served less than six years on bureaux. Comparatively, agricultural specialists have the best prospects for bureau longevity, with only 31 percent having been retained less than six years, 18 percent more than fifteen years. Yet there is no exact consistency even within these two functional types. Thirty-five percent of all cadre specialists are also bureau veterans with at least eleven years on the same bureau, while the percentage of agricultural specialists between eleven and fifteen years on the same bureau is the lowest for any functional type. A reflection of this inconsistency among types is the weaker measured association between functional specialization and bureau tenure in the table ($V = 0.13$).

Controlling party and bureau tenure by regional characteristics in Tables 1.11 and 1.12 magnifies some of these distinctions. In Table 1.11 nine of the eleven regional areas with magnitudes of association above 0.30 (Southeast Ukraine and Central Black Earth areas being the exceptions) have consistently recruited functional types who entered the party approximately the same number of years prior to first election. Consistency in recruitment has been the rule particularly for bureau members in North Caucasus. Although the twenty-four bureau members in the subsample for this area were elected at quite different times over the twenty-seven years, they have been remarkably similar by functional type in party tenure. All three of the agricultural specialists and seven of the nine industrial specialists had eleven to twenty years' party tenure; both cadre specialists and eight of the ten mixed generalists, a minimum of twenty-one years. The consistent pattern followed over twenty-seven years in North Caucasus and the eight other areas indicates that central cadre officials select candidates for various bureau positions only if they have passed a certain prescribed minimum period in the party considered essential for their particular functional responsibilities and for the particular area.

In addition to the regional area, central cadre officials appear to weigh the economic dimensions of a region in prescribing a minimum party tenure for certain functional specialists on a bureau. The party tenure of potential bureau members is likely to be scrutinized more for those in urban than in rural regions, with a higher magnitude of association for urban than rural regions in Table 1.11 (0.24 to 0.13). Not only is there less selectivity by party tenure in rural regions, but almost all five functional types in rural regions are much more likely to be veteran party members at the time of their first election. Eleven percent more rural than urban bureau members had been in the party a minimum of twenty-one years when first elected.

Table 1.11 Regional Association of Functional Specialists by Party Tenure when First Elected to Obkom Bureaux

	Cramer's V	N
Union republic		
Russian	0·19*	282
Ukrainian	0·23†	170
Urbanization		
rural	0·13	164
urban	0·24*	288
Historic-economic regional areas		
Southwest Ukraine	0·39	36
South Ukraine	0·39	49
Southeast Ukraine	0·29	85
Northwest	0·33	25
Central Industrial	0·31	74
Central Black Earth	0·28	39
Volga	0·32	40
Volga-Viatka	0·49	16
North Caucasus	0·69*	24
Urals	0·59	20
Western Siberia	0·31	44

* Derived from a chi-square value for this subtable statistically significant ($P < 0.01$).
† Derived from a chi-square value for this subtable statistically significant ($P < 0.05$).
Source: Compiled by author.

Table 1.12 Regional Association of Functional Specialists by Bureau Tenure

	Cramer's V	N
Union republic		
Russian	0·18*	407
Ukrainian	0·10	207
Urbanization		
rural	0·15	233
urban	0·14†	381
Historic-economic regional areas		
Southwest Ukraine	0·27	50
South Ukraine	0·27	56
Southeast Ukraine	0·18	101
Northwest	0·28	40
Central Industrial	0·20	100
Central Black Earth	0·24	64
Volga	0·29	60
Volga-Viatka	0·37	20
Urals	0·43	25
North Caucasus	0·40	32
Western Siberia	0·38*	66

* Derived from a chi-square value for this subtable statistically significant ($P < 0.01$).
† Derived from a chi-square value for this subtable statistically significant ($P < 0.05$).
Source: Compiled by author.

In contrast to party tenure there is hardly any measured association between bureau tenure by functional type and the different regional groupings. In Table 1.12 both rural and urban regions have the same low measured association between functional type and bureau tenure. The even marginal difference by Russian republic can be explained by the contrast on Russian bureaux between cadre and ideological specialists who have served less than six years and mixed generalists who have served more than ten years. Only four of the eleven regional areas have strong measured associations above 0·30, and none of the four approximate the magnitudes found for party tenure and regional areas in Table 1.11.

Of course, many political uncertainties determine the bureau tenure of any official or any subgroup of bureau officials identified by their common functional specialization. Despite these uncertainties, it is surprising that the four regional areas register strong measured associations in bureau tenure. The term 'tenure' in these regional areas may be quite appropriate, for the bureau member in a particular functional specialization in these four areas can reasonably expect the same relative length of time on the bureaux. Bureau members in Southeast Ukraine have the least predictable tenure by functional type in the table ($V = 0·18$). This inconsistency, however, has been far from a disincentive to bureau membership in Southeast Ukraine. As pointed out in the next section, bureau members from the Southeast Ukraine have also been the most successful of all areas in using their positions as political springboards to promotion beyond their regions. Their high probability of promotion has likely accounted for the absence of any pattern in bureau tenure for almost all functional specialists in this area.

Political mobility

Election to *obkom* bureau need not represent a terminal point, but a transitional stage in a political career. After their tenure, bureau members can at times be found in lower-level positions of the same regions fulfilling functional roles comparable to those with which they were associated prior to and during bureau membership.[37] For some, particularly female or non-Russian bureau members, their election may have constituted only a token gesture directed to their group; after serving a brief tenure in the *obkom* bureau, these token representatives will be transferred back to lower-level positions in the region only to be replaced on the bureau by another member of the group.[38]

For many more, however, bureau membership can represent an opportunity for career reassignment beyond their regional locales. In recent years several Western scholars have attempted to explain the factors affecting the probability of reassignment for Soviet regional officials. Particularly singled out has been the universe of *obkom* first secretaries, made most visible by published reports in the Soviet Union. Among the factors that apparently determine their reassignment (and whether a reassignment will mean a promotion or demotion) are performance in meeting industrial and agricultural quotas, political ties with patrons in the centre, regime changes in the centre and relative prestige of the region as a political base.[39]

As noted in the introductory section of this chapter, my previous research disclosed that officials transferred from these same twenty-five regions since 1954 have been reassigned over time to the same positions in other locales or to the central organs in Kiev and Moscow. A deviant case were officials from Dnepropetrovsk since 1965, whose functional backgrounds and promotion opportunities beyond their region did not seem constrained by the bureaucratic routines determining careers in the other twenty-four regions. On the basis of this deviant pattern and other comparative evidence I concluded that Dnepropetrovsk cohorts reassigned since 1965 had benefited from the close association of their region with their political patron, Brezhnev, and this association resulted in a wide range of functional specialists from Dnepropetrovsk gaining promotions.[40]

If we now examine the career patterns of the 614 bureau members in the present sample, we find that 203 were transferred outside their regions to at least one position after serving as bureau member. For several of these 203 since 1953, their first transfer was only an initial step before eventual advancement to several other posts of greater influence. Included among our 203 reassigned bureau members are those who in 1982 were the 'Second' Secretary of the All-Union Central Committee (Kirilenko), First Secretary of Ukraine (Shcherbitskii), Chairman of the All-Union Council of Ministers (Tikhonov) and other major party and government officials in the Central Committee and state ministries.[41] For others, their initial transfers outside their regions were the only positions that were identifiable subsequent to their bureau membership; in some instances their single reassignment symbolized the demise of their careers before disappearing in apparent political disgrace. Among these officials were the former *obkom* first secretaries of Odessa and

Kursk in 1970, who vanished into political obscurity after brief tenures in their new respective positions as head of the Ukrainian river-fleet administration and councillor in the Russian Republic Council of Ministers.[42]

If bureau membership does not guarantee a promotion for those reassigned outside their regions, membership on a bureau may not be a prerequisite to being reassigned and even promoted to positions outside a region. My research has uncovered the backgrounds and later positions of twenty-six individuals who originated in various lower-level positions below the *obkom* bureau level in these twenty-five regions since 1953. Although they never made it to bureau positions during their regional careers, all twenty-six somehow became recognizable enough to central cadre officials to prompt their reassignment beyond their regions. Included are A. I. Danilov, N. S. Priezzhev, L. A. Borodin and A. S. Kapto. Danilov, who rose to become rector of Tomsk State University at the pinnacle of his career, was reassigned from the region and since 1967 has been the Russian Republic Minister of Education.[43] Priezzhev, an agricultural party official whose last position in Saratov was as a rural party secretary, was reassigned from Saratov and in the last twenty years has held a series of agricultural positions as instructor-inspector in the Agricultural Department of the Central Committee, second secretary of the rural Riazan region and since 1967 first secretary of the same region.[44] Like Priezzhev, Borodin was an agricultural party official but in the Volgograd region; since the late 1950s he catapulted from his last regional position as a rural party secretary to become in succession secretary of the Chuvash Autonomous Republic, instructor in the Agricultural Department of the Central Committee, second secretary of the Bashkir Autonomous Republic and since 1967 first secretary of the Astrakhan region.[45] A classic example of an ideological specialist like Danilov, A. S. Kapto since 1966 has risen from a lower Komsomol official in Dnepropetrovsk to become editor of the Ukrainian Komsomol newspaper, then second and first secretary of the Ukrainian Komsomol, party ideology secretary of the Kiev *gorkom* and *obkom*, head of the Ukrainian Party Cultural Department and since 1979 Ukrainian party secretary for ideological-cultural affairs.[46]

Collectively, then, 229 officials originating from the twenty-five regions since 1953 have been reassigned outside their regions to at least one other position. By union republic and urbanization the 229 include 132 from Russian regions, 97 from Ukrainian regions, 73 from rural regions and 156 from urban regions. By regional areas the number reassigned ranged from 5 who originated in the Volga-Viatka area and 8 each in the Northwest and North Caucasus areas to the 52 who originated in Southeast Ukraine. By functional types the 229 included 52 agricultural specialists, 63 industrial specialists, 29 ideological specialists, 34 cadre specialists and 51 mixed generalists. For those who were bureau members, 71 at some time had been *obkom* first secretary, 36 cadres/second secretary and 33 *oblispolkom* chairman. At the opposite end of the political mobility spectrum only 3 had been chairman of the regional trade union council, and 1 each chairman of the regional control committee and head of the organizational-party work department. By total years in the *obkom* bureau, bureau longevity has not proven advantageous to any eventual reassignment. Ninety-seven of those reassigned had served less than six years on their bureaux, 72 had served six to ten years, 27 had served eleven to fifteen years and only 7 had served more than fifteen years. By geographical origin prior to their first bureau election 58 were regional natives elected to their bureaux from lower-level positions inside their regions, 21 were recruited to their bureaux from contiguous regions in the same area and 65 were designated to the bureau from outside.

Obviously, these absolute differences suggest that the very opportunities for reassignments to some extent depend on career characteristics and the nature of the region. As a composite the best opportunities for reassignment prevail for an industrial specialist designated to the bureau from outside and elected *obkom* first secretary within the five years which he served on the bureau of an urban region – especially in Southeast Ukraine. The worst opportunities for reassignment prevail for an ideological specialist transferred from another region in the area and elected control committee chairman after fifteen years in various positions of the same rural region – especially in the Volga-Viatka and Northwest.

Pertinent to our analysis is whether functional specialization by itself had any direct bearing on the kinds of positions to which these 229 were assigned at the time of their transfers from the twenty-five regions. Do officials vary in terms of their reassignments dependent on their functional specialization? And to what extent is this variation more pronounced for officials transferred from certain regions?

The answers can be found in Tables 1.13–1.16, where the 229 officials are differentiated by functional responsibilities and bureaucratic positions in their first reassignment following

Table 1.13 *Functional Specialists Reassigned from Regions by Functional Responsibilities of New Positions*

Functional specialists	Functional responsibilities of new positions (%)					
	Agricul- tural	Indus- trial	Ideo- logical	Cadre	Mixed General- ist	N
Agricultural	73	6		4	17	52
Industrial	3	69		15	13	62
Ideological			89	11		28
Cadre		6	3	88	3	34
Mixed generalists	12	27		27	35	40
Total bureau members	20	27	12	25	16	225*

$\chi^2 = 411 \cdot 54$, $P = 0 \cdot 0001$, $V = 0 \cdot 68$.
* Although there were 229 officials reassigned in 1953–79, the exact functional responsibilities of 4 in their new positions could not be ascertained.
Source: Compiled by author.

Table 1.17 *Regional Association of Functional Specialists Reassigned from Regions by Financial Responsibilities of New Positions*

	Cramer's V	N
Union republic		
Russian	0·67*	129
Ukrainian	0·71*	96
Urbanization		
rural	0·65*	72
urban	0·71*	153
Historic-economic regional areas		
Southwest Ukraine	0·82*	21
South Ukraine	0·63*	24
Southeast Ukraine	0·76*	51
Northwest	0·75	8
Central Industrial	0·69*	31
Central Black Earth	0·69*	18
Volga	0·81*	25
Volga-Viatka	1·00	4
North Caucasus	0·64	8
Urals	0·90*	8
Western Siberia	0·85*	27

* Derived from a chi-square value for this subtable statistically significant ($P < 0 \cdot 01$).
Source: Compiled by author.

departure from the region. In Tables 1.13 and 1.14 an over-whelming percentage of officials has been reassigned only to positions exactly related to long-term career specialization: 73 percent of agricultural specialists in agricultural positions, 69 percent of industrial specialists in industrial positions, 89 percent of ideological specialists in ideological positions and 88 percent of cadre specialists in cadre positions. Only mixed generalists have been exceptional; this exception itself reaffirms our logical distinction of mixed generalists as a regional career type, unique among bureau members by the diversity of functional positions over the span of their careers. The precise measured association between functional type and functional reassignment in Table 1.13 is a very high 0·68. Squared, this measure means that 46 percent of the variance in functional reassignments can be explained by differences in the career specialization of those reassigned. More simply, almost one out of every two times that officials have been transferred, the nature of their reassignment could be predicted on the basis of their functional type.

However we control for the nature of the region in Table 1.14, we find the same high association between functional type and functional reassignment. Admittedly, the measures of association for the regional areas have been derived from small subsamples in which statistical measures can be misleading. Yet the subtables for eight of the eleven regional areas produced chi-square values statistically significant, and none of the regional areas fell below a magnitude of 0·63. That the pattern is not just a statistical fluke can be clearly demonstrated by those twenty-seven officials reassigned from the Western Siberia regional area since 1953. Five each of the twenty-seven were agricultural specialists, ideological specialists, cadre specialists and mixed generalists; seven were industrial specialists. Of the twenty-seven officials, only three mixed generalists and one industrial specialist were *not* reassigned to functional positions exactly matching their long-term career specializations. It is important to consider that the twenty-seven include officials reassigned from the area as early as 1955 and as recently as 1977.[47]

Even the specific leadership positions of the reassigned officials closely parallel their different functional specializations. In Table 1.15 agricultural specialists and mixed generalists more than other types have been reassigned to leadership positions in regional-territorial party organs; transferred to the union republic or All-Union levels both functional types have generally been placed in state ministry posts. In contrast, half of all industrial specialists have been reassigned to state ministry posts, and the probability that industrial specialists would be transferred laterally to any position in local organs (party, state, or mass) has been 19–24 percent less than for agricultural

Table 1.15   Functional Specialists Reassigned from Regions by New Leadership Positions

| Functional specialists in old positions | New positions (%) | | | | | | |
| | Regional* official | | | All-Union/union republic official | | | |
	party	state	mass	party	state	mass	N
Agricultural	29	15		15	39	2	52
Industrial	10	10		24	50	7	62
Ideological	7	4		32	36	21	29
Cadre	6		6	20	11	57	34
Mixed generalist	31	8		16	31	14	51
Total bureau members	18	8	1	21	36	17	228†

$\chi^2 = 92.55$, $P = 0.0001$, $V = 0.32$.

* In this context region means either a region (*oblast*) or territory (*krai*).

† Although there were 229 officials reassigned in 1953–79, the exact position of one following his reassignment from the region could not be ascertained.

Source: Compiled by author.

Table 1.16   Regional Association of Functional Specialists Reassigned from Regions by New Leadership Position

	Cramer's V	N
Union republic		
Russian	0·38*	131
Ukrainian	0·30*	97
Urbanization		
rural	0·32	72
urban	0·34*	156
Historic-economic regional areas		
Southwest Ukraine	0·45	21
South Ukraine	0·37	24
Southeast Ukraine	0·38*	52
Northwest	0·59	8
Central Industrial	0·54†	31
Central Black Earth	0·62†	18
Volga	0·52†	25
Volga-Viatka	0·79	4
North Caucasus	0·75	8
Urals	0·43	10
Western Siberia	0·47	27

* Derived from a chi-square value for this subtable statistically significant ($P < 0.01$).

† Derived from a chi-square value for this subtable statistically significant ($P < 0.05$).

Source: Compiled by author.

specialists and mixed generalists. Nine of every ten ideological and cadre specialists have been designated solely to union republic and All-Union positions; a major difference between the two is the much higher percentage of ideological specialists assigned to state organs and the understandably higher percentage of cadre specialists to mass organs.

Table 1.16 reveals a bureaucratic routine in cadre reassignment effectively maintained over twenty-seven years, two regimes (Khrushchev and Brezhnev) and widely different regional contexts. The measured associations between functional type and position register almost equally strong magnitudes in Russian, Ukrainian, rural and urban regions. The determining importance of specialization has found even the fifty-two officials from Southeast Ukraine, by far the largest number reassigned from any area, transferred to positions relative to their functional type. Among the eleven former Southeast Ukrainian officials transferred to regional-territorial positions, 64 percent were either agricultural specialists or mixed generalists; among the fourteen transferred to state ministry posts, 64 percent were industrial specialists; and even among the eleven transferred to union republic or All-Union mass organs, 64 percent were cadre specialists. Thus, the large number of officials reassigned from Southeast Ukraine (especially from the Dnepropetrovsk region) may be explained by the capriciousness of a political patron like Brezhnev and the subjective features of elite advancement in Soviet politics dependent on informal patron–client networks, but even these fifty-two officials have been limited in the nature of their first reassignments by a procedure reflecting a predictable and formal bureaucratic continuity of the system over twenty-seven years.

Conclusion

The political fortunes of Soviet local cadres cannot be understood apart from the distinct specializations by which they have been marked since entering the party and embarking on full-time political careers. We can conclude from our analysis that their career specialization will affect their probability of election as *obkom* bureau member, the specific position which they hold as bureau member, the locale from which they have been recruited onto the bureaux, the number of years after entering the party before bureau election and, to some extent, the number of years they remain bureau members. Their specialization will also determine whether they are reassigned from a region and, once reassigned, the functional position in which they find themselves.

No less important than specialization has been the nature of the region in which they begin their careers. Bureau members elected first secretary, cadres/second secretary, chairman of the trade union council or control committee and Komsomol first secretary have not been the same in all regions, but different functional types have consistently held these positions dependent on the union republic or urban-rural context of the region. In urban regions industrial specialists are consistently recruited from lower-level cadres inside the region and enter the party fewer years before election than rural bureau members. And the very opportunities for advancement beyond a region have been best for industrial specialists in urban regions and worst for ideological specialists in rural regions.

Political fortunes also vary dependent on the particular regional area in which cadres originate. A comparison of statistical measures among regional areas in Tables 1.6, 1.8, 1.11 and 1.12 shows that bureau members in Southeast Ukraine differ less noticeably by functional type than bureau members in any of the other ten areas. The relative sameness of bureau members in Southeast Ukraine means that, in any regime period since 1953, a very high percentage has been industrial specialists recruited inside the region within eleven to twenty years of entering the party and with bureau tenures fluctuating randomly by functional type. In contrast, officials from the Western Siberia area – otherwise quite similar economically to the Southeast Ukraine – have varied quite predictably in their careers consistent with differences in functional specialization. All six measured associations between functional type and career dimensions in Western Siberia register a very strong interdependency, ranging from 0·31 (regime periods) to 0·85 (functional specialization of reassignment). The only measures above 0·29 for Southeast Ukrainian bureau members are those for functional specialization and position of reassigned official.

Products of a political system notorious for encouraging conformity and stifling initiative among its political subordinates Soviet local cadres have, none the less, been treated differently by central officials according to functional specialization and locale. Countering their normal reluctance to tolerate any diversity within the system central officials may have unintentionally fostered just that diversity within their own political ranks by the consistent manner in which local cadres have been differentially recruited and reassigned.

Central officials cannot remain indifferent to the potential uncertainties and long-range consequences of this cadre policy.

Role theory would lead us to speculate that, if their careers and very opportunities for advancement depend primarily on their functional specialization, Soviet cadres cannot but conceive of themselves less as interchangeable cogs in an authoritarian bureaucracy than as indispensable specialist subgroups in a political system. To the extent they subjectively identify themselves and their careers with their functional subgroups local cadres may have become more assertive in promoting policies directly beneficial in the long run to their particular functional subgroup. With their very careers at stake policy conflict among these specialized subgroups may have taken on an additional heated dimension.

We might also speculate that their early role identification with specific functional subgroups may further the process of institutional pluralism and coalitionbuilding within the Soviet political establishment. Cross-pressured by their career identification with their functional subgroups Soviet cadres promoted to positions in central organs may be less subject to rigid polarization along the ideological, ethnic, generational and factional lines which divide them. The potential for bargaining and compromise may have been enhanced by the degree to which these other cleavages overlap with the added functional career variance among Soviet cadres. Because of the overriding importance of functional specialization in their careers, a reform-minded Russian industrial specialist in his forties aligned with the Romanov faction in the central leadership may come to perceive more in common with a conservative Ukrainian industrial specialist in his sixties aligned with the Shcherbitskii faction in the central leadership than otherwise would be the case. Thus, in upgrading the specialized expertise of local cadres to preserve the authoritarian state, central officials may have institutionalized a basis for conflict in their own ranks that tempers the authoritarian rigidity and extremes of their leadership.

Notes: Chapter 1

This chapter is adapted from Joel C. Moses, 'The impact of nomenklatura in Soviet regional elite recruitment', *Soviet Union*, vol. 8, pt 1 (1981), pp. 62–102, and appears by permission. For financial support in research, I am indebted to Iowa State University for a foreign-travel grant and computer funding in 1979. I should also express my gratitude to Mr Keith Bush, director of the Radio Liberty Research Division in Munich, West Germany, who allowed me to utilize the Division's personnel files, and to Professor Mack Shelley, my colleague in political science at Iowa State University, who provided wise counsel in the statistical phase of my analysis.

1 George Fischer, *The Soviet System and Modern Society* (New York: Atherton Press, 1968); Frederic J. Fleron, 'Representation of career types in the Soviet leadership', in R. Barry Farrell (ed.), *Political Leadership in Eastern Europe and the Soviet Union* (Chicago: Aldine, 1971), pp. 108–39; Robert E. Blackwell, 'The Soviet political elite: alternative recruitment policies at the *obkom* level', *Comparative Politics*, vol. 6, no. 1 (1973), pp. 99–121; and Kenneth Jowitt, 'Inclusion and mobilization in European Leninist regimes', *World Politics*, vol. 28, no. 1 (1975), pp. 77–8, 82–4.

2 While Soviet officials have persistently denied any basis to claims of a division between specialists and non-specialists within the party bureaucracy, even General Secretary Leonid Brezhnev, in remarks on cadre policy during his Central Committee report to the Twenty-sixth CPSU Congress in 1981, criticized specialists recruited into party leadership positions for political insensitivity in the conduct of their new party positions and 'administrative-economic methods'; Brezhnev contrasted their insensitivity with the virtues of professional party politicians, who have demonstrated themselves more responsive to the demands and interests of workers because of their lifelong 'personal experience' in the 'school of life and practical work among the masses', *Pravda*, 24 February 1981, p. 8.

3 Joel C. Moses, 'Regional cohorts and political mobility in the USSR: the case of Dnepropetrovsk', *Soviet Union*, vol. 3, no. 1 (1976), pp. 63–91, and 'Women in political roles', in Dorothy Atkinson, Alexander Dallin and Gail Lapidus (eds), *Women in Russia* (Stanford, Calif.: Stanford University Press, 1977), pp. 333–53; John H. Miller, 'Cadres policy in nationality areas – recruitment of CPSU first and second secretaries in non-Russian republics of the USSR', *Soviet Studies*, vol. 29, no. 1 (1977), pp. 3–36; Robert E. Blackwell, 'Cadres policy in the Brezhnev era', *Problems of Communism*, vol. 28, no. 2 (1979), pp. 29–42; Seweryn Bialer, *Stalin's Successors: Leadership, Stability and Change in the Soviet Union* (New York: Cambridge University Press, 1980), pp. 65–126; and Jerry F. Hough, 'The generation gap and the Brezhnev succession', *Problems of Communism*, vol. 28, no. 4 (1979), pp. 1–16, and *Soviet Leadership in Transition* (Washington, DC: Brookings Institution, 1980), pp. 37–78.

4 Carl Linden, *Khrushchev and the Soviet Leadership, 1957–1964* (Baltimore, Md: Johns Hopkins University Press, 1966); Moshe Lewin, *Political Undercurrents in Soviet Economic Debates* (Princeton, NJ: Princeton University Press, 1974), pp. 300–55; Roy A. Medvedev, *On Socialist Democracy* (New York: Norton, 1977), pp. 48–65; Alexander Yanov, *Détente after Brezhnev: The Domestic Roots of Soviet Foreign Policy* (Berkeley, Calif.: Institute of International Studies, University of California, Berkeley, 1977), pp. 5–21, 43–73; and Stephen F. Cohen, 'The friends and foes of change: reformism and conservatism in the Soviet Union', *Slavic Review*, vol. 38, no. 2 (1979), pp. 187–202.

5 Jerry F. Hough, 'The party *apparatchiki*', in H. Gordon Skilling and Franklyn Griffiths (eds), *Interest Groups in Soviet Politics* (Princeton, NJ: Princeton University Press, 1971), pp. 47–92; Jerry F. Hough and Merle Fainsod, *How the Soviet Union is Governed* (Cambridge, Mass.: Harvard University Press, 1979), pp. 409–48, 491–510.

6 Hough and Fainsod, op. cit., pp. 424–9, 445–8, 497–505; Grey Hodnett,

Leadership in the Soviet National Republics: A Quantitative Study of Recruitment Policy (Oakville, Ontario: Mosaic Press, 1978), pp. 130–6, 177–94, 224–302, 395–6; Joel C. Moses, *Regional Party Leadership and Policy-Making in the USSR* (New York: Praeger, 1974), pp. 162–5, 179–80, 194–5, and 'Local leadership integration in the Soviet Union', in Daniel N. Nelson (ed.), *Local Politics in Communist Countries* (Lexington, Ky: University Press of Kentucky, 1980), pp. 34–9, 42–5.

7　Robert V. Daniels, 'Office holding and elite status: the Central Committee of the CPSU', in Paul Cocks, Robert V. Daniels and Nancy Whittier Heer (eds), *The Dynamics of Soviet Politics* (Cambridge, Mass.: Harvard University Press, 1976), pp. 77–95.

8　For previous research on bureau members in these twenty-five regions and my rationale in assuming that certain positions ascribe bureau membership, see my *Regional Party Leadership*, op. cit., pp. 159–246, and 'Local leadership integration', op. cit., pp. 23–45. On the composition of *obkom* bureaux, also see Philip D. Stewart, *Political Power in the Soviet Union: A Study of Decision-Making in Stalingrad* (New York: Bobbs-Merrill, 1968), pp. 88–133; and Jerry F. Hough, *The Soviet Prefects: The Local Party Organs in Industrial Decision-Making* (Cambridge, Mass.: Harvard University Press, 1969), p. 333, and 'The Generation Gap', op. cit.

9　As illustrative examples: (*a*) Iu. V. Sedykh – first deputy chairman (1966–8) and agriculture secretary (1969–71) – in Vologda and prior to 1966 director of the regional agricultural administration; (*b*) V. A. Belousov – agriculture secretary (1960–2) – in Volgograd and prior to 1960 chairman of a rural district, deputy director of the regional agricultural administration, first secretary of a rural district and head of the *obkom* agricultural department; (*c*) V. P. Borodin – agriculture secretary (1962–5) and chairman (1965–71) – in Volgograd and prior to 1962 instructor in the agricultural department, chairman and first secretary of a rural district and head of the *obkom* agricultural department.

10　Thus, with the exception of 1961–4, the Kursk chairman since 1954 has always been the head of the *obkom* agricultural department when first elected a bureau member: S. I. Cherepukhin (1954–61), I. I. Dudkin (1964–71), D. V. Kamynin (1971–6) and N. I. Zhurkin (1976–9). The same was true for the position of agriculture secretary in Volgograd in 1954–65: Belousov and Borodin (n. 9, above) and their predecessor in the position – N. A. Nepokupnoi (1954–60) – all headed the agricultural department before they were elected agriculture secretary.

11　Thus, Sedykh (n. 9, above) became deputy head of the CPSU Agricultural Department; Belousov (note 8, above), Kursk *oblispolkom* chairman and later USSR Deputy Agricultural Procurement Minister; Borodin (n. 9, above), deputy head of the CPSU Agricultural Department and later USSR First Deputy Agricultural Minister. Establishing the political legacy for agricultural specialists from Volgograd I. S. Pankin, a preceding Volgograd chairman (1950–61) was head of the CPSU Agricultural Department (RSFSR) in 1961–4.

12　As illustrative examples: (*a*) I. Ye. Liaboga – industry secretary (1962–73) – in Kharkov and prior to 1962 first secretary of the Ordzhonikdze borough in the capital and director of the Ballbearing Works Plant; (*b*) V. G. Boiko – first secretary of the regional capital (1974–6), second secretary (1976–8) and *oblispolkom* chairman (1979) – in Dnepropetrovsk and prior to 1974 instructor to head of the Krivoi Rog industrial-construction department, deputy head of the *obkom* construction-urban economy department, head of the *obkom* construction department and chairman of the regional capital; (*c*) A. V. Dynkin – industry secretary (1962–4) – in Volgograd and prior to 1962 head of the *obkom* construction department and chairman of the regional capital (and, after 1964, the deputy chairman for construction in the *oblispolkom*).

13 Thus, since 1960 two first secretaries and an industry secretary in Perm – K. T. Galanshin, B. F. Korotkov and L. A. Kondratov – had all been first secretaries of the Berezniki *gorkom* in the region when first elected bureau members. The current first secretary of Perm, B. V. Konoplev, entered the bureau in 1954 following two years as party organizer of a hydroelectric construction site on the Kama River, where Galanshin had also worked in the late 1940s.

14 Thus, Galanshin (n. 13, above) became the USSR Minister for the Paper-Cellulose Industry; K. K. Cherednichenko (a former first secretary of the regional capital and *obkom* first secretary in Volgograd), USSR Deputy Minister for the Chemical Industry; V. V. Listov (a former first secretary of the regional capital in Kemerovo), an unspecified position in the USSR Ministry for the Chemical Industry and later Head of the CPSU Chemical Industry Department; and B. A. Steshov (a former industry secretary in the Crimea), the industry secretary of Moldavia and later USSR Deputy Minister for Machine-Building in Light and Food Industry and Domestic Appliances.

15 As illustrative examples: (*a*) N. F. Pichugin – editor of the regional newspaper (1971–9) – in Perm and prior to 1971 a correspondent for the newspaper and chairman of the regional state committee for radio and television; (*b*) O. K. Sazonova – ideology secretary (1964–75) – in Tambov and prior to 1964 regional Komsomol first secretary of Kaluga; (*c*) V. E. Titov – editor of the regional newspaper (1970–3) and ideology secretary (1974–9) – in Smolensk. In Novosibirsk, several ideological specialists later promoted to head the *obkom* agitprop and science-educational institutions departments, the regional Komsomol, or the regional state cultural administration were first secretary of the Soviet borough early in their careers; the Soviet borough as a training-ground for ideological specialists encompasses several scientific-research institutes (the so-called 'Academic City' of Novosibirsk).

16 Thus, Iu. A. Skliarov (a former ideology secretary in Kharkov) became Deputy Head of the CPSU Propaganda Department; A. A. Nebenzia (a former ideology secretary in Volgograd), Deputy Chairman of the USSR State Publishing Committee; and V. K. Grudinin (a former editor of the regional newspaper in Kaliningrad), Director of *Sovetskaia Rossiia* and later First Deputy Chairman of the RSFSR State Publishing Committee.

17 As illustrative examples: (*a*) A. P. Trutnev, regional Komsomol first secretary (1956–61), chairman of the regional trade union council (1962–6) and cadres/second secretary (1966–71) in Zaporozhe; (*b*) V. A. Sviatotskii – chairman of the regional trade union council (1970–1) and cadres/second secretary (1971–9) – in Lvov and prior to 1970 second secretary of the regional capital; (*c*) S. D. Stepanov – chairman of the regional People's Control Committee (1976–9) – in Volgograd and prior to 1976 head of the *obkom* administrative organs department; (*d*) A. N. Kopychev – head of the organizational-party work department (1966–7) –in Tambov and subsequently secretary of the *oblispolkom*.

18   As illustrative examples: (*a*) A. A. Makarevskii, regional Komsomol
     first secretary (1957–8) and director of the regional MVD (1969–70) in
     Smolensk; (*b*) Iu. P. Tupchenko, regional Komsomol first secretary
     (1956–9) and chief of the regional KGB (1961–6) in Rostov; (*c*) F. P.
     Tkachenko, head of the *obkom* party organs department (1961) and
     director of the MVD (1970) in Lvov.
19   Thus, G. I. Dubrava (a former Komsomol first secretary in Kharkov)
     became head of the Union Republics Department of the Komsomol and
     later an instructor in the CPSU organizational-party work department;
     L. N. Kurzin (a former chairman of the trade union council in
     Kemerovo), chairman of the USSR Trade Union of Geological-Ex-
     ploration Workers; B. N. Rogatin (a former Komsomol first secretary in
     Kemerovo), head of the Sport and Mass-Defense Work Department of
     the Komsomol and later chairman of the Komsomol Auditing Commis-
     sion; and V. I. Zaluzhnyi (a former second secretary in Kemerovo),
     deputy chairman of the Party- State Control Committee and later first
     deputy chairman of the All-Union People's Control Committee.
20   As illustrative examples: (*a*) V. P. Rusin – *oblispolkom* chairman
     (1963–74) – in Transcarpathia and prior to 1963 the regional procurator
     and a member of the Ukrainian delegation to the United Nations; (*b*) I.
     Z. Komissarov, both ideology secretary (1955–8) and regional trade
     union council chairman (1966–70) in Tambov; (*c*) N. N. Semeniuk
     ideology secretary (1969–75, 1976–9) and head of the organizational-
     party work department (1975–6) – in Transcarpathia and prior to 1969 a
     regional Komsomol secretary and first secretary of a rural district; (*d*) V.
     A. Artamanov – cadres/second secretary (1973–7) – in Odessa and prior
     to 1973 first secretary of the Krivoi–Rog *gorkom* for six years in Dnep-
     ropetrovsk; (*e*) A. A. Ulanov – first secretary of the regional capital
     (1967–70) – in Dnepropetrovsk and prior to 1967 head of the *obkom*
     sciences and educational institutions department.
21   Thus, Rusin (n. 20, above) became Deputy Ukrainian Minister for
     Social Security and a member of the USSR Academy of Medical Sci-
     ences (!); Artamanov (n. 20, above), first deputy chairman of the Ukrai-
     nian People's Control Committee; and Ulanov (n. 20, above), head of
     the organizational-party work department for Ukraine, an *obkom* sec-
     retary in Voroshilovgrad and ambassador to Liberia.
22   Hough, 'The party *apparatchiki*', op. cit., pp. 72–87.
23   'Regional cohorts and political mobility in the USSR', op. cit., pp. 78–
     82.
24   'Local leadership integration in the Soviet Union', op. cit., pp. 42–5.
25   The positive benefits of cadre stability since 1965 and the more careful
     selection of local cadres relative to their prior administrative experience
     are central motifs to be found in the following as examples: P. A.
     Leonov, 'Razvitie XXIV s"ezdom KPSS leninskikh printsipov raboty s
     kadrami', *Kommunist*, no. 18 (December 1971) pp. 46–57; V. A.
     Kadeikin, A. D. Pedosov and V. M. Shapko (eds), *Voprosy vnutripar-
     tiinoi zhizni i rukovodiashchei deiatel-nosti KPSS na sovremennom etape*
     (Moscow: Mysl, 1974), pp. 183–202; D. M. Kukin, V. A. Kulinchenko,
     A. M. Musaev and V. A. Iatskov (eds), *Voprosy raboty KPSS s kadrami
     na sovremennom etape* (Moscow: Mysl, 1976), pp. 98–103, 164, 171–2;
     M. P. Trunov, *Organizatorskaia rabota partiinogo komiteta* (Moscow:
     Politizdat, 1978), pp. 55–64; and S. I. Surnichenko, *et al.*, *Organizat-
     sionnopartiinaia rabota* (Moscow: Mysl, 1978), pp. 325–7.

26 Kadeikin, *et al.*, *Voprosy*, op. cit., pp. 187–8; V. K. Beliakov and N. A. Zolotarev, *Organizatsiia udesiateriaet sily* (Moscow: Politizdat, 1975), p. 171; and V. V. Shcherbitskii, 'Podbor i vospitanie kadrov, povyshenie otvetstvennosti rukovoditilei', *Partiinaia zhizn*, no. 15 (1981), p. 9.

27 G. Vorob'ev and V. Loskutov, 'Sel'skokhoziaistvennyi otdel obkoma partii', *Partiinaia zhizn*, no. 15 (1974), pp. 31–41; Iu. Kuz'min, 'Promyshlenno-transportnyi otdel gorkoma partii', *Partiinaia zhizn*, no. 12 (1975), pp. 27–34; Iu. Litvintsev, 'Zabotimsia o stabil'nosti ideologicheskikh kadrov', *Partiinaia zhizn*, no. 12 (1975), pp. 64–9; N. Kudriashova, 'Biuro i apparat gorkoma partii', *Partiinaia zhizn*, no. 13 (1975), pp. 25–32; and F. Loshchenkov, 'Glavnoe zveno', *Izvestiia*, 12 November 1975.

28 A very good recent example of such a study is T. H. Rigby, 'The Soviet regional leadership: the Brezhnev generation', *Slavic Review*, vol. 37, no. 1 (1978), pp. 1–24. The 'regional leadership' in Rigby's title are the *obkom* first secretaries in the Russian Republic.

29 In the sense that the concept 'structure of political opportunities' has been employed by Western political scientists to analyze the formal and informal determinants and career patterns of political advancement by officials in a nation-state like those in the United States. The concept is most closely identified with Joseph A. Schlesinger, *Ambition and Politics* (Chicago: Rand McNally, 1966).

30 Space limitations prevent me from including my coding scheme by which I systematically classified the 614 bureau members. By written request, I shall be willing to send any interested reader a copy of the coding scheme, a computerized list of the 614 members by classified type, and examples of the sources which I used in determining the classification of different types. From these, the reader can judge the reliability of my coding and the validity of my classification. Examples include those cited in nn. 9–21 of this chapter.

31 See my *Regional Party Leadership*, op. cit., and 'Local leadership integration in the Soviet Union', op. cit. That the career patterns of local cadres may differ dependent on the republic or urban-rural context of the locale has been an underlying methodological assumption by most Western analysts of Soviet elites such as Robert Blackwell, Jerry Hough and Grey Hodnett cited in this chapter. The actual extent to which Soviet elites differ, seemingly in defiance of the highly centralized nature of the leadership-selection process, has been difficult to verify with our limited information and hard data about Soviet local officials.

32 For example, Jerry Hough contends that among other selections within the organizational-party work department of the Central Committee Secretariat are those based on a geographical division of responsibility for the Ukraine and Moldavia, the Baltic republics and Belorussia, Central Asia, Kazakhstan, Transcaucasia and specific major territories of the RSFSR; see Hough and Fainsod, op. cit., p. 421.

33 On the Cramer's statistic, see Hubert Blalock, *Social Statistics*, 2nd edn (New York: McGraw-Hill, 1972), pp. 295–8; William Buchanan, *Understanding Political Variables*, 2nd edn (New York: Scribner's, 1974), pp. 190–1; and Jean Dickinson Gibbons, *Nonparametric Methods for Quantitative Analysis* (New York: Holt, Rinehart & Winston, 1976), pp. 330–3.

34 In Kharkov N. K. Kirichenko had been first secretary of the regional capital Komsomol and second secretary of the *oblast* Komsomol before his tenure as regional first secretary (1950–5); following his tenure, he became second secretary of the Ukrainian Komsomol. Also from Khar-

kov G. I. Dubrava (1955–61) became head of the Komsomol Organs for Union Republic Department and later an instructor in the CPSU Party Organs Department following his regional tenure; and V. P. Duravkin was regional Komsomol second secretary for at least five years prior to his election as the first secretary in 1974. In Novosibirsk V. I. Koval as regional first secretary (1961–4) then became head of the Sport and Defense-Mass Work Department in the All-Union Komsomol before a series of parallel reassignments in the State Committee for Physical Culture and Sport; and the three most recent regional first secretaries – B. D. Namestnikov (1966–71), A. G. Shmaraev (1972–5) and I. P. Savenko (1976–9) – were all regional second or third secretaries for several years before accession to first secretary.

35   Typified by the trend among *obkom* bureau members in Rostov through-out the 1970s: I. A. Bondarenko – *obkom* first secretary (1966–81); N. M. Ivanitskii – capital *gorkom* first secretary (1970–3) and *obkom* second secretary (1973–9); I. N. Soldatov – *obkom* agriculture secretary (1969–79); M. E. Teslia – *obkom* ideology secretary (1967–79); N. D. Bekikov – head of *obkom* organizational-party work department (1970–81); S. N. Sabaneev capital *gorkom* first secretary (1966–70) and *oblispolkom* chairman (1970–9); N. I. Semeniuta – editor of regional newspaper (1971–9); and B. I. Golovets – capital *gorkom* first secretary (1973–9).

36   Bialer, *Stalin's Successors*, op. cit., pp. 120–2.

37   Moses, *Regional Party Leadership*, op. cit., pp. 179–81.

38   Moses, 'Women in political roles', op. cit., pp. 337–40.

39   Philip D. Stewart, *et al.*, 'Political mobility and the Soviet political process: a partial test of two models', *American Political Science Review*, vol. 66, no. 4 (1972), pp. 1269–94; Philip D. Stewart, 'Toward more adequate models of elite mobility in communist polities', paper presented at International Studies Association Convention, Dallas, Texas, USA, 15–18 March 1972; Robert E. Blackwell and William Hulbary, 'Political mobility among Soviet *obkom* elites: the effects of regime, social back-grounds and career development', *American Journal of Political Science*, vol. 17, no. 4 (1973), pp. 721–43; and Blackwell, 'Cadres policy in the Brezhnev era', op. cit., pp. 35–7.

40   'Regional cohorts and political mobility in the USSR', op. cit.

41   Among the 203 former bureau members are included (by regional origin and bureau tenure) in 1979 M. S. Solomentsev (Rostov, 1964–6), chair-man of the RSFSR Council of Ministers, N. K. Dybenko (Novosibirsk, 1962–77), second secretary of the Lithuanian Republic, A. I. Shibaev (Saratov, 1955–76), chairman of the All-Union Central Trade Union Council, G. S. Zolotukhin (Tambov, 1944–66), USSR Minister of Agri-cultural Procurements, A. I. Struev (Perm, 1954–8), USSR Minister of Trade and V. M. Chebrikov (Dnepropetrovsk, 1960–7), deputy chairman of the KGB.

42   Moses, *Regional Party Leadership*, op. cit., pp. 50–3, 75–81.

43   See *Deputaty Verkhovnogo Soveta SSSR* (1966), and *Current Soviet Leaders*, vol. 2, no. 2 (1975), p. 15.

44   See *Deputaty Verkhovnogo Soveta SSSR* (1974), and *Ezhegodnik Bol'shoi Sovetskoi Entsiklopedii* (1977).

45   See *Ezhegodnik* (1977).

46   See the biography of Kapto in *Pravda Ukrainy*, 27 April 1979.

47   In 1955 I. D. Iakovlev, *obkom* first secretary in Novosibirsk and classified

as an agricultural specialist in our study, was reassigned to the position of the Kazakhstan Second Secretary at the beginning of the Virgin Lands program. R. G. Ianovskii, the most recently transferred official from the area in our sample, was first secretary of the cultural-scientific Soviet borough (n. 15, above) through 1974, later served as head of the *obkom* science and educational institutions department, and some time after 1976 was transferred to the center, where he is currently the deputy head of the CPSU Department of Science and Educational Institutions. Ianovskii was classified as an ideological specialist in our sample.

2

Nomenklatura: Check on Localism?

JOHN MILLER

Introduction

This chapter is an investigation of the geographical dimension of central personnel policy in the USSR. About a thousand cases where Soviet officials were transferred from one province to another have been analyzed to see what light may be thrown on central policies and practices regarding regional specialization of officials.

Many large or heterogeneous political systems have practiced such things as the 'rule of avoidance' (forbidding official employment in one's place of birth), or systematic rotation of officials from a tour of duty in one place to a tour of duty in another.[1] The aim has been to reduce undue identification of officials with a region and hence the strengthening of regional interest representation or regional 'lobbies', with possibly destabilizing or even centrifugal tendencies entailed. It has been accepted that the price to be paid for such rotation or dispersal arrangements is a loss of specialist experience; indeed, in some such systems there has been an explicit policy of promoting generalists or amateurs.

A priori one would have expected such practices in the Soviet system.[2] Party supremacy (most of us would take for granted) has entailed the limitation and control of interest groups (inside or outside the party) and the important methods have included control of communications, association and staffing. In principle two of these methods, control of communications and association, should be much less effective against interest groups based on locality, because it is difficult to prevent administrators in the same place exchanging information and discussing common problems. So one might have expected that the third method, control of staffing, would be invoked the more thoroughly to keep locally based interest representation in hand. And there is ample evidence that the turnover and the local identifications of officials have been matters of concern and disagreement among the 'party managers'. The obligatory turnover provisions introduced into the Party Rules under Khrushchev, and speedily removed after his fall,[3] must have had the effect, *inter alia*, of promoting turnover from place to place. The Brezhnev administration inaugurated an era of 'stability of cadres' and, as an aspect of this, the General Secretary singled out at the 1971 Party Congress the cutback in the dispatch of first secretaries from the centre to *obkomy*;[4] that is, he virtually disavowed a Soviet 'rule of avoidance'.

Since it is *highly* unlikely that *obkom* authorities can get together to arrange transfers of personnel between *oblasti* (provinces), without reference to their administrative superiors,[5] by collecting transfers across *oblast* lines an analyst is collecting transfers which virtually by definition will fall into a *nomenklatura* at either All-Union or republic level.[6] And in the case of the RSFSR, which has no republic Central Committee or *apparat*, the assumption seems inescapable that personnel transfers between oblasti are arranged either at All-Union Central Committee level, or by some other body at higher than *oblast* level, of whose existence we know nothing. Exactly which posts are on the All-Union Central Committee *nomenklatura* and which on those of the republic Central Committees is a matter not yet sufficiently clarified. But it is difficult to imagine a post-*oblispolkom* chairman, for example – being on the All-Union Central Committee *nomenklatura* in the case of the RSFSR and on that of the republic Central Committee elsewhere; this would be to posit greater centralization of staffing decisions in the RSFSR than in the non-Russian republics. So the suggestion arises at the outset that cross-*oblast* transfers may almost all be matters for the All-Union Central Committee *nomenklatura*. It is a subsidiary purpose of this chapter to try to clarify the precise scope of the latter.

To pursue the chain of *a priori* reasoning the central authorities cannot afford a policy of complete *laissez-faire* toward regional lobbies, but neither can they prevent the accumulation of administrative experience and expertise. Indeed, certain types of experience or expertise will be welcome; so the center will have to live with a certain level of attempts to utilize this to strengthen the bargaining position of a region. One should expect to find a situation of balance between encouragement and discouragement of accumulated expertise in a region's problems; perhaps also one of checks on the deployment of this expertise. Depending on the strength of central distrust of regional pressure (potential or actual), one could envisage three patterns in which transfers from place to place might be distributed.

(1)   Transfers from one *oblast* to another might be, to a high degree, transfers to any other *oblast* in the Union, seemingly at random and cutting across geographical, economic, or cultural similarities. This would indicate a tough central policy against specialization by officials and the contribution such specialization can make to a region's bargaining position.

(2)   Frequent and perhaps even a statistically significant number of transfers might be observed between economically similar but widely separated *oblasti* – between Donetsk, Chelyabinsk and Kemerovo, for example, or between Tambov, Krasnodar and the wheatlands of North Kazakhstan. Like this, the center would be restricting careers based on a single region, but not specialization in particular sectors of the economy or of administration. This might indicate a more moderate level of concern to control regional interest representation. Personnel imported regularly from the outside would tend to act as a check on the coalescence of a lobby, but it would be a less serious check if the imported personnel were familiar with regional problems of a similar type.

(3)   Transfers might be frequently, even significantly, to a *neighboring oblast*, one which might often be economically similar, and one which in any case might be an ally in budgetary or other negotiations. This would seem to be the 'weakest' central policy toward regionalism in that little attempt was being made to combat it by systematic rotation. If observation suggested this pattern of cross-*oblast* transfers, it might invite a number of interpretations, for instance: (*a*) that regional lobbies do not pose the threat that many, including Chinese mandarins, have perceived in them and hence need little controlling; or (*b*) that regional interest representation is already immensely successful, and that in the center – willingly or reluctantly – accedes to regional demands in the personnel deployment field; or (*c*) that the center has found some other means of restraining regionalism. All these three interpretations would have in common that the All-Union party *nomenklatura* is more routine, and less interven-

tionist, than is generally supposed, or more routine than it used to be.

In what follows I hope to be able to show that some of these hypotheses are more plausible than others, and at the same time fill out our picture of how the *nomenklatura* process works in detail.

The Sample: Features, Limitations and Technical Terms

The aim was to collect at least 1,000 fully documented cases of personnel transfer from one *oblast* to another. The resulting data-set contained information on 1,069 such transfers, not all complete in every detail, involving 472 persons.[7] A 'transfer' was recorded whenever a person moved to a new job across the boundaries of an *oblast* or equivalent administrative unit, the latter including *kraia*, autonomous *oblasti* or autonomous Soviet Socialist Republics (ASSRs), union republics (if not subdivided into *oblasti*) and *oblasti* subordinate to *kraia*.[8] An attempt was made to let the sample be as representative a cross-section of such transfers as Soviet sources allow, with a minimum of exclusions imposed by the investigator. As regards occupation, no notice was taken of rank, promotion, or demotion, nor of task specialization, *except* that transfers within the armed forces and the KGB were excluded. The reasons for excluding these was that the military and state security almost certainly have staffing rules distinct from those applying to most administration, rules by which rotation would be the norm and local influence on central personnel deployment minimal.[9] As regards time, transfers since 1944 were collected, with a very small number (five) being accepted from the war period when not to do so would have broken up an interesting sequence of provincial appointments.

Two relevant avenues of inquiry had to be ignored and postponed for a more extensive study. First, place of birth was not recorded. Birthplaces are usually specified only in obituaries and the sample would have had to be considerably larger before a useful number of birthplaces could have been collected. So this study is one of geographical rotation, and not one of the 'rule of avoidance' in the strict Chinese sense. Secondly, no attempt was made to compare cross-*oblast* transfers with intra-*oblast* movement, with regard, for instance, to the relative frequency of either type of movement or to the specific rank,

Table 2.1 Transfers by Level and Sector of Position

Transfers of personnel
To Jobs
From Jobs
At level

From Jobs At level		All-Union			Republic			Oblast In task sector			City			Raion			Totals
		P	S	O	P	S	O	P	S	O	P	S	O	P	S	O	
All-Union	P	2	3		21	3		46	3		1			2			79
	S	2			1	2		4	21								30
	O					1		1									2
Republic	P	12	12	2	8	2		58	4		3			2			103
	S	2	7		4	7		29	23			2					74
	O		1	1				11	1								14
Oblast	P	62	16		56	50	8	194	39		5			3			433
	S	6	19		4	34	1	38	57		1			3			163
	O	3		2			3	2	1	5			1				17

															Total
City															
P	5	1	7	1	2	16	1	1	1	1					36
S	1	2	2	7											14
O		1	1	1											3
Raion															
P	8	7	2	1	18	4	8								48
S	1	1	1	1											4
O		1													1
Totals	100	60	5	110	104	16	418	156	7	12	10	1	21	1	1,021

P=party, S=state, O=other.

Note: Included at the All-Union level are attendance at the All-Union Higher Party Schools (under 'Party') and ambassadorships (under 'State'); at *oblast* level posts in the administration of republic capital cities; the *state* category includes economic administration; 'Other' are predominantly posts in the trade unions, the Komsomol, or the Academy of Sciences.

occupational, or nationality characteristics of each.[10] This is a study of cross-*oblast* transfers only, and of the sorts of jobs or careers in which the cross-*oblast* transfer occurs.

Talking succinctly about the analysis of these data involves a certain amount of shorthand. The conventions regarding the words 'transfer' and '*oblast*' have been explained above. In addition, a distinction will be made between 'supplier' and 'recipient' regions or offices. And it becomes important to distinguish between provincial posts in an administrative sense – for instance, in the administration of Moscow City – and posts at the 'center', that is, in the All-Union Central Committee, Council of Ministers, or other All-Union level institutions; similarly, union republic level administration needs to be distinguished from *oblast* or lower-level administration in that republic. So frequent reference will be made to the All-Union or republic 'center', and the label 'province' or 'provincial' will be applied to all posts not at one of the 'centers', even if they are in the administration of Moscow or Kiev cities.

Analysis of Transfers by Occupation

A complete matrix of the transfers in the sample specifying the task sector, administrative level and rank of the posts to and from which personnel moved would be as large as a room. So Table 2.1 summarizes the transfers by task sector and administrative level only; by itself it prompts more questions than it answers but it provides a useful framework in which some important issues concerning interregional transfers and the central *nomenklatura* can be examined in more detail.

The broad implications of Table 2.1 are not surprising. Because it is a classification of transfers across *oblast* lines, and therefore of transfers effected by authorities at *higher* than *oblast* level, at least 95 percent of the transfers are *to* positions at *oblast* level or higher, and 90 percent are *from* such positions. (The remainder, transfers to and from positions at city or *raion* level, will be examined below.) Nearly 60 percent of transfers are to posts at *oblast* administrative level, slightly more than 20 percent to posts at republic level and 16 percent to All-Union level. The most common transfer is to another position at the same administrative level, but transfers to a *higher* level exceed transfers to a *lower* level, that is, overall this is a sample of upwardly mobile careers.[11]

Approximately 30 percent of transfers are to or from a 'state' position, that is, one in a Council of Ministers, an *ispolkom* (soviet executive committee) or economic management, and about two-thirds are transfers to or from party positions. It would be tempting to draw the conclusion that transfers across *oblast* lines are more prevalent in the party task sector than elsewhere and that this reflects a more centralized and interventionist staffing policy about party positions. This *may* be correct, but we cannot be sure on the basis of the available information. This is because the bulk of Soviet prosopographical data are derived from membership of Supreme Soviets or Central Committees[12] and below the republic administrative level party positions would be more likely than any other to be represented in these bodies. This feature of Soviet career data in general is reflected in Table 2.1, where state positions are nearly but not quite as numerous as party positions at republic level, but only a third as frequent at *oblast* level and below.

From the point of view of task sector, the most common form of transfer in Table 2.1 is to another position in the same sector, rather than between sectors. But nearly a quarter of the transfers are between party and state posts, and within this category, transfers from party to state are more common than the reverse. Overall the party is thus a net supplier of staff to other positions.

The transfers in Table 2.1 involving the lower – city and *raion*-administrative levels may cause puzzlement. Transfers from *raion* and city-level positions to the All-Union or republic levels are principally (more than 70 percent) cases of recruitment of junior officials (instructors or inspectors) to the relevant Central Committees, and comparable movement into Councils of Ministers and Central Committees of the Komsomol also occurs. There is no doubt that some mechanism for talent-spotting and recommendation to Central Committee work must exist down to urban and rural *raion* level, but whether this is run by central or local personnel is thus far unclear. To some extent such recruits, after a spell in a Central Committee *apparat*, are redeployed in provincial posts again.

There are also twenty-two cases in Table 2.1 in which personnel were moved from one post to another at city or *raion* level, but across *oblast* boundaries. Eighteen of these fall into two clearly definable groups. First, in small republics such as Kirghizia, Turkmenistan, or Tadzhikistan, transfers would seem to be arranged freely between *raiony* irrespective of the (small number of) *oblast* boundaries. The number of *raiony* in such republics is comparable to the number of *oblasti* in large republics; it is plausible that we are dealing here with posts on the republican *nomenklatura*, and that in the smaller republics the *raion* is perceived as the basic administrative subdivision. Secondly, there are eight cases in which specialist economic administrators (factory directors, mining or construction engineers) are moved across *oblast* or republic boundaries to new projects in their area of specialization.[13] It is likely here that the specialist tasks of the ministry that employs them entail a high degree of geographical mobility of personnel.

The principal variable left unclassified in Table 2.1 is the *rank* of the positions held at the various administrative levels and in different task sectors. To process rank the following equivalencies between party and state posts at *oblast* level have been postulated:

rank	party	state
(1)	first secretary	chairman of *ispolkom*
(2)	second secretary	first deputy chairman
(3)	ordinary secretary	deputy chairman
(4)	department head	department head, nachal'nik upravleniia
(5)	first deputy department head, or lower	deputy head of department or upravlenie, or lower

Table 2.2   Rank of Supplier and Recipient Posts at Oblast Level

Supplier posts rank	party	state	other
1	229	99	13
2	96	15	—
3	87	15	—
4	16	12	1
5	5	22	1
	433	163	15
Recipient posts rank	party	state	other
1	272	100	4
2	81	11	1
3	51	12	—
4	11	14	—
5	3	19	1
	418	156	6

Note: Supplier posts exceed recipient posts because of net mobility upward from the *oblast* level.

Table 2.3   *Most Frequent Transfers*

	Old post	New post	Cases
1	First secretary, *obkom*	First secretary, *obkom*	84
2	Second secretary, *obkom*	First secretary, *obkom*	37
3	Chairman, *oblispolkom*	First secretary, *obkom*	28
4	Chairman, *oblispolkom*	Chairman, *oblispolkom*	24
5	Ordinary secretary, *obkom*	First secretary, *obkom*	23
6	First secretary, *obkom*	Ordinary secretary, Republic CC	23
7	Ordinary secretary, Republic CC	First secretary, *obkom*	14
8	Second secretary, *obkom*	Second secretary, *obkom*	14
9	Department head, Republic CC	First secretary, *obkom*	12
10	First secretary, *obkom*	Minister, Republic C of M	12
11	Instructor/inspector, All-Union CC	Second secretary, *obkom*	10
12	First secretary, *obkom*	Chairman, *oblispolkom*	10
13	Minister, Republic C of M	First secretary, *obkom*	10
14	Chairman, *oblispolkom*	Minister, Republic C of M	10
15	Ordinary secretary, *obkom*	Second secretary, *obkom*	10
16	First secretary, *obkom*	Secretary, All-Union CC	9
17	First secretary, *obkom*	Chairman, Republic C of M	9
18	Ordinary secretary, *obkom*	Instructor/inspector, All-Union CC	8
19	Sector head, All-Union CC	Second secretary, Republic CC	8
20	Deputy minister, All-Union C of M	Chairman, *oblispolkom*	8
21	Second secretary, *obkom*	Chairman, *oblispolkom*	8
22	Ordinary secretary, *obkom*	Chairman, *oblispolkom*	8
		Total	379

Table 2.2 distributes supplier and recipient offices at *oblast* level according to rank and task sector. *Oblast*-level transfers were selected for Table 2.2 both because this is the level at which the largest number of transfers occur, and because the sources on the *nomenklatura* of the All-Union Central Committee[14] are agreed that, in the main, the scope of this *nomenklatura* extends to some, but not all, posts at the *oblast* level of administration.

It will be clear from Table 2.2 that more than 95 percent of transfers to and from party positions at the *oblast* level concern *obkom* secretaries, that is, the senior party appointment and his immediate deputies. Of the remaining thirty-five party cases, twenty-five are cross-*oblast* transfers in small republics, or recruitment into junior Central Committee positions, both of a type just discussed. Whichever *nomenklatura* authority handles party transfer from *oblast* to *oblast* in the larger republics, it is clear that its scope does not extend seriously below secretarial rank.

The situation is otherwise regarding state and economic management positions. Here more than 20 percent of transfers concern persons ranking junior to deputy chairman of an *oblispolkom*. The posts concerned are ones such as *nachal'nik upravleniia, zaveduiushchii otdelom, nachal'nik ob''edineniia, nachal'nik kombinata*, directors and chief engineers of factories, and directors of *sovkhozy*. Here again the suggestion naturally arises that we are dealing with the personnel deployments of those economic ministries for whose tasks specialist expertise outweighs local knowledge. In other words, we are dealing with posts on the ministerial *nomenklatura*, possibly but not necessarily ratified also in the All-Union Central Committee.[15] As a further supplement to Table 2.1 and guide to the sort of posts with which this chapter is concerned, Table 2.3 gives details of the twenty-two most frequent transfers by administrative level, task sector and rank; they account for more than a third of all the cases considered.

The Scope of Central *Nomenklatura*

It has been suggested that the posts under investigation in this chapter are principally posts on the *nomenklatura* of the All-Union Central Committee or those of republican Central Committees. What further light is thrown on the scope of these *nomenklatury* by the data described in the preceding section, particularly on the more junior levels of their operation?

First, we have seen that concerning relatively junior posts – those at city and *raion* level, and the lower-ranking state posts at *oblast* level – three distinct types of transfer can be isolated.

(1) Transfers to and from posts at *raion* level in the smaller republics. Since these do not occur across the boundaries of republics (with two exceptions which will be discussed below) and are much more frequent in the smaller than in the larger republics, it seems sensible to interpret them as transfers arranged by the Central Committee *apparat* of the republic concerned.

(2) Transfers of specialized economic personnel. It seems reasonable to postulate that some ministries have *nomen-*

klatury extending more deeply into the formal administrative structure than does the All-Union Central Committee.

(3) Recruitment into junior posts in the *apparaty* of the All-Union or republic Central Committees can occur from virtually any level of administration, certainly from urban or rural *raikomy*.[16]

Now, it follows from this last point that lists of (and files on) personnel held at All-Union level are very extensive indeed, including, for instance, the first secretaries of the 2,000 or so *raikomy* in the RSFSR.[17] Over some matters – admission into Higher Party Schools, for instance – the All-Union center might be happy to accept *obkom* or republic recommendations, but for entry into an *apparat* post they would surely evaluate qualifications and provide themselves with the means to do this.

The All-Union center recruits freely *from* the *raikom* and *gorkom* levels. Does it also deploy people with central experience *to* these levels? Except for one unusual case,[18] the answer would seem to be no. We seem to be dealing here with a *nomenklatura* used for co-optation, but not for deployment purposes. This fits well with Harasymiw's account of the *uchetnaia nomenklatura*: 'a supplementary list of likely candidates for future vacancies . . . [they] are in the *osnovnaia* (basic) *nomenklatura* of some lower body, and the superior party committee keeps track of their progress in the event it has an opening in its own basic list.'[19] The *uchetnaia nomenklatura* of the All-Union center would seem to include *raikom* first secretaries; the lower boundaries of its basic *nomenklatura* to lie at a somewhat higher administrative level. One might supplement Harasymiw's account with the suggestion that the elevation of *raikom* first secretaries to the central *apparat* is unlikely to be because the center lacks for suitable candidates higher up; it is much more likely that we see here cases of a conscious policy of giving very junior officials central experience.

Apart from following up cases of officials co-opted into, and then transferred from the All-Union central *apparat*, we seem to have only one other way of identifying the operations of the All-Union *nomenklatura* with any certainty, and of distinguishing them from those of republic *nomenklatury*. This is to investigate transfers from one provincial post to another *across republic boundaries*, or across *oblast* boundaries in the case of the RSFSR; such transfers must have been arranged by the All-Union center, simply because there is no other administrative superior which could have arranged them. Table 2.4 classifies

Table 2.4 Low-Echelon Transfers Arranged by All-Union Center

Person	Date	Supplier post	Recipient post
From the post of:			
(a) Rural raikom			
T. K. Mal'bakhov	1949	RK 1st secretary, Azerbaidzhan	secretary, Kabarda *obkom*
F. K. Kniazev	1955	RK 1st secretary, Tambov *oblast*	secretary, Kurgan *obkom*
L. A. Borodin	1959	RK 1st secretary, Volgograd *oblast*	secretary, Chuvash *obkom*
I. S. Morozov	*ca* 1962	RK 1st secretary, Vladimir *oblast*	1st secretary, Ivanovo agricultural *obkom*
(b) Urban raikom			
V. P. Kuzmin	*ca* 1959	RK secretary, Irkutsk	deputy head, Samarkand *obkom*
V. G. Lomonosov	1962	RK 1st secretary, Moscow	chairman, Central Asian Bureau, CC, CPSU
V. N. Ptitsyn	1959	RK 2nd secretary, Leningrad	deputy head, Murmansk *obkom*
(c) Gorkom			
V. K. Akulintsev	1951	1st secretary, Enakievo GK, Donetsk *oblast*	deputy head, CC, Turkmenistan
Yu. N. Vladychin	1952	deputy head, Orekhovo-Zuevo GK	instructor, CC, Estonia
G. A. Kozlov	1958	1st secretary, Sverdlovsk GK	1st secretary, East Kazakhstan *obkom*
N. V. Bannikov	1959	1st secretary, Kuibyshev GK	2nd secretary, Karaganda *obkom*
I. V. Bondaletov	1962	1st secretary, Zaporozhe GK	deputy bureau head, CC, Latvia
V. V. Mitiushkin	1955	1st secretary, Barnaul GK	2nd secretary, Iakut *obkom*
V. V. Vorob'ev	*ca* 1979	1st secretary, Tikhvin GK, Leningrad *oblast*	2nd secretary, Daghestan *obkom*
			To the post of:
(d) Rural raikom			
G. R. o. Gasanov	*ca* 1971	editor, Azeri newspaper, Armenia	RK 1st secretary, Azerbaidzhan
(e) Gorkom			
S. F. Medunov	1959	1st deputy chairman, Crimean *oblispolkom*	1st secretary, Sochi GK, Krasnodar *krai*

RK=*raikom*, GK=*gorkom*.

transfers of this kind to or from relatively low levels in the administration, with the aim of clarifying the putative lower limit of All-Union staffing activity. It includes all the cases of the relevant types that could be identified in the sample.

Four points can be made about Table 2.4. First, the absolute number of low-echelon provincial transfers that we can attribute to the All-Union center is small. Secondly, they are overwhelmingly cases where a vacancy which is probably on the All-Union *osnovnaia nomenklatura* (that is, one at *oblast* level or higher) is filled by promoting someone from below this level; again we would seem to be witnessing the use of the *uchetnaia nomenklatura*, this time more strictly as a reserve of promising personnel. Thirdly, the transfers in Table 2.4 are principally from the Khrushchev period or earlier, and Harasymiw reports that the scope of the senior *nomenklatury* was being cut back in the late 1960s.[20] Finally, special circumstances probably affect the two most junior transfers in Table 2.4, those of T. K. Mal'bakhov and G. R.o. Gasanov. Mal'bakhov is a Kabarda, and Gasanov an Azeri working among the Azeri minority in Armenia. It is not inconceivable, simply on the ground of their nationality, that their names were listed on an *uchetnaia nomenklatura* of non-Russians outside their native areas and to be considered for a post back in that native area.[21]

The tentative conclusion is, therefore, that the All-Union center does not appoint to posts at *raion* or city level, or, if it once did, does not any more. The corollary of this is that these appointments are on the *nomenklatura* of the republic Central Committee, or in the case of the RSFSR, on that of the *obkom*.[22] This is a somewhat surprising conclusion, because there are many cities which are larger than the smaller *oblasti*, and which one might have surmised present more important staffing problems to the center. But if there is evidence to falsify this conclusion, it must await future study.

If the lower boundaries of the basic *nomenklatura* of the All-Union Central Committee lie at *oblast* level, they do not embrace absolutely every post tenable at that level. Avtorkhanov (followed by the others in n. 6) lists secretaries and department heads of *obkomy*, but by implication no lower-ranking party posts, as being All-Union appointments. Harasymiw adds chairmen of *oblispolkomy* in the RSFSR to this list. How do the present data fit in with this delineation?

First, as regards party positions at *oblast* level, Table 2.2 suggested that there is very much less transfer activity touching department heads than there is involving secretaries. And only four cases of transfer *to* the position of *obkom* department head seem to be clear examples of All-Union central appointment, using the criteria invoked above. These are V. P. Kuz'min and V. N. Ptitsyn, mentioned in Table 2.4, K. A. Novikov (transferred from Riga to be department head, Krasnodar *kraikom* in 1953) and A. A. Kochetov (moved from the All-Union Central Committee to be department head in Karelia in 1956).[23] All four are from the 1950s; their early date and small number make it doubtful whether *obkom* department head is any longer an All-Union appointment.

There are ample cases of appointments to *oblispolkom* chairman across *oblast* lines both in the RSFSR and in the other republics; but hardly any to this post across republic boundaries.[24] This bears out Harasymiw's view that this is an All-Union appointment only in the case of the RSFSR, but it also presents us with a difficulty. Transfer from the position of first, second, or ordinary *obkom* secretary to that of *oblispolkom* chairman is quite common, as attested in Table 2.3, and more than half of these cases are in republics other than the RSFSR. Transfer from an All-Union *nomenklatura* post to a republic one must surely be a demotion, but this is what would be entailed, following Harasymiw's position, in a transfer in the non-Russian republics from *obkom* secretary to *oblispolkom* chairman. The same difficulty arises concerning the transfer from *obkom* secretary to member of a Council of Ministers outside the RSFSR. Avtorkhanov and Lebed (but not Harasymiw in his 1977 article) omit the post of union republic minister from their listing of All-Union *nomenklatura* posts; but a transfer to this position from an *obkom* secretaryship is quite common, particularly outside the RSFSR. If a transfer is in any sense a routine and publicized one, it is difficult to regard it as a demotion. For this reason, it would seem sensible to *retain oblispolkom* chairman and union republic minister on the postulated list of All-Union *nomenklatura* posts, outside as well as within the RSFSR.

Finally, there does *not* seem to be a case for treating *deputy* chairmen of *oblispolkomy* or their equivalents as All-Union appointments. Only four cases occur in the present sample crossing republic boundaries,[25] and they present unusual features, consistent only with the idea that there can be All-Union intervention at this rank in special circumstances.

The working assumption of the rest of this chapter, therefore, is that the All-Union *nomenklatura* extends at least to the following posts in the party and state sectors (and to their equivalents elsewhere): members of Councils of Ministers in the union republics, *obkom* secretaries and *oblispolkom* chairmen. Probably beyond the All-Union scope, and therefore on the *nomenklatura* of republic Central Committees – or of *obkomy* in the RSFSR? – are department heads of *obkomy*, deputy chairmen of *oblispolkomy* and all staff of *gorkomy* and *gorispolkomy* (excepting capital cities of republics). In terms of this delineation approximately 87 percent of the transfers in the sample would seem to be to positions on the All-Union *nomenklatura*, and 13 percent to lower ones. Of the transfers to positions on the All-Union *nomenklatura*, about 69 percent are to party posts, about 28 percent to 'state' posts and about 3 percent to other miscellaneous positions. This is clearly not a fair cross-section of official employment in the USSR; rather, by selecting transfers from province to province, the author has obtained a sample in which party posts in the gift of the All-Union authorities are unduly represented.

Analysis of Transfers by Region

General Issues

Table 2.5 is an attempt to discern the kind of patterns foreshadowed in the introduction, by tabulating the broad region to and from which cross-*oblast* transfers are made. The broad regions selected are the nineteen economic regions (*krupnye ekonomicheskie raiony*) familiar from Soviet statistics, with modifications, and increased in number to thirty-three as follows.

(1)   Since it is of interest to know the extent of transfer *between* republics in cases where several republics are in one economic region, and this is particularly so in the economically and culturally homogeneous regions of Central Asia and Transcaucasia, these regions have been divided into their constituent republics.[26]

(2)   In this author's opinion there are two economic regions of the USSR which group artificially into a single region *oblasti* that are very dissimilar. These are the 'Southwestern' region of Ukraine, and Kazakhstan. The former has therefore been divided into a 'Western' region consisting of those *oblasti* wholly or partly outside Soviet control before 1939–40,[27] and a 'Central' region of Kiev and its hinterland.[28] Kazakhstan has been divided into a 'Southwestern' majority non-European group of *oblasti*, and a 'Northeastern' predominantly European region.[29]

Table 2.5 *Cross-Oblast Transfers by Broad Regions*

Transfers from:	to:	(1)	(2)	(3)	(4)	(5)	(6)	(7)	(8)	(9)	(10)	(11)	(12)	(13)
1	Belorussia	52	1			1	1				1			
2	Baltic	1	1	1	1				1					
3	Northwest		1	4	3	1	2		1	2		1		2
4	Central		1	1	8	1	2		1	1	2			2
5	Volga-Viatka		1	1		3								4
6	Central Black Earth				1	2	3		3	2				2
7	Volga	1		1	2	3	3	9	1	1	3			
8	North Caucasus	1		1	2	1	1	3	16		1	1		1
9	Urals		1		2	1		1	2	2	5			
10	West Siberia				3				1	1	3	2	3	
11	East Siberia							1		3	2	2	3	
12	Far East				2		2					1	10	
13	RSFSR: center		1	1	1				5		2		1	
14	Moldavia													
15	Donets-Dnieper		1		1	1	1			1				
16	South Ukraine				1				1	1	1			
17	Central Ukraine													
18	West Ukraine													
19	Ukraine: center								2					
20	NE Kazakhstan			2							1	1		
21	SW Kazakhstan													
22	Kazakhstan: center		1						1	1				
23	Uzbekistan					1								
24	Kirghizia													
25	Tadzhikistan													
26	Turkmenistan								2	1				
27	Central Asia													
28	Georgia													
29	Azerbaidzhan					1			1					
30	Armenia													
31	Transcaucasia													
32	Abroad				1				1					
33	All-Union center	3	7	8	10	5	3	14	9	9	5	2	5	
34	TOTALS	58	16	20	40	20	17	32	46	23	26	10	22	2

If patterns in cross-*oblast* transfers occur, these modifications may serve as a test of whether the patterns occur independently of formal administrative boundaries.

(3) In the case of the three republics which transcend the regional subdivisions established (RSFSR, Ukraine and Kazakhstan) further 'regions' denoting posts at the republican 'center' have been set up. Posts at the All-Union center also have their own category.

(14)	Ukraine					Kaz			Central Asia					Transcaucasia						(34)
	(15)	(16)	(17)	(18)	(19)	(20)	(21)	(22)	(23)	(24)	(25)	(26)	(27)	(28)	(29)	(30)	(31)	(32)	(33)	(34)
						1			1									3	6	67
1																			1	7
1										1				1				1	13	34
							1		3			1						2	20	46
	1																		9	19
						1													4	18
						2												2	12	44
		1				3	1												18	51
	1					1			1		1		1						17	36
	1					2		1						1				1	7	30
										2								1	6	22
	1																		6	24
								1										2	2	16
																			1	1
1	14	6	1	4	16	1			1		1								5	55
1	3	5	1	1	7	1								1						24
	3	4	4	1	7														1	20
	1	4	1	12	5															23
	8·	1	7	6														2	4	31
						24	15	16											6	65
						6	23	17											3	49
						15	12		1								1		4	36
						1		1	110				3						9	125
					1					16					1					19
										8		1							1	11
										1	24	2							1	31
									2		1	2							2	7
														10			1		2	13
															1	14			1	18
																1				1
																				0
																			2	4
	3	2		1		5	2	4	8	3	1			2	1	3		3		122
	33	24	16	24	37	63	55	39	129	19	13	30	7	13	18	5	1	18	163	1,069

(4) A separate category has been created for work abroad, principally diplomatic.

Two things stand out from an initial examination of Table 2.5. The first is that the majority of transfers from one *oblast* to another are transfers *inside* the given republic; 666 (62 percent) of all transfers recorded are of this type. A further 307 (29 percent) are transfers between the provinces and the All-Union center (including positions abroad). Only 9 percent are transfers from one republic to another.

This is particularly noteworthy in respect of Kazakhstan and the republics of Central Asia. One might have expected a fair amount of job mobility between the republics of Central Asia and Kazakhstan on the part both of native Central Asians and of Europeans employed there; one might also have expected Europeans employed in these regions to move with ease between Kazakhstan plus Central Asia and the European USSR or Siberia. But transfers from republic to republic within Central Asia plus Kazakhstan are minute in number, and half of them are connected with the establishment and dissolution of the short-lived Central Asian Bureau of the Central Committee (1962–5).[30] And while movement between Central Asia plus Kazakhstan and the rest of the union does occur, it is principally by Europeans (the few native Central Asians who make such moves are transferred to and from the All-Union center) and even then more than half the Europeans recorded as moving to another *oblast* from one in Central Asia or Kazakhstan go on to another part of the same republic and not beyond.[31]

The center, of course, might have special reasons in Central Asia for retaining personnel, both European and native, largely in one republic. But it is noticeable how little personnel interchange there is even between the Slavonic-speaking republics. It has been postulated above that more than 85 percent of cross-*oblast* transfers are made by the All-Union center. In which case, why are there not more transfers between say, Belorussia and the neighboring Pskov, Smolensk, or Briansk *oblasti*, between the grain-growing areas of Ukraine and of South Russia, or between the Donbass and Rostov *oblast*? Like this (one might expect), occupational expertise could be promoted with a reduced risk of fostering articulate regionalism. Such transfers between economically related places with different administrative subordination are very infrequent,[32] and this prompts an alternative line of thought. If transfers are confined noticeably within republics, and particularly in republics other than the RSFSR which have their own Central Committee *apparaty* and Departments of Organizational-Party Work (while the RSFSR shares the All-Union facilities), may this not be a *republic* preference? It could well be in the perceived interest of a republic to retain experienced personnel, both native and Russian, within the republic to increase its negotiating 'clout' with the center. This is not, of course, to contradict earlier evidence about the *nomenklatura* scope of the All-Union center, but rather to suggest an adjustment to the way we visualize its working, namely, that the initiative in a staffing change may be taken by the republic *nomenklatura* officials, and that the All-Union center may accede to this advice (though it reserves the right to overrule it).

The second salient point arising from Table 2.5 is that the rate of transfer recorded to and from positions in the RSFSR is surprisingly low, and that to and from positions elsewhere in the union are surprisingly high. Basically staff have been transferred across *oblast* lines two or three times more frequently in some non-Russian republics than in the RSFSR, and this is so whether one reckons transfers per administrative unit or per unit population. The difference is even more striking when it is noted that a high proportion of staff transfers in the RSFSR are transfers into and out of the All-Union center; transfers strictly within the RSFSR as a republic are a quarter as frequent in the period as they are in Kazakhstan or Uzbekistan, and a third as frequent as in Belorussia. Some, but not all, of this difference is removed when one takes into account that the RSFSR, having no Central Committee, has a much smaller 'republican center' and many transfers between RSFSR provincial positions and the All-Union center would in other republics be transfers between a province and the republic center. But even when one reckons only transfers from one 'provincial' position to another within the various republics, the RSFSR has a transfer rate nearly half that of most other republics.

There seem to be three lines of explanation for this: they are not mutually exclusive and each probably contributes in some measure to the discrepancy.

(1) As noted above, membership lists of republic Supreme Soviets make a crucial contribution to Soviet prosopography. The RSFSR is bigger than all the other republics combined but it does not have a correspondingly larger Supreme Soviet. Personnel, therefore, need to be much more senior in the RSFSR before they have prospects of *ex officio* membership of the republic Supreme Soviet, and the external student learns fewer details of the early and middle stages of RSFSR careers than he does in the case of, say, Belorussia or Kazakhstan.[33]

(2) Against a background in which the average tenure of office is getting longer and turnover decreasing, it may well be that this process has been more marked in the RSFSR than elsewhere.[34]

(3) It may be that more people make a career staying in one place and not crossing *oblast* lines in the RSFSR than in other

republics; possibly also that they are allowed to reach higher levels of seniority in a Russian *oblast* before transfer is considered.[35] This would be a probable outcome if, in the RSFSR, *obkomy* control some appointments that are elsewhere the business of a republic Central Committee.

Transfers by Region: the RSFSR

The share of the RSFSR in total transfer activity is small. This is an interesting observation in itself but it makes it more difficult to say things of significance about internal processes in the RSFSR, because the overall sample for the republic (and therefore the distribution that might be expected in various subcategories) is too small. But the RSFSR portion of Table 2.5 does prompt some tentative discussion along three lines.

(1) First, if one runs one's eyes down the diagonal, there is the clear suggestion that cross-*oblast* transfers are more likely to be *to an adjacent place* than to one far away; of all destinations except the All-Union center the most likely one is another *oblast* in the same economic region. Chi-square testing (after some collapsing of the cells in Table 2.5) gives a probability of less than 0·001 that this distribution could have occurred by accident.[36] It will also be noticeable that it is transfers within four economic regions, the Central, the Volga, the North Caucasian and the Far Eastern, that contribute a great deal to the significance of the result. Because of conventions adopted in the processing of transfers, the last three regions will be looked at a bit more closely.

In the cases of the North Caucasian, Far Eastern and Volga regions Table 2.5 might present a somewhat misleading picture. This is because it counts as transfers, movement between Stavropol *krai* and the Karachai-Cherkessk autonomous *oblast* (AO) (eight cases), between Khabarovsk *krai* and the Jewish AO (four cases), and between Khabarovsk *krai* and the Lower Amur and Kamchatka *oblasti* at a time when the latter were subordinate to Khabarovsk *krai* (two cases). Further, it might be argued that movement from Rostov *oblast* to Kamensk *oblast* in 1954,[37] from Riazan *oblast* to Lipetsk *oblast* in 1954,[38] from Saratov and Stalingrad *oblasti* to Balashov *oblast* in 1954,[39] and Khabarovsk *krai* to Magadan (1953) and to Kamchatka (1956)[40] – six cases in all – should not be treated as cross-*oblast* transfers in the strict sense. They occurred during the setting up of a new *oblast* by the subdivision of one or more old ones and it is hardly surprising that existing staff were reallocated along with territory. When these twenty cases are removed from the table, the chi-square value for the cells of Table 2.5 concerning the provincial part of the RSFSR is reduced, but the probability remains below the 0·001 level.[41]

The above comments, although introducing a note of caution into the observation that transfers tend to be to places relatively close at hand, prompt a further digression as they may suggest a clue to a process affecting *nomenklatura* decisions. When a larger administrative unit is divided into smaller ones, the officials of the newly established administrative units not unnaturally include many officials of the old unit, moving simply to another base in the area where they are already active. Examples of this are the breakup of the vast administrative empire based on Khabarovsk in 1947–56,[42] the breakup of the short-lived *krai* organizations in Kazakhstan in 1964–5, the separation of Arzamas *oblast* from Gorky in 1954, the carving out of four new *oblasti*[43] in the Central Black Earth–Don area in 1954 and the separation of the Kalmyk ASSR from Stavropol *krai* in 1959. Clearly, in so far as locally derived information was used for the selection of personnel for new or reformed *oblasti*, it must have been information from the center of the old administrative unit – from cities like Khabarovsk, Voronezh, Rostov, Gorky, or Tselinograd. Although the posts in question were on an *osnovnaia nomenklatura* in Moscow, relevant information on the recent record of candidates had to come from such provincial centers. It would be sensible to assume that Khabarovsk, Voronezh, and so on, took copies of their staff files and did not send the only copy to Moscow and I think not fanciful to suggest that they held onto these files after administrative rearrangement; they would then be in a good position to try and exert influence on appointments in neighboring *oblasti*[44]. Is it possible that the 'regionalism' we have detected in cross-*oblast* transfers is connected not only with a central policy to promote or permit such specialization, but also with the informal influence of regional 'capitals'?[45]

(2) In the sample under study there were 163 transfers to the All-Union center from somewhere else. Of these, 114 (70 percent) were from the RSFSR, and 93 (57 percent) from the seven economic regions of European Russia. Transfers from a provincial position to the All-Union center represented one-third of all transfers from positions in the RSFSR; the comparable figure for the other republics is 8 percent. Now, it is true that the RSFSR possesses no Central Committee of its own and

when staff are transferred to the All-Union Central Committee, some of them will be employed in tasks concerning the RSFSR which in Ukraine would be handled by a Central Committee official in Kiev. But while about 30 percent of transfers from Ukraine, Belorussia, Kazakhstan and Uzbekistan are to positions either in the republics or in the All-Union center, the corresponding figure for the RSFSR is 40 percent. It is no exaggeration to say that the RSFSR, and particularly European Russia, supply personnel to the All-Union center to a degree unwarranted by their size, and to surmise (this is nothing new) that they are the major suppliers of personnel to the federal and international level of Soviet politics.

By contrast, when we look at the All-Union center as supplier rather than recipient, only 57 percent (70 out of 122) are transferred from the All-Union center to positions in the RSFSR. The All-Union center acts as a clearing-house (perhaps also retraining center) for the net transfer of staff from the RSFSR to other republics, principally non-Slavonic ones, and the RSFSR is a net exporter of personnel. So too are Ukraine and Belorussia, though not on the same scale as the RSFSR. The other republics are net importers.

(3)   Are there any regions of the RSFSR that play a distinct role in personnel deployment, for instance, by exhibiting more rapid turnover of staff, or by supplying or receiving staff in characteristic patterns?

On the first score one's initial impression is that the Central, the Volga and the North Caucasus regions show a higher degree of transfer activity, whether internally, between themselves and other regions, or between themselves and the All-Union center. But each of these economic regions is large, both in population and in administrative subdivisions. When transfers are reckoned as a rate per administrative unit, or per million population, these three regions do not stand out from the others significantly. In other words, the comparatively slow rate of transfer in the RSFSR appears to apply equally all over the republic, or at least it would take a larger sample to reveal any areas of special treatment.

Some regions do seem to diverge from the RSFSR norm regarding the typical source and destination of their personnel; the absolute numbers involved are small and difficult to test statistically, so I shall merely note three tendencies that may be suggestive. Moscow and its hinterland (the central economic region) seems to supply fewer personnel than average to other parts of the RSFSR, and rather more to the All-Union center and to the other union republics. One can imagine that in the *oblasti* around Moscow promising officials more readily 'catch the eye' of the Department of Organizational-Party Work, and the latter may feel that its judgements on people working near Moscow are more reliable and, hence, be more inclined to appoint them into the All-Union center or directly to remote and demanding assignments.[46] The Volga, Central Black Earth, Urals, West and East Siberian regions provide personnel freely for other provincial areas of the RSFSR – but not the Volga-Viatka region, which seems to have relatively exclusive relationships with the RSFSR and All-Union centers. Is it that Volga-Viatka (consisting of the highly specialized industrial area of Gorky, Kirov *oblast* and three ASSRs) is not thought an appropriate training for, or stage in, a career of general provincial administration? Finally, the Urals and West Siberian regions look to be a somewhat more fruitful supplier of personnel to other union republics and the North Caucasus a somewhat more hospitable recipient of people transferred from other republics. Two other regions, mentioned below, share this tendency to be better integrated into unionwide transfer activity.

Transfers by Region: Ukraine

Five observations can be made about the Ukrainian portion of Table 2.5.

(1)   As with the RSFSR, there is the clear suggestion that cross-*oblast* transfers are more likely to be neighboring *oblasti* within the republic.[47] This observation depends on the fact that the Donets–Dnieper economic region and West Ukraine behave as relatively distinct and self-contained *nomenklatura* regions. Each could be said to be an area requiring distinct policy from the point of view of Kiev and Moscow; Donets–Dnieper on account of its high component of heavy industry and of Russian speakers, and West Ukraine because of its late incorporation into the Union, its low levels of economic development and size of religious minorities.

(2)   In particular, it has proved justified to distinguish between the eight (formerly nine) *oblasti* of West Ukraine and the Kiev hinterland. There is relatively little transfer of personnel between these two groups of *oblasti*, despite their unification in one economic region in Soviet statistics.

(3)   Not only is there substantial movement from *oblast* to *oblast* within the Donets–Dnieper region, but it receives and supplies personnel to and from the rest of the USSR more than other parts of Ukraine. Indeed, along with three regions of the RSFSR just mentioned and along with North Kazakhstan, it stands out as a region with a high degree of personnel interchange with other parts of the Union (including the All-Union center) and a low degree of encapsulation within its republic boundaries. Its heavy industrial emphasis (which associates it more with areas such as the Urals, the Kuzbass, or Karaganda) and its large proportion of Russian speakers would have suggested in any case that it might be broader in the scope of its relationships than the rest of Ukraine.

(4)   By contrast, the West Ukraine region is revealed as very cut off from the rest of the Union. It has a high degree of transfers within the region,[48] a fair degree of interchange with the rest of Ukraine, and no recorded transfers to or from anywhere else, even the All-Union center. One can conclude two things: that West Ukraine is thought of as an area with special features requiring personnel with previous experience of the area (seemingly no attempt to counter regional lobbies here!) and also that this experience is of little relevance elsewhere in the Union; and secondly, that Moscow has made this area the responsibility of Ukraine, sending no personnel there from the All-Union center as it does to virtually all other nationality areas.[49]

(5)   Finally, although the absolute figures are very small, it is worth noting that three out of the seven recorded transfers to Moldavia are from Ukraine.[50] More evidence could be collected of the disproportionate role that Ukraine has played in Moldavian personnel affairs; Moldavia was, of course, an ASSR within Ukraine before 1940 and there were many Moldavians resident in Ukraine outside the ASSR, particularly in Odessa *oblast*. But (unlike the case of West Ukraine above) the All-Union center also sends its own people to Moldavia – in this sample three second secretaries.[51]

Transfers by Region: Kazakhstan

(1)   For analytical purposes, Kazakhstan was divided into three 'regions': the republic 'center'; Northeast Kazakhstan; and Southwest Kazakhstan. As can be seen, there is again a tendency to transfer staff to adjacent *oblasti* and the probability is low (just less than $0·001$)[52] that this is accidental. And as was

the case with Ukraine, this tendency reflects administrative boundaries only partially; Kazakhstan had internal boundaries roughly coinciding with those of the regions defined for a short period only, in the early 1960s.[53] In cases where they were not working within administrative boundaries, personnel officials are most likely to have been influenced by economic or cultural similarities between *oblasti*, or by simple proximity. This is the kind of factor which would be more likely to appeal to republic than central officials; again the balance of probability would seem to be that we are seeing the outcome of local, not central, initiatives.

(2) The northeastern part of Kazakhstan is distinctive for the large input it receives from outside the republic; if one disregards movement to and from the All-Union center, it is the most pronounced set of transfers across republican lines. A lot of it comes from the southeast of European Russia, the Urals, or West Siberia. The conclusion is unavoidable that this inflow reflects the opening up of North Kazakhstan under Khrushchev, and the areas of the RSFSR that particularly supply personnel are just the areas one would have expected to be in a position to offer experience relevant to the Virgin Lands scheme. In time, too, transfers to *oblasti* in Northeast Kazakhstan are more than half in the period 1957–64, a period of heightened transfer activity all over the Union (see Table 2.6) but disproportionately so in Kazakhstan.

Transfers over Time

Table 2.6 distributes recorded transfers by period and by republic (or group thereof). One thing stands out strikingly from this table, and that is some sort of watershed in transfer activity in or around 1961–2. After that time, the share taken by the RSFSR of total transfers declines to a fraction of what it had been, and the share taken by the other republics (except Belorussia) rises. There are only temporary exceptions to this pattern: Kazakhstan (as just described) experienced a massive boost in personnel turnover for the whole of the 1957–64 period; and Ukraine and Belorussia do not share in the general upswing in transfers in the late 1950s, but make up for this in the 1962–4 period instead. One gets a vivid sense that, as regards direct central intervention in provincial personnel matters, the RSFSR succeeded in coming to terms with it, or controlling it, or deflecting it onto other republics sometime in the late Khrushchev period.

Table 2.6   *Transfers by Period and Republic*

Transferred in the period	1946–52	1953–6	1957–61	1962–4	1965–70	1971–9	Total
To:							
RSFSR	52	58	105	14	28	19	276
	(35·9)	(31·0)	(33·7)	(12·6)	(17·8)	(13·9)	(26·3)
Ukraine	18	24	27	20	22	19	130
	(12·4)	(12·8)	(8·7)	(18·0)	(14·0)	(13·9)	(12·4)
Belorussia	13	13	9	11	5	6	57
	(9·0)	(7·0)	(2·9)	(9·9)	(3·2)	(4·4)	(5·4)
Kazakhstan	7	20	59	22	26	23	157
	(4·8)	(10·7)	(18·9)	(19·8)	(16·6)	(16·8)	(15·0)
Uzbekistan	12	18	31	17	30	21	129
	(8·3)	(9·6)	(9·9)	(15·3)	(19·1)	(15·3)	(12·3)
Other Central Asian republics	3	6	22	4	13	13	61
	(2·1)	(3·2)	(7·1)	(3·6)	(8·3)	(9·5)	(5·8)
Other republics	6	15	14	4	9	12	60
	(4·1)	(8·0)	(4·5)	(3·6)	(5·7)	(8·8)	(5·7)
All-Union center	34	33	45	19	24	24	179
	(23·4)	(17·6)	(14·4)	(17·1)	(15·3)	(17·5)	(17·1)
Total	145	187	312	111	157	137	1,049

Note: Figures in brackets are percentages of *column* totals, that is, of the total number of transfers recorded in the relevant time period.

The interlocking issues of job tenure and promotion of local people which have clearly been the subject of a lot of political pressure since Stalin died are cast in an interesting light; it looks suspiciously as if the pressures in favor of tenure and local promotions came particularly from Russians and that they achieved a change of practice toward the RSFSR. It needs to be said that the RSFSR was not subject to a higher degree of cross-*oblast* transfers than the other republics in the 1950s – quite the contrary, when with more than half the population they received about a third of the transfers! – but by the 1970s the former discrepancy had been vastly increased.

It might seem puzzling that this change of practice seems to occur around 1961–2, and not three years later when a new leadership initiated policies with a similar aim and left the distinct impression that they were in reaction to Khrushchev. But we do have evidence of a shift in the direction of personnel policy in the early 1960s, and one precisely associated with heightened central interventionism toward the republics and a freer rein for the RSFSR. This was the replacement in May 1960 of the Ukrainian A. I. Kirichenko by the Russian F. R. Kozlov as head of the Department of Organizational-Party Work.[54]

Transfers by Way of the All-Union Center

Out of the whole sample, 163 transfers (15 percent) were transfers from the republics to the All-Union center; 122 were from the All-Union center to positions in the republics. It has already been noted that in this process the Slavonic republics were net exporters and the non-Slavonic republics net importers of staff and that, therefore, the All-Union center functions as a redeployment center and possibly also a center for training and retraining. Can anything unusual be detected in the deployment of people who moved from a provincial position to a spell in the All-Union center, and then on to another provincial position? One hundred such cases occur in the sample. A simplified distribution of these (to superimpose them on Table 2.5 would be too cumbersome) is given in Table 2.7.[55]

Table 2.7   *Transfers by Way of The All-Union Center*

	To the RSFSR	*To other republics*	*Total*
From the RSFSR	47	29	76
From other republics	8	16	24
Total	55	45	100

The table reveals some of the same tendencies that have emerged earlier in the chapter, but in stronger measure. Personnel from the RSFSR are more likely to be appointed to positions in other republics than are personnel from other republics to be transferred to the RSFSR, but in either direction such movement is increased if the staff in question have spent an interval at the All-Union center, presumably because the latter serves to brief people in very different cultures. Even so, only three[56] of the twenty-four who move from non-Russian republics to the All-Union center and back to a provincial post are non-Slavs; the rest are the type of Slav with experience of work in several republics, often senior work in Central Asia or Kazakhstan.[57]

Staff moving from the RSFSR to new posts by way of a spell in the All-Union center are deployed with remarkable evenness throughout both the RSFSR and the other union republics (this is not in Table 2.7). Within the RSFSR a slight tendency to return to the region which they originally left can be discerned, but in general one would conclude that here at least is a case of the Central Committee maximizing dispersal in order to mini-mize regionalism; the overwhelming majority of these cases occur before 1962. And, of course, the wide deployment of RSFSR personnel throughout the other republics – that is, almost always, the introduction of Russians into predomi-nantly non-Russian groups of administrators – is also a prac-tice designed to counter regionalism.

Conclusions and Further Speculation

Both the tendency, observed in several republics, to transfer personnel to nearby rather than remote places, and the cut-back overall in cross-*oblast* transfers in the RSFSR, suggest that the All-Union center does not have a strategy of combat-ing regionalism by the maximum dispersal of staff throughout the union. In so far as it seeks to counter regionalism using staffing policies, these are, instead, of two kinds. The first is the placement in key positions in local administration of a small number of personnel from the All-Union center, usually Russians, often very experienced. The second is to limit the experience of officials (apart from the group just mentioned) to work in a single republic, and thereby to limit the building up of comparative experience of regional problems.

Yet the All-Union center undoubtedly has the power to arrange the systematic rotation of officials from place to place, and it is interesting to speculate why it has not exer-cised it, or is exercising it less than it used to. The reason seems to lie in the imperatives of rapid economic growth. A system of fixed tours of duty and of regular rotation and redeployment is not one which seeks to match expertise or experience with variety of, or changes of, need; its image of society is a static one, and its solutions to problems standard solutions which can be implemented by anyone. Hence, the historical associations of this type of system with amateurism. A program for social change on the other hand cannot go far before it is faced with the *specificity* of problems, and with the possibility of overcoming them by matching specific problems with specific expertise or experience. Once this strategy is entertained, the center comes to rely on a flow of accurate information from the 'localities' on the success or failure of its programs, and this includes information on the qualities and performance of its personnel. In this sense, once the specific-ity of problems is recognized, solutions can no longer be standardized, and policy can no longer in an absolute sense be centralized.

The All-Union *nomenklatura* is still a relatively centralized system but it cannot work without inputs of locally aggregated information. In concrete terms people do not get on to the *uchetnaia nomenklatura* of the All-Union Central Committee unless a republic or an *obkom* – using its own *osnovnaia nomenklatura* – puts them there; and the monitoring and assessment of their performance that determine whether they are promoted to the All-Union *osnovnaia nomenklatura* can be greatly influenced at the local level. So a central policy of taking local conditions into account entails an undertaking to be influenced in some measure by local input on personnel matters. To what extent is this so, currently? The picture which has emerged from the foregoing study is that personnel deployment shows a regional bias, because it is largely the outcome of local recommendations; for the most part, it would seem, the center endorses nominations sent up from the republics or *oblasti*, and only in a minority of cases does it replace these with nominations of its own. One might almost begin to speak of an 'inner' All-Union *nomenklatura*, consisting of those posts – second secretaries in nationality areas, for example – which the center insists on retaining in its direct control.

This picture entails a further difficulty, of a simply mechanical nature. It is easy to visualize the institutional framework within which a recommendation could be drawn up that, say, the vacant post of first secretary in Vitebsk *obkom* should go to the incumbent chairman of Gomel *oblispolkom*; relevant personnel are familiar with each other from meetings of the Belorussian Central Committee, and officials of that Central Committee are in a position to collate opinions and submit a proposal. That is the situation in the non-Russian republics.[58] In the RSFSR the evidence is also for transfers to geographically adjacent *oblasti*, but how are we to visualize the pooling and collation of information and judgements on junior officials, and who submits the suggestions? It is difficult to resist the idea that some formal arrangements must exist for this. In which case they might take one of two forms. The first is some kind of regional meeting of *oblast* officials, a regional tier between the *oblast* and the All-Union levels of administration. The *krupnye ekonomicheskie raiony* of Soviet statistics (regions which formed the basis for the classification in Table 2.5) come to mind as such a regional tier; and it is noteworthy that their capitals are often the former capitals of large, now dismantled administrative units, as described in an earlier section. The problem with this hypothesis is that we have very little evidence that the Large Economic Regions have any permanent organization or staff.[59]

The other alternative is that arrangements for coordinating the personnel affairs of groups of RSFSR *oblasti* exist within the Department of Organizational-Party Work of the All-Union Central Committee. We know that sectors of this department have exactly this task concerning groups of non-Russian republics,[60] and J. F. Hough has suggested that similar sectors exist grouping regions within the RSFSR;[61] however, he cites no confirmatory evidence for this. Their existence would be intrinsically likely, but it is odd, if they do exist, that information about them has not been more prominent.

Notes: Chapter 2

1 The rule of avoidance in classical China prohibited appointment not only to one's native province, but also to the native provinces of specified paternal and maternal relatives. For this and the three-year tour of duty, see T'ung-tsu Ch'ü, *Local Government in China under the Ch'ing* (Cambridge, Mass.: Harvard University Press, 1962), pp. 21–2, 32; and J. R. Watt, *The District Magistrate in Late Imperial China* (New York: Columbia University Press, 1972), pp. 20–1, 59–67. Watt points out that magistrates, though transferred from district to district, might frequently stay in the same province.

2 For another posing of this question, and provisional reasoning, see Grey Hodnett, *Leadership in the Soviet National Republics: A Quantitative Study of Recruitment Policy* (Oakville, Ontario: Mosaic Press, 1978), pp. 62–9.

3 Party Rule no. 25 in the version current, 1961–66.

4 See *XXIV s''ezd KPSS, stenograficheskii otchet* (Moscow: Politizdat, 1971), Vol. I, p. 124.

5 This course of action might conceivably be permissible in the case of very junior vacancies in an *oblast*. But then one is bound to ask what would be the mechanisms for learning about and assessing candidates from outside one's own region. And the answer is, a 'clearing-house' of personnel information – at republic level at least.

6 The basic accounts of the scope of *nomenklatura* are B. Harasymiw, 'Nomenklatura: the Soviet Communist Party's leadership recruitment system', *Canadian Journal of Political Science*, vol. II, no. 4 (December 1969), pp. 493–512, and 'Die sowjetische Nomenklatur', *Osteuropa*, vol. 27, no. 7 (1977), pp. 583–98; A. Avtorkhanov, *The Communist Party Apparatus* (Chicago: Henry Regnery, 1966), pp. 211–12; and A. I. Lebed, 'Vysshie organy SSSR opredeliaiushchie politiku i podbor rukovodiashchikh kadrov dlia nikh', Institute for the Study of the USSR, Munich, 1965; mimeo. All three authors draw on an unpublished manuscript by Avtorkhanov, which I have been unable to consult; in his 1966 work he does not cite any source for his categorization. It is reproduced without modification from Lebed by G. Ionescu, *The Politics of the European Communist States* (London: Weidenfeld & Nicolson, 1967),

pp. 61–3; for a general summary, see J. F. Hough and M. Fainsod, *How the Soviet Union Is Governed* (Cambridge, Mass.: Harvard University Press, 1979), pp. 430–2.

7   Data were collected on persons with surnames beginning with the letters A–P from a card-index of Soviet biographical data, compiled with the generous assistance of the Australian Research Grants Committee and of the Social Sciences Research Committee, La Trobe University. Principal sources for the index were: (*a*) *Deputaty Verkhovnogo Soveta SSSR*, 1958, 1962, 1966, 1970, 1974 and 1979; (*b*) lists of deputies to the Supreme Soviets of the union republics, taken from union republic newspapers of 1955, 1959, 1963, 1967, 1971 and 1975; (*c*) *Ezhegodnik Bol'shoi Sovetskoi Entsiklopedii*, 1958, 1962, 1966, 1972 and 1977; (*d*) *XXII s"ezd KPSS: stenograficheskii otchet* (Moscow: Politizdat, 1962), Vol. 2, pp. 363–584; *XXIII s"ezd* (1966), Vol. 2, pp. 389–623; *XXV s"ezd* (1976), Vol. 2, pp. 329–596; and (*e*) *Deputaty Verkhovnogo Soveta Latviiskoi SSR, vos'moi sozyv* (Riga: Izdatel'stvo Liesma, 1972), *Deputaty Verkhovnogo Soveta Uzbekskoi SSR, deviatyi sozyv* (Tashkent: Izdatel'stvo Uzbekistan, 1976), *Verkhovnyi Sovet Estonskoi SSR, deviatyi sozyv, kratkii biograficheskii spravochnik* (Tallin: Eesti Raamat, 1976) and *Deputaty Verkhovnogo Soveta Moldavskoi SSR, deviatyi sozyv* (Kishinev, 1976).

8   Examples of the last are the majority of *oblasti* in Kazakhstan in the late Khrushchev period, when South Kazakhstan, West Kazakhstan and Tselinnyi *kraia* formed an administrative level between *oblasti* and the union republic; also Kamchatka, Magadan, Amur and Sakhalin *oblasti* which were subordinate to Khabarovsk *krai* until the end of the Stalin period.

9   Hodnett, op. cit., p. 304 makes the same point concerning the KGB. This is not to deny that regional specialization may occur among security officials, as the career of A. S. Boiko, currently KGB chairman in Turkmenistan, shows, but to claim that regional influence on such specialization must be minimal.

10 Visual observation suggests that transfers within the same *oblast* are becoming increasingly frequent, and have become virtually the norm in the RSFSR.

11 Because persons who have been demoted would be less likely to figure in Supreme Soviets and Central Committees, this tendency is implicit in the sort of biographical data we possess.

12 See n. 7, above.

13 The careers of V. E. Bulat and P. I. Kavtarov, both in *Dep. V. S. Uzb.* (1976), are particularly good examples of this sort of mobility.

14 See n. 6, above.

15 For the ministerial *nomenklatury*, see Harasymiw, 'Die sowjetische Nomenklatur', op. cit. pp. 592–3; for party supervision of managerial appointments, see Harasymiw, '*Nomenklatura*', op. cit., pp. 498, 506.

16 Thus the following, all easily traceable in *Deputaty V. S. SSSR*, moved from the position of *raikom* first secretary to that of *instruktor otdela* of the All-Union Central Committee: O. A. Basiev (from Rostov *oblast* 1961), P. V. Guzenko (Krasnodar, 1954), L. B. Ermin (Rostov, 1959), A. A. Kochetov (Voronezh, 1952), L. G. Monashev (Stavropol, 1954) and N. S. Priezzhev (Saratov, 1959).

17 Noticeably, the examples given in n. 16 and other similar cases are all from the RSFSR. When we consider All-Union central deployment of *gorkom* first secretaries, a few cases from Ukraine come to light.

18   This is the case of G. S. Pavlov, moved in 1949 from an unspecified position in the Central Committee *apparat* to be first secretary, Magnitogorsk *gorkom*. It is an early date; staffing policies might well have been more centralized then than later. More importantly, Magnitogorsk was then a town of peculiar importance and might well have been in a higher *nomenklatura* category than other *gorkomy*.

19   Harasymiw, '*Nomenklatura*', op. cit., p. 496 with n. 13.

20   Harasymiw, '*Nomenklatura*', op. cit., p. 498, and 'Die sowjetische Nomenklatur', op. cit., pp. 584–6.

21   Similarly, Ya. N. Zarobian, G. A. Martirosian and O. A. Basiev move to posts in their native areas after considerable periods away from them, and by no obvious process, unless a register of 'natives abroad' was being kept. The best example of the principle is the substantial number of Balts who were émigrés in the USSR before 1940, and were then deployed in the administration of the Baltic States after 1944.

22   Harasymiw, '*Nomenklatura*', op. cit., p. 498, comes to this conclusion also, citing a case in which the Georgian Central Committee dismissed the first secretary of Gori *gorkom*; he does not mention the difficulty entailed concerning the RSFSR. Republic capital cities are exceptions to all the above, being treated, according to all the authorities, as the equivalents of *oblasti*. Avtorkhanov, indeed, names *raikom* secretaries in these capital cities as being on the All-Union CC *nomenklatura*; in which case, V. G. Lomonosov's position in Table 2.4 is explained.

23   In addition, three *obkom* department heads in the RSFSR moved from this position to that of *obkom* secretary somewhere else. These were K. A. Novikov (1956), V. G. Agibalov (1960) and I. G. Baliasinsky (1961).

24   V. N. Korneev became chairman, Tselinograd *oblispolkom ca*1960, from Voronezh, and V. V. Matskevich, chairman, Tselinnyi *kraiispolkom* in 1961, from USSR Gosplan; the Virgin Lands scheme may have involved more than usual All-Union supervision of appointments. P. A. Levitsky became chairman, Mogilev *oblispolkom ca*1958, after being first deputy chairman, Council of Ministers, Lithuania.

25   S. F. Medunov (see Table 2.4), S. D. Elagin (moved in 1955 from deputy chairman, Samarkand *oblispolkom* to first secretary, Pavlodar *obkom*), A. N. Bykov (*ca*1961 from first deputy chairman, Krasnodar *kraiispolkom*, to first deputy chairman, Tselinnyi *kraiispolkom*) and G. V. Kochkin (*ca*1965 from secretary, Tselinnyi *kraikom*, to first deputy chairman, Leningrad *gorispolkom*). Note again the unusual personnel arrangements associated with the *krai* organizations in Kazakhstan.

26   All but one of these, Armenia, are republics with an *oblast* or ASSR organization. In consequence, all except Armenia show transfers within the 'region' as defined, that is, between *oblasti*, ASSRs, or *raiony respublikanskogo podchineniya* within the republic.

27   Volhynia, Transcarpathia, Ivano-Frankovsk (formerly Stanislav), Lvov, Rovno, Ternopol, Khmelnitsky (formerly Kamenets-Podolsky), Chernovtsy and Drogobych (abolished in 1959). These *oblasti* did not come under substantial Soviet influence before 1944 and many of the population are not of the Russian Orthodox faith. On many socioeconomic indicators they form an internally coherent region very different from the Kiev hinterland or the Ukrainian average.

28   Kiev, Vinnitsa, Zhitomir, Cherkassy and Chernigov.

29   The 'Northeastern' region of Kazakhstan consists of East Kazakhstan, Karaganda, Kokchetav, Kustanai, Pavlodar, North Kazakhstan, Semi-

palatinsk, Turgai and Tselinograd *oblasti*. The 'Southwestern' region is Aktyubinsk, Alma-Ata, Gurev, Dzhambul, Dzhezkazgan, Kzyl-Orda, Mangyshlak, Taldy-Kurgan, Uralsk and Chimkent. The latter, even including the city of Alma-Ata, has a bare majority of non-Europeans.

30 V. K. Akulintsev moved from Turkmenistan in 1962 and S. M. Veselov from Uzbekistan in 1963, each to become deputy chairman of the *Sredazbiuro*. V. A. Ponomarev and R. Nabiev were both inspectors of the *Sredazbiuro*, the former from Uzbekistan, the latter from Tadzhikistan; Nabiev returned to his former post as head of the Central Committee department of agriculture in Tadzhikistan in 1965 and Ponomarev became deputy chairman of the Council of Ministers in Turkmenistan. The chairman of *Sredazbiuro*, V. G. Lomonosov, became second secretary in Uzbekistan in 1965. S. K. Kalizhniuk (*ca*1953–4) held a construction post which seems to have been of Central Asian rather than of republic scope, and the same seems to be the case with the scientific institute of which Kh. A. Irgashev was director (*ca*1958–60). Kalizhniuk returned to Turkmenistan and Irgashev to Uzbekistan. Kalizhniuk was later (1961) transferred from Turkmenistan to Tadzhikistan. I. V. Martsiniuk was deputy Minister of Construction of Metallurgical and Chemical Enterprises in Kazakhstan *ca*1956–7; this was an interval between construction posts in the Tashkent region. S. D. Elagin was deputy chairman of Samarkand *oblispolkom* in 1955 and then became first secretary of Pavlodar *obkom*. Apart from the staff of the *Sredazbiuro* this is a very heterogeneous grouping!

31 The figures: 52 percent of European transfers are to another post in the same republic, and so are 58 percent of individual Europeans transferred. For Kazakhstan and Uzbekistan the figures are 57 percent (transfers) and 66 percent (persons). Some Europeans – an example is N. I. Zhurin – spend all their careers in a succession of posts in Kazakhstan or Central Asia.

32 Rare examples of the type are: P. A. Levitsky, 1956–9 first deputy chairman, Council of Ministers, Lithuania, 1959–? chairman, Mogilev *oblispolkom*; V. S. Markov, in 1950 secretary, Poltava *obkom*, in 1955 first secretary, Orel *obkom*; N. F. Vasil'ev, 1961–4 chairman, Dnepropetrovsk *oblispolkom*, 1964–71 first secretary, Belgorod *obkom*; S. F. Medunov, 1951–8 first secretary, Yalta *gorkom*, 1959–69 first secretary, Sochi *gorkom*; A. M. Maliutin, 1952–9 chief editor, *Bakinskii rabochii*, 1959–69 chief editor, *Turkmenskaia iskra*; F. S. Kolomiets, 1960–2 chairman, Krasnodar *kraiispolkom*, 1962–3 first secretary, West Kazakhstan *kraikom*; A. K. Protozanov, 1964–9 second secretary, Tiumen *obkom*, 1969–? first secretary, East Kazakhstan *obkom*.

33 It is an odd side-effect of Soviet nationalities policy that it should provide us with much fuller data for the study of administration in the non-Russian republics than in the RSFSR (outside Moscow and Leningrad); it is the RSFSR which is the inscrutable area for outside students!

34 This has not been explicitly demonstrated to this author's knowledge, but it would seem to be entailed, for instance, in the widening discrepancy between the ages of RSFSR and non-RSFSR officials. For this information in the case of *obkom* first secretaries, see J. F. Hough, *Soviet Leadership in Transition* (Washington, DC: Brookings Institution, 1980), p. 70. If, as has sometimes been suggested, a longer term in office was one of the benefits that full Central Committee members were working for when they voted Khrushchev out and Brezhnev in, then it would not be

surprising if the debt were repaid, particularly in the RSFSR, whose representatives greatly outnumber the representatives of other regions among full Central Committee members.

35   J. F. Hough, *The Soviet Union and Social Science Theory* (Cambridge, Mass.: Harvard University Press, 1977), p. 30 and n. 32 (data concerning first secretaries only).

36   Chi-square value: 87·6 with nine degrees of freedom.

37   N. E. Kruchina, both Komsomol posts.

38   G. P. Pavlov, probably moving from *raikom* first secretary to department head in the new *obkom*.

39   A. S. Borisenko (*oblispolkom* chairman in both *oblasti*) and V. A. Karlov (second secretary in both *obkomy*).

40   P. Ya. Afanas'ev (from deputy chairman of the *kraiispolkom* to chairman of the *oblispolkom*) and M. A. Orlov (from *kraikom* secretary to *obkom* first secretary).

41   Chi-square value: 55·4 with nine degrees of freedom.

42   Sakhalin became an independent *oblast* (that is, one of republic subordination) in 1947, Amur in 1948, Magadan in 1953 and Kamchatka in 1956; see *SSSR: Administrativno-territorial'noe delenie soiuznykh respublik*, 9th edn (Moscow: Izdatel'stvo 'Izvestiia', 1958), pp. 47, 92, 118, 165.

43   Balashov, Belgorod, Kamensk and Lipetsk; Voronezh contributed territory to all four of them.

44   Interestingly Arzamas, Balashov and Kamensk were all abolished again in 1957, with territory (and some personnel?) returning to its former subordination.

45   It is perhaps not inapposite to note the influence that Kiev has over appointments to Moldavia, and Leningrad (less certainly) over appointments to the Baltic States.

46   V. G. Lomonosov (details above in Table 2.4) would be a very good example of the latter. Other cases, where one might otherwise have expected an appointment from inside the *apparat*, are L. I. Grekov (second secretary, Uzbekistan, 1976), and V. Ya. Pavlov (ambassador to Hungary, 1971).

47   Chi-square testing of the cells in Table 2.5 representing the provincial parts of Ukraine gives (after collapsing of some cells) a value of 26·9. With four degrees of freedom, the probability of accidental distribution is less than 0·001.

48   One notes a tendency for careers to be based almost wholly in West Ukraine; I. S. Grushetsky and Yu. V. Il'nitsky are examples.

49   The Census figures for the 1959–79 period do not show any sign of Russian immigration into West Ukraine such as there has been to other parts of Ukraine, and even more into Belorussia, Moldavia and the Baltic States.

50   Namely, L. I. Brezhnev transferred in 1950 from Dnepropetrovsk, V. A. Arpent'ev transferred from Kherson *oblast* to be Minister of Finance in Moldavia in 1955, and N. N. Kurilenko shifted from the Ukrainian to the Moldavian Central Committee *apparat ca*1960.

51   N. A. Mel'nikov (appointed 1961), Yu. D. Mel'kov (1967) and N. V. Merenishchev (1973).

52   Chi-square value: 11·3 with one degree of freedom.

53   Tselinny *kraia* existed 1960–5, and West and South Kazakhstan *krai* 1962–4: *Bol'shaia Sovetskaia Entsiklopediia*, 3rd edn (Moscow: Izdatel'stvo Sovetskaia Entsiklopediia, 1973), Vol. II, p. 153.

54   Hough and Fainsod, op. cit., pp. 223, 230–2. It is possible to see in Kozlov

a harbinger of the policy pursued under Brezhnev; but saying this, as Hough argues cogently, does not entail saying that Khrushchev 'stood for' an opposite policy and was defeated. For the date 1961, see also J. H. Miller, 'Cadres policy in nationality areas', *Soviet Studies*, vol. XXIX, no. 1 (1977), pp. 19–20.

55 The chi-square value of Table 2.7 is 4·9 after the application of Yates' correction, giving a probability greater than 0·02 but less than 0·05 that it is an accidental distribution.

56 S. K. Kamalov (Uzbek), K. Murtazaev (Uzbek) and S. B. Niiazbekov (Kazakh) each of whom returns to his home republic, two after courses at the Higher Party School and one after a spell in the All-Union Komsomol apparatus.

57 For instance, Brezhnev himself, V. K. Akulintsev, S. M. Veselov, S. D. Ignat'ev, B. V. Popov and A. K. Protozanov.

58 This probably explains why transfers between economically similar areas but across republic borders (see n. 30, above) occur, though relatively infrequently. If the initiative for regional specialization in appointments lay with the center, we might have expected rather more such cases where specialization ignored administrative boundaries. A fuller list could have been given of staff transferred across administrative borders to the Virgin Lands scheme and it is significant that this was the sort of occasion which called for a departure from normal practice.

59 *Pravda*, 23 February 1962, attests that they *had* an organizational structure and staff in their heyday in the late Khrushchev period. But there is no evidence that these were maintained, and the officials named in the article in question never achieved prominence.

60 See Miller, op. cit., p. 29 and n. 64.

61 Hough and Fainsod, op. cit., p. 421.

3

Regional Elites in Socialist Yugoslavia: Changing Patterns of Recruitment and Composition

LENARD COHEN

Introduction

For the first time in thirty-five years the key question asked of specialists on Yugoslav political development is not who will succeed Tito, but whether his successors having initially maintained their own authority, can preserve the regime's rather unique and well-known distinguishing features. The skills, attitudes and performance of the individuals who occupy important positions of political authority and societal activity – the political and social elites – are major factors affecting the continuation and vitality of the Yugoslav socialist 'experiment'. Although a great deal of attention has recently been directed to the identity and characteristics of the new and relatively small 'collective' party and state leadership, there has been almost no systematic analysis of Yugoslav elites below the federal (central) level of the political system. Those studies which have been done focus exclusively on elites at the local (communal, municipal and enterprise) level rather than the middle (republic and provincial) levels of the political system. Over the last several years the incumbents of posts at the federal level have been regularly selected or 'delegated' from those 'middle-level' elite groups and have generally returned to them after a limited term of service at the 'center'. Moreover, the importance accorded to 'harmonizing' divergent ethnic and regional interests prior to the formulation of federal policy – a practice now firmly institutionalized in the constitution and in elite political culture – adds even more significance to the selection, characteristics and preferences of middle-level elites. Indeed, the degree of cleavage and consensus among such elites, and their propensity to cooperate or conflict in the decisionmaking process, is probably the most crucial datum for any assessment of stability in post-Tito Yugoslavia.

This chapter will examine the recruitment and sociopolitical composition of political elites on the regional level of the Yugoslav system, that is, in the six republics and two provinces (hereafter called regional elites). Four institutionally distinct regional elites will be considered:

(1) the *party elite*, including (*a*) members of the presidencies, and (*b*) executive secretaries of the regional central committees of the League of Communists (SKJ);
(2) the *state administrative elite*, including secretaries and directors of the various secretariats, committees and institutes that constitute the state (public) administration in each republic and province;
(3) the *state executive elite*, that is, members of the state executive councils responsible to the assemblies (the equivalent of the Cabinet in each region);
(4) the *legislative elite*, including the presidents and vice-presidents of the regional assemblies.

In view of present and potential modes of elite recruitment at both the middle and top levels of the federal structure (see below), it appears very likely that the individuals who comprise these four regional elites will exercise an important influence on the operation of the Yugoslav political system over the next decade.

In order to examine systematically the political and social characteristics of the various regional elite groups biographical information concerning 423 individuals was obtained and then transferred to a computer-readable format for analysis.[1] Except for a few missing cases, the study embraces the entire universe of elite members in these regional positions at the beginning of 1980. In order to provide a background to the examination of elite composition the first part of the chapter surveys changing trends and issues in the recruitment of Yugoslav political decisionmakers over the past thirty-five years. The second section presents the findings from the analysis of those elite characteristics for which information was available: age, political generation (party membership and participation in the partisan struggle), level and type of education, and ethnic background. Although it is impossible to extrapolate elite attitudes and behavior from data on sociopolitical background, such information can provide valuable empirical insights regarding the potential character and magnitude of cleavages within and among different subelites. The absence of current survey data on Yugoslav political elites, and the probable unlikelihood of obtaining such information in the near future, makes such background data even more useful as a departure-point for the analysis of 'self-managed socialism'. The present study of elite backgrounds is based entirely on empirical data not previously available or analyzed and is part of this author's broader research project on elites in Yugoslav society.

Patterns of Elite Recruitment, 1945-81

The institutional methods and screening criteria for selecting governing elites in Yugoslavia, that is, the process of elite recruitment, can be differentiated into a number of patterns since the end of World War II. Each pattern of recruitment is generally related to a specific stage of the regime's political history, although far less closely than has sometimes been recognized by observers. Despite the variation among the patterns and stages of elite recruitment, three issues appear to be very significant throughout the entire course of postwar political development:

(1)   *the scope* of party influence over the selection of non-party elites, that is, both the extent of party influence over recruitment decisions in other sectors of obvious political authority (legislatures, executive organs, the state administration and mass sociopolitical organizations) and also over less directly political sectors such as the economy, the arts, the universities, and so on;

(2)   *the centralization* of party influence over its own and other elite personnel, that is, the extent to which influence over elite recruitment is concentrated in central (federal-level) party organs;

(3)   *the professionalization* of political elites, that is, the extent to which political officeholding constitutes a full-time career as opposed to an episodic and avocational form of activity.

This section of the study offers an examination of the successive phases and patterns of elite recruitment paying particular attention to the regime's approach to the preceding issues.

(a)   Partisan Ascendency and Elite Formation, 1945–9

The first period begins with the political ascendency of a relatively young, politically cohesive and ethnically diverse group of partisan leaders who had emerged victorious in a civil war and national liberation struggle and ends in the wake of the rift between the 'Soviet bloc' and Yugoslavia. Recruitment throughout the period was characterized by highly centralized and pervasive party control of elite personnel including the preferential allocation of elite-level jobs to professional party functionaries and 'tested' political activists who had served in the partisan movement. The routine supervision of recruitment was carried out by the Personnel Department of the Central Committee's apparatus in Belgrade. The scope of the Personnel Department and also its close resemblance to Soviet institutions of the time is best described by an authoritative political history of the period:

> The Personnel Department was head by an organisational secretary of the Central Committee under whose jurisdiction were the leading personnel in the party and the youth organisations. Other members of this department were responsible for personnel questions in non-party institutions, the apparatus of the government and its institutions, the security services, and the selection of specialised personnel. The prerogatives of the department also extended to lower level party committees, the sending of students to party schools and courses, the revision of party penalties, the personnel services of the state organs, questions of personnel in sensitive services (Post, Telephone, and Telegraph, etc.) ... The higher leadership was not elected, but entirely chosen by the method of co-optation. For lower leaderships, the proposals for new committee members were compiled by higher committees and their personnel commissions. The criteria for selection included, however, that proposed candidates be authentic fighters both in the war and in the peacetime construction of the country, with long party seniority and a clean past ... In leaderships Communists were elected according to their '*partijnost*' and not according to functions in the state apparatus.[2]

Other factors contributing to the centralized operation of the party and recruitment policy in this early period were the complete absence of regular plenary meetings of the regional Central Committee memberships, and the extreme secrecy surrounding the activities and meetings of the top leadership in each region of the country.

Despite the rigid hierarchical and 'conspiratorial' procedures, internal criticism was soon raised about the 'degradation of specialised skills' in personnel selection to the state apparatus, and its consequences for economic development. As early as September 1946, for example, a government commission proposed 'the re-education of older specialists, correct relations towards specialists, and the improvement of their material position'. A campaign was also launched to improve the geographical distribution of specialists and to discourage their outmigration from the poorest and most devastated regions of the country.[3] Politics and the central party functionaries remained firmly in command of recruitment, but the imperatives of economic development and economic planning were quickly leading to demands for the increased utilization and expansion of the technical intelligentsia. Indeed, it was even acknowledged that professional revolutionaries (partisan fighters) did not always make the best professional (ideologically well-educated and administratively qualified) politicians.[4] The Yugoslav regime's major answer to such personnel deficiencies was the educational system which was mobilized both to train a new generation of professionals in political and non-political fields, and also retrain existing cadres to aid in the 'construction of socialism'.

(b)   Elite Consolidation and Resocialization, 1950–65

After an initial period of disorientation and reflection (1948–50) the Tito–Stalin break precipitated a major institutional transformation of the Yugoslav political system. There is no question that measures such as the creation of workers' councils, the elimination of central planning, the decentralization of the state apparatus, the enhanced position of local governments and legislative bodies, and the reorganization of the Communist Party (renamed the League of Communists in 1952), to mention the most important changes, introduced an entirely new basis for socialist development in Yugoslavia. The actual impact of this new 'model' (the details of which have been described many times elsewhere) on elite recruitment is far less dramatic, however, than the character of changes in other areas. Although the party, for example, underwent a striking change in its name, operational principles[5] and the relative size of its bureaucratic apparatus (Table 3.1), these changes had rather a negligible effect on the process of elite recruitment. The selection of personnel to fill top positions in the party and other sectors

Table 3.1 Size of the Yugoslav League of Communists and the Party Apparatus, 1950–81

Year	Number of party members	Central apparatus Function-aries*	Central apparatus Workers†	Central apparatus Total	Regional (republican and provincial) apparatus Function-aries	Regional Workers	Regional Total	Total party apparatus (central and regional) Function-aries	Total Workers	Total Total	Total party apparatus as a percentage of total party membership
1950	607,443	n.a.	n.a.	n.a.	n.a.	n.a.	n.a.	11,930	n.a.	n.a.	n.a.
1952	772,920	n.a.	n.a.	n.a.	n.a.	n.a.	n.a.	n.a.	n.a.	5,156	0·67
1957	755,066	n.a.	n.a.	n.a.	n.a.	n.a.	n.a.	n.a.	n.a.	2,579	0·34
1958	829,953	n.a.	n.a.	n.a.	n.a.	n.a.	n.a.	n.a.	n.a.	2,860	0·34
1963	1,019,013	n.a.	n.a.	n.a.	n.a.	n.a.	n.a.	n.a.	n.a.	3,339	0·32
1965	1,046,262	58	88	146	1,311	2,026	3,337	1,369	2,114	3,482	0·33
1966	1,006,285	19	131	150	1,090	1,990	3,080	1,109	2,121	3,230	0·32
1967	1,013,500	11	137	148	1,112	1,822	2,934	1,123	1,959	3,082	0·30
1968	1,146,084	13	148	161	791	2,099	2,890	804	2,247	3,051	0·27
1969	1,111,682	14	189	203	671	2,244	2,915	685	2,433	3,118	0·28
1970	1,049,184	13	213	216	758	2,346	3,104	771	2,559	3,330	0·32
1971	1,025,476	14	205	219	748	2,284	3,032	762	2,489	3,251	0·31
1972	1,009,947	15	198	213	796	2,364	3,160	811	2,562	3,373	0·33
1973	1,076,711	15	199	214	938	2,468	3,406	953	2,667	3,620	0·34
1974	1,192,466	17	234/10	261	1,127	2,550	3,677	1,114	2,794	3,938	0·33
1975	1,302,843	18/1‡	240/13	272	1,130	2,861	3,991	1,149	3,114	4,263	0·33
1976	1,460,267	18/1	245/13	277	1,216	3,265	4,481	1,235	3,523	4,758	0·33
1977	1,623,735	17/2	267/13	299	1,290	3,514	4,804	1,309	3,794	5,103	0·31
1980	1,950,000	n.a.	n.a.	n.a.	n.a.	n.a.	n.a.	ca1,500	n.a.	n.a.	n.a.
1981	2,117,083	25	n.a.	n.a.	1,489	n.a.	n.a.	1,514	4,358	5,872	0·28

* Elected functionaries and 'professional sociopolitical workers' on the payroll of the Central Committee.
† Employees in the 'specialized services' of the Central Committee; in the middle of 1971, for example, 22 percent of these employees were 'specialized political workers' and the remainder workers in analytical-statistical, technical and auxiliary affairs.
‡ Individuals working in the Committee of the Conference of the Central Committee in Organizations of the Federation.
Source: Lenard Cohen, 'Elites in Yugoslav society' (forthcoming).

remained highly centralized and limited largely to individuals with professional political experience.[6]

One change during this period which does, in retrospect, seem to represent at least an incremental shift in the basis of power, if not a fundamental change in the pattern of personnel selection, was the increased role of the central state security apparatus and especially its chief, Alexander Ranković. As Ranković remained an organizational secretary of the League of Communists and a member of its Politburo, in addition to his post as Minister of State Security, it is difficult to view his now well-documented domination over elite recruitment up until 1966 as exemplifying a reduction of the scope of party control. Moreover, party pronouncements (particularly after the adoption of a new program in 1958) which encouraged greater independence and control by non-party organizations and sectors over their own personnel recruitment, do not appear to have had much effect. Even the official party and constitutional endorsements (1963) of new provisions to discourage the professionalization of political activity, such as limitations on the occupancy of governmental positions and prohibitions on simultaneous officeholding in party and state bodies, do not seem to have had much influence above the local level of the political system. Looking back at the remarks made by Alexander Ranković at the Eighth Party Congress in 1964 (where he gave the major speech concerning personnel questions) it is now easier to see his lukewarm support for what he then lauded as the 'democratisation of cadre policy'. His comments were undoubtedly a signal to the partisan generation that as far as he was concerned at least, they had little to fear from the new personnel measures, and perhaps even something to gain from them. For example, he pointed out that one of the positive effects of 'rotation' was that there would be more people available to fill the plethora of political and governmental jobs, thereby lessening the pressure on a small number of aging individuals to conduct several jobs at the same time. Or considered in another way (as it undoubtedly was by his audience), since there were plenty of jobs to go around, rotation could provide less strain and more variety in one's work.[7] It was only at the Fourth Plenum in July 1966, and after the removal of Ranković and his allies in the security service, that a more candid appraisal of recruitment policy was given:

Up to the Fourth Plenum conservative forces had a considerable influence on personnel policy in the League of Communists which, in different ways, contradicted proclaimed principles. In personnel policy and in practice, there were many different phenomena, solving personnel questions in closed circles, subjectivism, bureaucratic conservative relations, etc. The characteristics of individual members and leaders of the League of Communists often was based on data from the organs of state security which contained simplistic, manufactured, and subjective interpretations, behind which were concealed a definite political background ... Rotation was applied chiefly on the occasion of electing communal leadership, while the republic leaderships and the organs on the federal level of the League were renewed by broadening the size of their composition.[8]

It is important to add that alongside the often overlooked continuities in recruitment policy during the Ranković era profound changes were, nevertheless, taking place in society, and also that these changes were beginning to have at least an indirect effect on personnel selection. In fact, to a certain extent, these changes may have even contributed to the successful implementation of the 'anti-bureaucratic' decisions taken at the Fourth Plenum. For one thing, during the same years that the Ranković forces had monopolized elite recruitment a massive expansion and transformation of the educational system produced a large new generation of trained specialists. These university graduates were now seeking advancement and the adoption of policies which responded to their newly acquired occupational perspectives. For example, the total number of individuals classified as 'specialists and artists' grew from 222,000 in 1953 to 490,000 in 1961, or an increase of around 120 percent. While in 1919–40 two-thirds of all university graduates were in the field of law and philosophy, only 27 percent graduated in those fields in 1945–61. The number of students receiving diplomas in economics and in the engineering faculties alone doubled in 1945–61.[9] The goals and expectations of the new intelligentsia were molded during the more stable and 'promising' years of emergent self-management after 1950, rather than by the sacrifices and solidarity of the earlier revolutionary struggle. Although the removal of Ranković took everyone by surprise, the new generation of specialists undoubtedly regarded the event as a positive signal (an observation deserving of more research).

A second and closely related change was the growing professionalization of occupations, a development which affected both the political and non-political sectors of society. Younger and even older individuals in different specialized fields of work now identified more closely with certain standardized modes of behavior and ways of performing tasks (for instance, managers). Such professionalization also led to a greater differentiation between political subsectors such as legislative work, the state administration, journalism and party affairs (ironically, even affecting the security services because of their great institutional exclusivity and conspiratorial methods). Each political subsector began to see its respective field of work as a professional and distinct branch of 'sociopolitical activity'.[10] Elite positions within each political and non-political sector were still within the scope of the central party apparatus and the security organs, but each sphere was becoming relatively more specialized and differentiated both in outlook and interests.

Finally, and again related, the successful modernization and industrialization of the country itself meant that decisionmaking was far more complex and technical in nature and, therefore, required more sophisticated political and economic management skills. Taken together all three of the above changes created a climate, a constituency and a pressure for the reform of 'personnel policy', namely, for less arbitrary, centralized and personalized forms of selection, with less deference to 'ascribed' political credentials (service in the partisans) and increased opportunities for the influence and advancement of the newer generation of specialists. Since many of the advocates and potential beneficiaries of such changes (although by no means all of them) were located in the more economically developed regions of the country (that is, the northwestern, dissident, less partisan and more religious areas), their views of reform often became intermingled with demands for greater regional and ethnic autonomy. The 'collective' threat of several different and sometimes unrelated reforms was enough to provoke a strong challenge from the older and more conservative party leaders at the end of the next stage of Yugoslav political development.

(c)   *Elite Modernization and Elite Succession, 1966–71*

The reorganization of the League of Communists which resulted from the Ranković affair led to a substantial change in elite recruitment and personnel policy. These changes involved all three aspects of personnel selection which we have been discussing, the scope of party control, centralization and professionalization. New policy guidelines stipulated that the party organs, and certainly the security organs, would no longer dominate or manipulate the recruitment of leading political and non-political personnel.

The impact of this change, for example, allowed the Commission for Elections and Appointments in the Federal Assembly to assume a greater role over personnel policy within the assembly system (that is, leadership posts in the legislature, and in federal executive and administrative organs). It may be interesting to note that a normative and operational shift of control over personnel decisions from the Federal Executive Council to the Federal Assembly had begun as early as 1963. It was only in 1967, however, (after the Fourth Plenum) that the Assembly's commission was given the authority to formulate the proposals for higher administrative appointments and dismissal, 'after hearing the opinion' of the Federal Executive Council. This was a complete reversal of earlier procedure and practice whereby proposals on personnel were submitted by the executive organs after simply consulting with the Assembly. This shift in jurisdiction was not insignificant from the point of view of legislative institutionalization or personnel recruitment.[11] Increasingly, for example, elected members of legislative assemblies attempted to recruit higher civil servants and legislative staff personnel whose professional credentials were relevant to the specific tasks they were selected to perform. An interesting exchange in a plenary session of the Federal Assembly's Economic Chamber (composed, at the time, mainly of members of the managerial and technical intelligentsia) illustrates the new official outlook toward political recruitment, and the reaction to it. The question at issue was no longer, as after the war, whether higher civil servants should be technically qualified (or only politically qualified), but just how specialized an official's background had to be for the job. The fact that such questions could be raised by Yugoslav legislators is also an important development in this period:

Agenda (Dec. 4, 1971): A Proposal by the President of the Federal Government (Federal Executive Council) to appoint a new Federal Secretary for Transportation.
Question by a federal deputy: Has the proposed candidate for the job of Federal Secretary of Transportation 'had any experience in transportation or any connection with it?'
Answer by a spokesman for the Government: 'The function of the head of a department calls for: competence, knowledge of things, affinity, and consultations with the republics and provinces. Hence the proposal to appoint as a federal secretary ... an economist, a man versed in economics, as a member of our

government. But, is he an expert in transport? This question has not been posed quite correctly. He will have experts in his secretariat'.

Comment by a second federal deputy in support of the government's position: 'Something which we have not had in post-war practice has cropped up: we have to discuss the professional skill of a minister . . . this could lead to exclusion; no worker could be a member of the Federal Executive Council. Unfortunately such is the case now . . . for many years now we have not had a worker in the highest organs'.[12]

The role of the central party organs in the appointments of higher legislative and administrative personnel was not completely eliminated in this period, but the extent and method of party influence changed in a manner which tended to disperse (pluralize) control over elite recruitment. The decline in party interference and the use of political criteria in personnel selection was even more noticeable on the local level of the system, especially in the recruitment of enterprise management. A new generation of more professionalized managerial functionaries and technical intelligentsia began to predominate in both the operation of the economy and as part-time political decision-makers in representative assemblies.[13]

Perhaps the most striking change in recruitment policy was the decentralization of authority over personnel selection within the League of Communists itself. New policy guidelines gave responsibility to regional party organs for the selection of their own officials. After 1966, the personnel commission of the central committee in Belgrade was discontinued, although such commissions remained in some of the republics and provinces. Beginning in 1968 as part of the effort to increase the influence of regional party organizations over federal party decision-making republic and provincial congresses of the League of Communists were held before rather than after the central party congress. The latter change, although not unlike procedures in other communist countries, represented more than a simply symbolic gesture. More open and conflictual discussions began to occur in the republics and provinces concerning the criteria and methods used in elite recruitment. At the Sixth Congress of the League of Communists of Croatia in December 1968, for example, one delegate argued quite vigorously and in a manner far more candid than the practice in past years that local personnel and regional interests had been insufficiently accommodated in the recruitment process (actual names are replaced by letters in the passage quoted below):

I would like someone to explain why there are so many directors, legislators, and professional functionaries from socio-political organizations on the list of candidates and people who live outside of Croatia.

I would like someone to explain how the following people got on the list to be permanent members of the Conference of the League of Croatian Communists: 'A', director of the Ship-building Industry in Split, 'B', a federal legislator and president of a committee in the Federal Assembly who lives in Belgrade. These people were not proposed and not elected by the Communal Conference of the League in Split. Why aren't direct producers, workers and specialists, mainly young people, on the list such as, 'C', a highly skilled worker in the ship-building enterprise in Split, 'D', a highly skilled worker in the water works in Split . . . 'E', a vice-admiral and commandant of the Split army district, 'F', an engineer . . .

All these comrades were proposed and elected as candidates for organs of the Yugoslav League of Communists and the Croatian League of Communists. It is simply unacceptable that the Central Committee discards them and places on the list people who the Conference of the League in Split, and their basic organizations have not proposed. How can we explain this to the membership of the League and Conference?[14]

A new generation of regional political activists also began to make their appearance in this period. For example, about 90 percent of the delegates elected to regional congresses in 1968 and 1969 were at their first congress, and about 69 percent of the individuals elected to the new regional central committees were new members.[15] A history of the League of Communists emphasizes the significant impact of these and other changes 'after the fall of the group around Alexander Ranković':

Namely, until Brioni (the Fourth Plenum) of the Central Committee of the League of Communists, the nomination, appointment, and replacement of higher and middle range cadre often was exercised by the (federal) Central Committee of the League of Communists. Such practice created bureaucratic obedience to the leading officials who posted and changed them. This meant obedience to the organs of the federation. After the Fourth Plenum of the Central Committee that right completely shifted to organs of the republics. It strengthened the power of republican factors, turning the organs of the federation to the republics because public leadership functions frequently represented the only source of personal (private) existence of public functionaries . . . Now that important decisions were no longer taken on the federal summit, contact among representatives of the republics

were strengthened in the form of bilateral and multilateral visits
of state and party delegations. Consequently, a significant role
was played by Josip Broz Tito. Increasingly he entered into
political conversations with republican delegations and in that
way created a basis for political decisions. In daily political life the
slogan of unity was replaced by the slogan equality, negotiations,
and agreements between republics.[16]

The reduction and devolution of party control over personnel
selection in the years after 1966 was also accompanied by
important changes concerning the professionalization of political and non-political work. Briefly, a dual process was taking
place: first, a reduction of political professionalization, or in
other words, an increase in party and mass organization officeholding on an amateur or avocational basis; and secondly, a
greater emphasis on professionalization in areas that were
formerly very closely related to the party apparatus (managerial, legislative, higher civil service, journalistic and military
positions), as well as in more explicitly non-political sectors
(engineering, teaching, medicine, and so on). The latter development represented an intensification of a trend which, as we
noted above, had begun earlier. The increased deprofessionalization of careers in the party and mass organizations represented, however, the first really significant transformation of these
job areas since the war. Although the introduction of measures
during the early 1950s had considerably reduced the overall
number of political officials and the relative size of the party
apparatus (Table 3.1), other developments were also at work.
Thus, the expansion of special schools for political-administra-
tive education (including the re-education or degree completion
of activists from the partisan movement) and the multiplication
of political jobs at the communal level of the federation, along
with the increased differentiation and complexity of all political
roles in society, had gradually contributed to a growth in
political professionalism by the late 1950s.[17] It was only during
the two years after the party reorganization of 1967 that the
relative size of the central and regional party apparatus again
began to decline (Table 3.1).

Increasingly leadership posts in the party and mass organizations were filled on either a part-time or amateur basis, and
often by individuals whose major field of work was in non-
political sectors.[18] Separate Higher Party Schools – the traditional vehicle for elite political education – were discontinued
and such institutions became regular university faculties (a
change which ostensibly eliminated party training as a distinct

field but actually tended to professionalize political training). Not surprisingly, as a result of the above changes, fewer younger people during this period aspired to a career in politics. Without its earlier status, security and influence, it seemed that political work had simply lost most of its glamor and appeal to the brightest members of the younger generation, a development which did not go unnoticed by those who were already anxious about the course of political development.

Party leaders also worried about the class composition of elite recruitment in this period. Despite pronouncements and token efforts to forestall the steady decline in the number of 'direct producers' in positions of political leadership during the 1950s and 1960s, party leaders continued tacitly to encourage and to rationalize the overwhelming predominance of professionally trained personnel in political decisionmaking bodies. At the Sixth Congress of the League of Communists of Croatia in December 1968, for example, a proposal (originating outside the ranks of the party) was adopted by a large majority of votes in a Congress Commission session to the effect that three-fourths of the members of the forums and organs to the League of Communists be made up of 'communists from the working collectives of economic and societal spheres of activity' who would continue to remain on their jobs. This motion was defeated by a majority of delegates to a plenary session of the Congress at the insistence of the prominent Croatian leader Vladamir Bakaric.[19]

According to Bakaric, the reasons it was necessary to defeat the motion were as follows: (i) in some organizations the working class was actually in the minority, so its numerical predominance in party forums would be unjustified; (ii) a direct producers' majority in the Central Committee would tend to strengthen the influence of the permanent bureaucratic apparatus since the tasks confronting the Central Committee are very complex, especially with respect to foreign affairs; (iii) the preoccupation of workers with their immediate experience would promote the transformation of the League of Communists into an organization concerned exclusively with instrumental (economic) matters; and (iv) such a large representation of workers in the League of Communists would be tantamount to the introduction of a form of dictatorship not of the proletariat, but of the direct producers, which would signify a slowdown in the rate of growth that Yugoslavia has so far enjoyed. Bakaric's argument was a fascinating commentary not only on the broadened and modernized definition of the 'working class' in Yugoslavia and other socialist states, but also on the salient role played by the political and non-political (technical and 'humanistic') professional intelligentsia in that *new class*.

(d) Elite Retrenchment and Anxiety, 1972–81

Recruitment policy underwent a basic change following Tito's vigorous campaign against the supporters of liberalism, nationalism and technocracy in the regional party organizations at the end of 1971. The shift in policy was premissed on a disavowal of the centrifugal and devolutionary trends in party development which had begun at the Sixth Congress in 1952, but had been considerably accelerated after 1967. More specifically, party organs were again to monitor and actively to influence the appointment of personnel in all important political and non-political posts. Control of personnel appointments in the assemblies and the state administration once again reverted to the strengthened executive branch of the governmental structure – despite, and partially because of, the introduction of the much-heralded 'delegate system'.[20] The growth in executive control meant indirectly and directly greater influence by the League of Communists since the earlier prohibition on simultaneous officeholding in the state and party was now also relaxed, and party members were urged to work for the new policies of the party organization wherever they were employed. The new slogan was the 'party within the system' and not as earlier a League 'divorced from power'. As one regional party functionary observed,

> whenever the executive bodies of the state become stronger, that means that something similar is taking place in the party as well. And conversely: when the government executive is 'weakening' then the party is 'weakening' as well. Sometimes the tie-up gives strength to centralistic tendencies, and sometimes to particularistic tendencies.[21]

Another manifestation of the new recruitment policy was the growing interference of party organizations over appointments in the universities (most explicitly in Belgrade and Ljubljana), the media, cultural institutions and industrial enterprises.[22] The following exchange during an interview with Stane Dolanc, a member of the Presidency of the League of Communists, illustrates current elite views regarding the scope of party involvement in personnel decisions:

Interviewer:	A certain high official has told us the following anecdote: Participating in discussion at a session, he asked why the party is interfering in everything and even dismisses and replaces directors. Another participant in the same discussion replied: It is natural that the party is dismissing and replacing people because it appointed them in the first place. That was naturally said in jest but it did point out a serious problem. Do you agree?
Dolanc:	This question is now frequently raised in various ways and in various places. I think that the League of Communists has the right not to dismiss and replace but to provide the initiative for replacing a director, a minister or some office-holder. It has that right even under the Constitution, as a sociopolitical organization.[23]

After 1971 a renewed emphasis was also placed on the 'moral-political qualities and suitability' of candidates for important posts, in addition to their specialized qualifications. It was not so much a question of selecting 'reds' instead of experts (to use the somewhat oversimplified analytical dichotomy of elite studies on communist regimes), but of selecting the proper *red-experts*. A campaign was also launched to improve the class composition of the League of Communists, and striking if basically token successes were soon recorded in the number of direct producers enrolled as party members and elected to party organs. At the Tenth Party Congress in 1974 Tito sharply criticized the earlier emphasis on the 'renewal of cadres' urging that 'everyone who is fit to do so should continue to be active in every way, for communists must work in the interest of the revolution to the very end'. The composition of the new party Central Committees elected in 1974 and 1978 reflected this view and included in their membership a core group of loyal professional politicians from the partisan generation, and even some individuals who had retired from active political work during the elite succession policy of the late 1960s.[24] Beginning in 1972 the absolute number of professional functionaries and workers in the party apparatus also began to increase, as did the size of the party membership, a trend which continued unabated through 1980 (see Table 3.1). One recent analysis noted that Yugoslavia in mid-1981 had more than 10,000 politicians and that 'experience up to now shows that the delegate system can't secure an automatic reduction in the force and influence of political professionalism. On the contrary, in everyday life we often can see that such influence increases as do the number of professionals'.[25] Although elaborate provisions were adopted in the spring of 1981 to accelerate the rotation (or reduce the tenure) of Yugoslav politicians in most elite positions, past experience suggests that this will probably do more to speed up interorganizational or interapparatus mobility than to reduce the number of career politicians.[26]

One expression of the renewed party interest in recruitment was the reintroduction of personnel commissions in the federal and in all regional party organizations. The task of the personnel commissions was to ensure that 'all those selected for responsible and leading functions in society would give the highest guarantee that they will create the new course of the League of Communists'.[27] The Tenth Congress of the League of Communists condemned the

> earlier dilemma concerning 'non-interference' which in fact had served as a smoke screen for blocking out the League of Communists in the area of personnel policy . . . [O]rgans of the League have begun concretely to involve themselves in questions of personnel policy and directly to engage in their solution.[28]

In order to combat 'party federalism' and the 'political disintegration of the League of Communists' measures were also taken to 'restore the firm connections and responsibilities in the spirit of democratic centralism between the leadership of the League of Communists of the republics and the leadership of the [federal] organs of the League'.[29] The practice of ensuring equitable (usually parity) nationality and regional representation in all federal party organs was continued (the so-called ethnic 'key' in recruitment), but the new policy stressed the responsibility of all party officials to behave as members of a single (cross-nationality and cross-regional) political organization and not, as earlier, to function as delegated ambassadors of republic and provincial party machines. In effect, the 'new course' contributed to greater centralization of personnel policy both within and outside the party.

The effort by the League of Communists to consolidate its control over the political system during the 1970s can be illustrated by new data based on the organizational history and circulation of elite members on the regional level of the political system. Specifically by comparing two personnel directories which list all of the occupants of federal and regional political positions – published in 1972 and 1980 respectively[30] – it is possible to ascertain the organizational background of current elite incumbents. Briefly what positions in 1972, if any, were held by the current (1980) members of the regional political elites? The particular span of time (1972–80) was chosen for two reasons: first, the period begins right after Tito's purge of Croatian elite officials and thereby opens the most recent phase of Yugoslav political development (prior to Tito's death in May 1980); secondly, it covers a period in which, at least theoretically, there should have been a good deal of interorganizational rotation and personnel movement (two state elections and two party congresses, 1974 and 1978). Following this approach, information was generated for more than 600 officials serving in four elite sectors during 1980 (Table 3.2). Although the method of analysis is less than desirable (precise data on the career changes and chronology of each person are not available), it does provide some very interesting and important insights concerning the circulation of persons within and among different organizational sectors.

As Table 3.2 indicates, just over two-thirds of the individuals serving in the current regional party elites were also in elite positions either on the regional or federal level in 1972. This contrasts sharply with members of the other three regional subelites in the state sectors (top administrators, executives and legislators), who were either outside or below the political elite in 1972 (working in the economy, finishing education, in temporary retirement, working on the communal and municipal level, and so on). Moreover, of those members of the regional party elites who were already in elite activities in 1972, 58 percent were working in the same or a very closely related elite sector, that is, some position in the League of Communists or other mass sociopolitical organization. In other words, on the eve of Tito's death the regional party elites were composed largely of individuals with considerable elite-level political experience and organizational specialization. The much smaller group of regional state executives and top legislators with earlier elite-level political experience also had most of their major previous organizational affiliations in the party and mass sociopolitical organizations, a fact which reflects the increased party control of the assembly system in the period after 1971.

The most interesting subelite, however, is composed of the regional administrative functionaries in the state bureaucracy. This group had the highest percentage of new recruits to the elite level (78·4 percent), and among those civil servants with

Table 3.2 Organizational Background and Circulation of Yugoslav Regional Political Elites, 1972–80

	I	Sector of elite activities in 1980 (%)			
		II	III	IV	V
	party elite*	state administration elite	state executive elites	legislative elite	total
(a) *Activity in 1972*					
Activities outside of the political elite†	32·6	78·4	74·7	62·2	65·0
Elite activities (regional or federal)	67·4	22·4	25·3	37·8	35·0
Total	100·0	100·0	100·0	100·0	100·0
N	138	250	150	74	614
(b) *Sector of elite activities in 1972*					
Party (SKJ) and mass sociopolitical organizations	58·0	33·9	47·3	60·8	50·2
State administration	9·7	53·6	21·1	7·1	27·0
State executive bodies‡	18·3	1·8	18·4	25·0	10·7
Legislatures	10·8	10·7	13·2	7·1	10·7
Other elite activities§	3·2	—	—	—	1·4
Total	100·0	100·0	100·0	100·0	100·0
N	93	56	38	28	215

* This subelite includes the members of the Presidency of the Central Committee for each of the 8 republics and provinces; in each of those areas it includes the President of the Executive Council (state) and legislative assembly (state) and thus in 16 cases overlaps with subelites III and IV.
† Work on the communal and municipal level, working in the economy, finishing education, in temporary retirement, etc.
‡ Includes members of state executive councils, state presidencies and the Council for the Federation.
§ Administrators of mass media, etc.

earlier elite-level experience, a very high percentage (54 percent) was recruited from within the administrative sector. Only the party elite shows a higher level of intrasectoral recruitment. The regional administrative elite appears to be the subgroup most open to new talent (a trait which also shows up in the data on the state executive elite) and the only political subgroup other than the party elite with a real basis for organizational 'solidarity'. Data not shown also indicate that among all of the 1980 regional-elite members who earlier were serving on the federal level, the state administrators tend most frequently to return to their own organizational sector (that is, going from federal administrative work to regional administrative jobs). These findings tend to support other observations concerning the less 'partisanized' but still 'politicized' and highly techno-bureaucratic outlook in the state administration,[31] a feature which may have continued even after the resurgence of party influence in the 1970s. The next section offers a more detailed consideration of elite characteristics on the regional level.

The Composition of Yugoslav Regional Elites

(a) *Age Structure and Political Generations*

Generational cleavage and generational succession to elite positions have been important problems for communist political systems.[32] The age and generational structure of regional elites in Yugoslavia illustrates in a particular manner the dynamics of continuity and change which characterize most societies governed by an aging revolutionary elite which has transformed its environment. Each regional subelite includes a cross-section of different age cohorts within its ranks, but there are important modal tendencies within each elite group and interesting contrasts among the different elites.

One of the most striking tendencies revealed in the data on age composition (Table 3.3) is the diminished representation of the older generation of political leaders, that is, those who were at least 21 on the eve of World War II. Only seventeen out of 391 elite members (4·3 percent) in the whole regional sample were over 60 years of age. Most older individuals are concentrated in either the influential party presidencies or the more symbolic top legislative positions. The older character of the party and legislative presidencies is also revealed by the large number of individuals in the 50–60-year-old age cohort. An equally striking

Table 3.3 Age Structure of Yugoslav Regional Elites, 1980 (%)

Age in 1980	Years of birth	Regional elite groups — Party elites		State elites			total
		members of party presidencies	party secretaries	state administrative secretaries	members of state executive councils	legislative functionaries	
−35	since 1945	2·9	8·0	2·3	1·3	1·9	3·1
36–40	1940–4	8·7	12·9	5·5	3·8	5·8	6·9
41–45	1935–9	5·8	50·0	23·4	10·0	11·5	20·2
46–50	1930–4	26·1	19·4	21·9	37·5	13·5	24·3
51–55	1925–9	20·3	8·0	31·3	30·0	30·8	25·3
56–60	1920–4	29·0	—	13·3	13·8	26·9	13·9
61+	1919 and earlier	7·2	1·6	2·3	3·8	9·6	4·3
Total		100·0	100·0	100·0	100·0	100·0	100·0
N		69	62	128	80	52	391

contrast is the extreme youth of the party secretaries, a group which is now entrusted with the routine management of the party apparatus. While the party presidencies have the oldest composition of any subelite, the party secretaries comprise the youngest group in the sample.

Perhaps the most important age cohorts in considering Yugoslavia's immediate future development, however, are the two subgroups between 46 and 55 years of age in 1980. Individuals in these two cohorts who might be called 'children of the revolution' constitute the bulk of the entire elite sample, and of each subelite as well, except for the very young party secretaries. Indeed, the cohort of individuals between 51 and 55 years of age constitutes the largest subgroup within the administrative and legislative elites. The members of that age group were born in 1925–9 and were, therefore, 12–16 years old when the war started. Only 50 percent of the group participated in the partisan movement, and most of those joined in 1943–4.

The succession of the late partisan and postpartisan generation on the regional level is also revealed in the comparative data on political generations (Table 3.4). Fewer than one-third of all regional elite members served in the partisans, and those who did were mainly concentrated in the party and legislative presidencies. The data on affiliation with the party shows a similar tendency in contrast. Only two individuals joined the party before Tito became head of the organization in 1937. Except for the party and legislative presidencies, the majority of regional elite members joined the party in the period of self-management after 1950. In contrast to the late 1960s when the representative assemblies had acquired a good deal of political vitality, legislative leadership in particular seems to have again become a sinecure or an 'exit' arena for older politicians. The party secretaries stand out as the least 'partisan' subelite and the group whose members have most recently joined the League of Communists.

(b) Educational Background

Overall Yugoslavia's regional elites are very highly educated (Table 3.5). This generalization is even more true of the state administrative secretaries and the members of the state executive councils who have two to three times as many doctorates in their ranks as the party and legislative elites. The data on educational level also reveals that the young, new generation of party secretaries is not that well educated compared to the other

Table 3.4 *Yugoslav Regional Elites by Political Generation*

			Regional elite groups	members of state		
	members of party presidencies	*party secretaries*	*state administrative secretaries*	*executive councils*	*legislative functionaries*	*total*
(a) Participated in the National Liberation Movement (partisans) (%)						
Yes	49·3	3·2	24·8	21·3	56·6	29·3
No	50·7	96·8	75·2	78·7	43·4	90·7
Total	100·0	100·0	100·0	100·0	100·0	100·0
N	69	62	129	80	53	393
(b) Year of joining party (%)						
−1936	—	1·8	—	—	—	0·3
1937–40	6·1	1·8	0·9	1·3	6·1	2·8
1941–4	39·4	1·8	18·1	14·5	40·8	21·8
1945–8	16·7	10·7	21·6	28·9	24·5	20·9
1949–58	25·8	50·0	37·9	46·1	20·4	36·9
1959–63	6·1	25·0	14·7	6·6	6·1	11·8
1964+	6·1	8·9	6·9	2·6	2·0	5·5
Total	100·0	100·0	100·0	100·0	100·0	100·0
N	66	56	116	76	49	363

Table 3.5 *Yugoslav Regional Elites by Level and Type of Education*

| | Regional elite groups | | | | | |
	members of party presidencies	party secretaries	State administrative secretaries	members of state executive councils	legislative functionaries	total
Level of education (%)						
No higher education	4·7	13·6	0·8	—	4·3	3·9
Higher education	92·2	81·4	87·3	91·5	91·5	88·6
Higher education with doctorate	3·1	5·1	11·9	8·5	4·3	7·5
Total	100·0	100·0	100·0	100·0	100·0	100·0
N	64	59	118	71	47	359
Type of higher education (%)						
Political science, journalism	19·7	9·8	7·7	7·0	24·4	12·2
Administration and security	—	2·0	7·7	4·2	6·7	4·6
Law	9·8	25·5	24·0	18·3	17·8	19·7
Philosophy	6·6	11·8	7·7	8·5	—	7·2
Economic	18·0	11·8	24·0	33·8	20·0	22·6
Technical	1·6	2·0	23·1	16·9	17·8	14·2
Arts and sciences	3·3	7·8	—	2·8	2·2	2·6
Unknown*	41·0	29·4	5·9	8·5	11·1	16·8
Total	100·0	100·0	100·0	100·0	100·0	100·0
N	61	51	117	71	45	345

* Mainly unfinished higher education, 2-year 'higher schools', and political schooling, etc.

subelites, and particularly in contrast to the also relatively young state secretaries. This finding may partially be due to the age structure of the party secretaries, but very likely also reflects the party's incomplete success in attracting a new generation of functionaries who combine both political commitment and educational achievements. The insecurity and negative perceptions of professional political work (often officially encouraged, as already shown), as well as the availability of safer and more prestigious avenues of opportunity outside politics would tend to support the latter explanation.

The party's deficiencies in the area of educational specialization also emerge from the data on types of educational background. Not surprisingly, individuals with technical and economic training seem to be concentrated mainly in the state administration and the executive council, while those persons having political, administrative, military and journalistic training are more typically found in the party and legislative presidencies (although a good number of the vice-presidents of assemblies have economic and technical education). A large number of the younger group of party secretaries have been trained in law and philosophy. The very large percentage of 'unknown' higher educations revealed in both party subelites further accentuates the contrast in specialization between the party and state sectors. It is quite possible that the very different attitudes and modes of behavior usually resulting from such different training will create interelite conflicts during the next phase of Yugoslav development.

Type of education also bears an interesting relationship to age and political generations in a way which suggests that cleavages derived from training are both interelite and intraelite phenomena. Thus, further analysis of the entire sample reveals that nearly a third of those individuals who served in the partisan movement had educational training in politics, administration and security, while this was the case with fewer than a fifth of the non-participants. Close to half of all those who were not in the partisans had higher technical and economic training. Those individuals with technical and economic training who were in the partisans tended to join the movement rather late (in 1942–4), while those with political science, administration and military training mostly joined during 1941 (although such education may not have been acquired until after the war). The data also indicate that among younger elite members, those individuals with technical and economic education tended to join the party at a slightly older age, that is, after they had finished their education.

(c) Ethnic background

The official use of ethnic arithmetic in elite recruitment is an already well-understood feature of Yugoslav political life. Indeed, at least over the last fifteen years, the responsibility for maintaining such ethnic balance in regional and federal elite contingents has been left mainly to party organizations in the republics and provinces. Consequently, political subelites in all sections of Yugoslavia reveal considerable superficial representativeness in terms of their nationality composition relative to the general population. Despite this policy, however, certain interesting features and trends still require consideration. For one thing, although the ethnic representativeness of elites is only of rather minimal interest and sensitivity within the more homogeneous regions of the country (Slovenia, Montenegro, Serbia proper and Macedonia), it becomes a more important and controversial matter in the more ethnically diverse regions. Secondly, there appear to be significantly different degrees of representativeness depending on the specific subelite in question.

Table 3.6 offers data on the nationality composition of subelites in three of Yugoslavia's most sensitive areas of cultural diversity. In these regions – Croatia, Bosnia and Kosovo – there are large Serbian ethnic communities, ranking second in size to the region's principal nationality. Although the ethnic identities of a considerable number of elite members is unknown (particularly in Croatia and Bosnia), some generalizations can still be made.

Although Serbians are overrepresented in the party membership of each region relative to population size (a residue of the Serbs' disproportionately high participation in the partisan movement of all regions), the same extent of overrepresentation is not characteristic of the regional elite as a whole. It is probable, however, that greater Serbian elite overrepresentation would emerge if the ethnic identities of the unknown category were available (that is most likely in Bosnia where the partial data incorrectly make the Serbs appear very underrepresented). Data on party membership does indicate a considerable decline of Serbian representation compared with the immediate postwar years, although the recent decrease (1973–8) is very small except in Bosnia.

A noticeable contrast exists between the ethnic composition of the party elite and the state elite. In each multiethnic region Serbs are more overrepresented in the party elites (in Kosovo,

Table 3.6   *Ethnic Composition of Selected Yugoslav Regional Elites (%)*

Region and ethnic group		Total population (1971)	Party membership (1973)	(1978)	Party elite (1980)	State elites (1980)	Total regional elite (1980)
Croatia							
Serbs		14·2	24·7	24·2	26·3	18·2	21·2
Croats		79·4	64·8	64·2	57·9	63·6	61·5
Others		6·0	10·5	11·6	—	6·1	3·8
Unknown		0·4	—	—	15·8	12·1	13·5
	Total	100·0	100·0	100·0	100·0	100·0	100·0
					N=19	33	52
Bosnia							
Serbs		37·3	52·1	47·0	31·8	30·2	30·8
Croats		20·6	10·9	11·9	13·6	16·2	13·4
Muslims		39·6	31·1	33·9	31·8	41·9	38·5
Others		2·2	5·9	7·2	9·1	—	3·0
Unknown		0·3	—	—	13·6	11·6	12·3
	Total	100·0	100·0	100·0	100·0	100·0	100·0
					N=22	43	65
Kosovo							
Serbs		18·4	26·2	25·7	20·0	18·5	19·1
Montenegrins		2·5	8·0	7·0	10·0	3·7	6·4
Albanians		73·7	61·7	62·8	65·0	70·4	68·1
Muslims		2·1	1·7	2·3	5·0	3·7	4·2
Others		3·2	2·4	2·2	—	—	—
Unknown		0·1	—	—	—	3·7	2·1
	Total	100·0	100·0	100·0	100·0	100·0	100·0
					N=20	27	47

Montenegrins should be considered along with Serbs), while the principal ethnic group of each region has a 5–10 percent better representation in the state elite. Thus, in the case of each region's principal ethnic group, representation in the party elite bears a closer resemblance to its 'contribution' to party membership, rather than to proportion in the general population. The source of Serbian overrepresentation in the party elite of multiethnic regions (including Vojdvidina) emerges from another finding not shown: 50 percent (ninety-one individuals) out of all those regional elite members in the sample who were in the partisan movement were Serbs and Montenegrins, a figure which increases considerably if Bosnia, Croatia and Kosovo are considered separately. Among younger elite members, both in the party and the state subelites, the representation of individuals from the principal ethnic groups corresponds much more closely to the ethnic composition of each region. There is no doubt that such generational and interelite ethnic differences could be a source of considerable tension in the years ahead.[33] One regional political functionary noted in 1979 that the 'complex and delicate subject' of disproportion in the national structure of the League of Communists in Croatia is a very important 'ideopolitical question':

> Let us not forget that even today the Croatian nationalists have not abandoned their thesis that the Serbian nationality in Croatia has a dominant influence and that the Croats are in a subordinate position ... It is not a question of the need to reduce the number of the representatives of those nationalities that until now have been more strongly represented in the League of Communists of Croatia, but one should concentrate more on the inclusion of the representatives of those nationalities whose participation lags behind their share in the national structure of the population.[34]

Conclusion: Recruitment Imperatives and Elite Cleavages

The skills, values and behavior of regional political elites are key factors affecting the political stability of post-Tito Yugoslavia. Such elites not only have a significant influence on their respective republics and provinces, but they must also coordinate and compromise their views in the process of intraregional decisionmaking. Middle-level regional elites are also the primary source for the selection of federal-level officials who make the most important 'systematic' decisions in the system of self-management.[35]

The survey of elite recruitment in the first section of this chapter reveals important changes and continuities in the selection of political decisionmakers and other strategic leaders. After a five-year period (1966–7 to 1971) in which the pattern of elite recruitment was more pluralistic, decentralized and depoliticized, the last decade has witnessed a return to greater interference of party agencies over personnel selection, within and outside the party organization. At both the Tenth and Eleventh Congresses (1974 and 1978) of the League of Communists the slogan 'moral-political fitness', terminology reminiscent of the very early years of Yugoslav socialism and of other socialist states, again assumed prominence as a criterion for the recruitment of elite personnel.

It would be, however, incorrect to conclude from the preceding analysis that recruitment policy in the years after 1971 simply represented a throwback to the period of 'statist' or 'administrative' socialism. Although the policy of political deprofessionalization slowed considerably, and the absolute number of persons employed in the party apparatus nearly reached the same level as in 1952, it is also significant that the party had more than doubled in size in the intervening period (Table 3.1). Thus, the ratio of professional party functionaries to members has not changed appreciably over the last decade (there is even a slight decrease in 1981; see Table 3.1) and is possibly the lowest of any communist state. It is not surprising, therefore, that many seasoned party officials felt that the League of Communists was in danger of losing its firm control of society during the halcyon days of political pluralism and political deprofessionalization in the late 1960s.

More important than the size of the party apparatus is how that apparatus actually operates in the political system. A second distinguishing feature of elite recruitment in recent years has been the new methods by which the party attempts to wield influence over personnel selection in other sectors. In contrast to the comprehensive and centralized *nomenklatura*-type of system described in the early postwar years the party now utilizes greater persuasion and the mobilization of consensus to formulate criteria for personnel appointments in each elite sector. 'Cadre policy' is now based on 'social accords' worked out by the League with other mass sociopolitical organizations and specialists in personnel selection. Formulated at each level of the federal system the accords serve as a programmatic basis for the screening and final selection of job applicants. The implementation and monitoring of such personnel agreements fall within the jurisdiction of the Socialist Alliance (SSRNJ – a broad, mass sociopolitical organization) rather than the League of Communists, although the connection between the two organizations is very close. For example, on the central level the implementation of the social accords on cadre policy is controlled by the Coordination Committee for Cadre Policy in the Federation of the SSRNJ Federal Conference, a body composed of and headed by experienced professional political functionaries. While the locus of organizational control may only have shifted slightly, federal appointment procedures do give attention to the genuine coordination of regional views and peculiarities (recent accords, however, stress the need for regional recruits to maintain a cross-national perspective during their term of service in federal agencies). There is also considerable competition for federal governmental and political positions, a practice which although not quite as politically open as in the late 1960s, appears to be quite firmly institutionalized.[36]

Finally, although the 'moral-political suitability' of candidates for positions of leadership has been a central consideration during the last decade of political development, it has been impossible for the regime to ignore a tremendous pressure to recruit highly specialized and technically qualified individuals for important posts throughout the society. Thus, there has been official and unofficial resistance to any overly 'sectarian', or rigid tests of political 'fitness' which would exclude competent job applicants whose professional experience or training does not include political work. Social accords on cadre policy in the mid-1970s, for example, emphasized that it was a person's overall 'political and action orientation' toward self-management and 'not membership in the League of Communists alone' which constituted a 'true gauge for the evaluation of cadres', and also that personnel policy should 'strengthen even more the interconnection and unity of the moral-political, working, and vocational qualities'.[37] The general requirement that applicants for all leading posts be party members also has been frequently attacked in recent years (as in the late 1960s) for encouraging 'careerism' and the pursuit of privileges as a basis of party affiliation.[38] One political functionary in Croatia created quite a controversy by even suggesting that in a self-managing society trying to minimize political officeholding on a professional basis, special university faculties for political science may be unnecessary. In his opinion special 'cadre faculties' for political work and analysis are superfluous, since all working people and citizens are political 'cadre'.[39]

The abandonment of the formula 'moral-political qualities and suitability' in the federal personnel accords proposed immediately after Tito's death[40] may indicate the depth of reservations regarding the overt use and frequent misuse of political criteria in personnel selection after 1971.[41] Recent Yugoslav studies continue to indicate that 'moral-political fitness' and political experience are the most significant criteria in elite recruitment even on the local level of the political system (Table 3.7). Such research also reveals, however, that many other factors are considered in the recruitment process and that the criterion of moral-political 'fitness' is often very broadly interpreted and flexibly utilized by participants in the recruitment process.[42] Today the most successful candidates for leading

Table 3.7   *Perceptions of Communal Legislators in Croatia, concerning the Main Criterion which Determined their Own Nomination (%)*

| Criteria | Delegates in the Communal Assemblies by chamber | | |
	Chamber of Associated Labor	Chamber of Local Communities	Socio-political Chambers
Age	2·21	2·16	1·47
Sex	1·47	4·32	2·21
Education	4·41	1·44	—
Position in production	8·09	2·16	0·74
Nationality	1·47	0·72	2·21
Moral-political fitness	20·59	12·95	32·35
Local reputation	5·15	17·27	6·62
Connection with the interests of the locality	7·25	15·83	10·29
Responsibility and independence	7·35	5·04	4·41
Knowledge	5·88	5·76	4·41
Previous success in the delegate system	14·71	22·30	21·32
Involvement in self-management	12·50	5·04	11·03
Other	—	—	—
Don't know or no response	8·79	5·04	2·93
Total	100·0	100·0	100·0

Source: Ivan Grdešić, *Neki Aspekti Izbora Delegata u Općinsku Skupštinu*, Zagreb, Institut za Političke Nauke Fakulteta Političkih Nauka, 1980, p. 47; the precise number of delegates interviewed and actual responses was not given.

positions in Yugoslavia are typically individuals who can demonstrate both political reliability *and* professional credentials or a reputation outside the political sector. As has recently been pointed out with respect to the members of the intelligentsia in the other European socialist states, those two sets of qualifications create a new privileged group – 'pluralists of jobholding' – within the new class: 'Anyone lucky enough to possess this double seal of approval can be as secure as a person with dual citizenship.'[43]

The analysis of elite composition in the second part of the chapter reveals some interesting potential sources of cohesion and consensus among Yugoslav regional decisionmakers. Despite the pattern of elite retrenchment and political anxiety in the 1970s, the postpartisan elite generation seems to be well ensconced on the regional level. In terms of their sociopolitical

characteristics the political subelites in the republics and provinces appear to be relatively young, highly educated, with a
variety of skills, and ethnically well balanced.

There are also, however, indicators of potential elite
conflict which may cause problems in the post-Tito period.
The juxtaposition of different generational cohorts, with different formative experiences and different levels and types of
skills, emerges very clearly in the data on each subelite, and
in the contrast among subelites. Thus, in the case of the
party, a clear distinction appears between a relatively older
group of professional revolutionaries having only incomplete
higher education or a very general political training, and
another group of much younger and more broadly specialized
functionaries. The former group of party officials are concentrated in the presidencies of the League of Communists within
each region and include a disproportionately high number of
Serbs and Montenegrins, while the latter group consists
mainly of the party secretaries, a subgroup more ethnically
representative of the regional population. The party secretaries almost totally are a subgroup prominently defined by their
not having participated in the partisan struggle.

Another potential source of interelite cleavage is the
generational and educational contrast between the administrative secretaries in the state bureaucracies on the one hand,
and the members of the party subelites on the other. Much
younger and more technically proficient than the party decisionmakers, most of the state secretaries joined the party
after the war, and generally at an older age (usually after
finishing higher education). Even when compared to the party
executive secretaries, who are the most youthful group in the
whole elite sample, the administrative secretaries emerge as
the group most qualified to manage a technically complex and
modernized economy. While highly specialized expertise is
generally recognized by all Yugoslav leaders to be indispensable for the successful management of their society, individuals having technical and modern administrative skills are
frequently and perhaps conveniently charged with being a
threat to the continuation of the self-management system as
conceived and guided by the less technically educated and
more 'partisan' (in terms of their generational cohort and
organizational commitment) politicians. Less than six months
after Tito's death one top party official predicted, for
example, that imminent interelite conflict was unavoidable
and necessary:

> The power of the technocrats in the administrative and political bureaucracy is very great. For this reason any further postpone-ment of a decisive conflict between the League of Communists and other organized socialist forces with the holders of this [technical and administrative] power is impossible. Without such a conflict even greater difficulties could emerge.[44]

Different elite backgrounds and skills do not automatically, of course, get translated into elite conflict, but under certain circumstances – for example, a revival of the vigorous anti-technocratic and highly conservative ideological thrust of the early and mid-1970s – they might become a serious source of tension. Thus, the apparent succession of new skill groups, generational cohorts and ethnic spokesmen on the regional level may preview future pressure for the acceleration of recent recruitment imperatives, such as the increased abandonment of explicit political criteria and greater ethnic proportionality in the formation of regional party elites (which if strictly calculated on the basis of population would mean a further reduction of Serbs in leadership posts outside Serbia).

Recruitment policy and elite characteristics will have an important impact on the political viability and dynamics of Yugoslav socialism in the post-Tito era. Issues concerning the methods and criteria of personnel selection are likely to evoke lively disputes as the imperatives of economic and political management confront the strong anti-elitist and anti-bureau-cratic impulses of self-management theory. Any satisfactory recruitment formula must also balance the political anxieties of the older partisan generation against the claims of the new professional intelligentsia. As John Campbell has recently sug-gested with respect to Tito's heirs in the top federal posts,

> ability to change may be more significant than the ability to maintain. Actually, the new men are less attached than Tito to the mystique of certain Leninist principles and forms that Tito, with his Moscow background, never lost. They have made their careers in post-1948 Yugoslavia . . . [T]hey may also find that they can build solidly on popular support only by enlarging the area of real political freedom which the system permits, and by drawing back into public life some of the talented leaders whose taint of liberalism or nationalism kept them on the outside so long as Tito himself was in charge.[45]

On the whole Tito's personal reputation is likely to remain intact much longer than Stalin's or Mao's, and for good reasons, but the Yugoslav leader's final stand against the tide of 'techno-managerial', 'liberal' and 'nationalist' subelites may eventually suffer the same fate as the cultural revolution in China.

Notes: Chapter 3

1 The biographical information was taken from *Politički i poslovni imenik, III Deo, Biografije* (Belgrade: Dokumentacija Tanjuga, 15 October 1978, 12 December 1979), pp. 1–102.
2 B. Petranović, *Politička i ekonomska osnova narodna vlasti u Jugoslaviji za vreme obnove* (Belgrade: Institut za Savremenu Istoriju, 1969), pp. 51–2 and 57.
3 ibid., p. 269.
4 Public party leaders regarded such problems as temporary. At the Fifth Party Congress in 1948, Alexander Ranković remarked that 'The workers, peasants and a large number of intellectuals found themselves doing work they had never done before. This explains a certain rigidness and inflexibility which existed in the very beginning as regards complex economic and administrative problems. But they overcame these difficulties and introduced a new creative elan ... [O]ur enemies said that we knew how to wage war but that we would not know how to organize a state. Practice has shown that it was precisely the cadre that passed through the difficult school of war that was also the best bearer of the building up of the new state', A. Ranković, *Report of the Central Committee of the Communist Party of Yugoslavia on the Organizational Work of the CPY* (Belgrade: n.p., 1948), pp. 53, 56.
5 F. Neal, 'The Communist Party of Yugoslavia', *American Political Science Review*, vol. 51, no. 1 (1957), pp. 88–111; and P. Shoup, 'Problems of party reform in Yugoslavia', *American Slavic and East European Review*, vol. 18, no. 3 (1959), pp. 334–50.
6 R. Radonjić, *Sukob KPJ s Kominform i društveni razvoj Jugoslavie (1948–1950)* (Zagreb: Centar za kulturnu djelatnost, 1979), pp. 146–7, 178–80.
7 Ranković explained that 'rotation does not mean demotion or the "replacement of the older generation" but the normal reconstitution of executive bodies ... [N]evertheless there has been some uneasiness among some of the senior cadres who played a part in the revolution ... [E]ven some of relatively young people who took part in the People's Liberation War have been somewhat inclined to feel that retirement or pension is the only way out ... [I]t would be neither expedient nor wise to settle the question of the veterans merely by pensioning them off ... it would be extremely difficult for them today to go back to their original occupations ... Although the principle of obligatory rotation has not been finally inserted into the Statute of the League of Communists it has also been carried out to a certain extent. Of course the principle as it is applied to the representative bodies and central government organs cannot be automatically transferred to the League of Communists', Ranković, 'Current problem in relation to the work and role of the League of Communists of Yugoslavia', in *VIIIth Congress of the League of Communists of Yugoslavia* (Belgrade: Medjunarodna Politika, 1965), pp. 148–9, 151–2.

8 *Deveti Kongres Saveza Komunista Jugoslavie* (Belgrade: Komunist, 1970), pp. 151–2.

9 M. Janičijević, 'Osvrt na Strokturalne Promene Jugoslovenskug Drustva', *Promena Klasne Strukture Savremenog Jugoslovenskog Drustva* (Belgrade: Jugoslovensko Udruženje za Sociologiju, 1967), pp. 283–312; and R. Aleksic, 'Inteligencija u jugoslovenskom društvu', *Sociologija*, vol. 6, no. 1–2 (1964), pp. 115–33. Changing occupational demography aside, the growing political and social influence of the technical intelligentsia in the decade before 1966 has also been suggested by Yugoslav authors: Janičijević, 'Jedan pogled na karaktenstike nastanka i ravitka jugoslovenske inteligentije', *Gledišta*, vol. 1, no. 2 (1959), pp. 31–45; and I. Perić, 'Neke karakteristike socijalne strukture Saveza, Komunista Hrvatska', *Reforma Saveza Komunista Hrvatska* (Zagreb: Centar za Aktualni Politicki Studij, 1970), pp. 42–69.

10 Lenard Cohen, 'Yugoslavia: the political role of the administrative elite', in Charles Gati (ed.), *The Politics of Modernization in Eastern Europe* (New York: Praeger, 1974), pp. 160–99, and 'Devolutionary socialism: the political institutionalization of the Yugoslav assembly system, 1963–1973', doctoral dissertation, Columbia University, New York, USA, 1978.

11 Cohen, 'Devolutionary socialism', op. cit., and 'Politics as an avocation: legislative professionalization and participation in Yugoslavia', *Legislative Studies Quarterly*, vol. 5, no. 2 (1980), pp. 446–78.

12 *Politika* (Belgrade), 1971, p. 7.

13 J. Županov, 'Da li se rukovodenje preduzecem profesionalizira?', *Moderna organizacija*, no. 10 (1968), pp. 803–23; Z. Tanić, 'Direktori i predstavnici samoupravnih tela', *Naše Teme*, vol. 13, no. 2 (1969), pp. 186–206; and Cohen, 'Partisans, professionals, and proletarians: elite change in Yugosla·/ia, 1952–1978', *Canadian Slavonic Papers*, vol. 21, no. 4 (1979), pp. 175–207.

14 *Šesti Kongres Saveza Komunista Hrvatske, Stenografske Belješke, Zagreb 5–7 December 1968* (Zagreb: Komunist, 1969), Vol. 3, p. 120.

15 D. Bilandžić, 'SKJ u Borbi za Transformacija Državno-Centralističkog Sistema u Samoupravnu Organizaciju Društva (1961–1970)', in Pero Morača, Dusan Bilandžić and Stanislav Stojanović (eds), *Istorija Saveza komunista Jugoslavije* (Beograd: Rad, 1976), p. 280.

16 ibid., pp. 281–2.

17 Dj. Knežević, 'Kadrovska politika: politički profesionalizam u Savezu Komunista', *Socijalizam*, vol. 22, no. 11 (1979), pp. 138–53.

18 A communal party functionary explained the change from professional to 'deprofessionalized' political work on the local level in the period just before the removal of Ranković: 'When I was elected secretary of the communal committee four years ago, it didn't seem right to me that I had to give up my specialization . . . Right from the start I confronted difficult tasks, mainly in the economy. People referred their biggest and smallest problems to the committee, generally to the secretary . . . [T]he secretary was asked and expected to give his opinion and judgement about everything, to be everywhere. Others hid themselves behind him and fled from responsibility. In concrete political work, many obligations and tasks were heaped upon the secretary. Since he was a paid official, many people thought he was required to accept the duties of other members of the communal committees and other socio-political activists, to write papers, reports, and analyses, to prepare and organize all meetings of the

committee, to attend meetings of primary organizations of the League, etc. . . . [W]hether he wished it or not the secretary became a professional practitioner and administrator and his colleagues hid themselves behind him, as passive spectators . . . Two years ago I was again elected as secretary but this time as a non-professional . . . I am performing the duty of secretary while simultaneously working at my profession. I can't say it is easy because it requires great physical and psychological effort . . . It allows the secretary to pay more attention to real political work . . . Since there isn't a 'principal' personality in the person of the paid secretary collective leadership (*kolektivnost*) is more apparent in the work of the committee . . . That also assumes an equitable division of functions and tasks among a greater number of people, each of them assuming responsibility for their implementation', *Komunist*, 2 June 1960, p. 4.

19   Šesti Kongres, op. cit., pp. 200–2, 205.
20   Cohen, 'Politics as an avocation', op. cit.
21   *Nedelnje Informativne Novine* (Belgrade) (hereafter *NIN*), 29 May 1977, pp. 6–8.
22   A director of a Belgrade enterprise with twenty-five years' experience recently explained the nature of the political pressure in his job: 'The director is located between two social forces whose interests are not the same. On one side is the enterprise, or the workers employed in it, and on the other, the socio-political organizations – the [party] committee, communal assembly, trade union . . . To whom should one look for royal assent when there are sharp differences of opinion . . . to the members of the [workers'] collective, at the head of which I sit . . . or the president of the commune, the secretary of the committee . . . ? It is more honorable to respond to my collective, but many directors do the opposite, conscious of the fact that their place, their business career depends more on socio-political workers, or even exclusively depends upon them', *NIN*, 31 August 1980, p. 16.
23   *NIN*, 18 January 1981, p. 10.
24   Cohen, 'Partisans, professionals, and proletarians', op. cit.
25   *NIN*, 4 January 1981, p. 22.
26   Cohen, 'Politics as an avocation', op. cit.
27   Bilandžić, p. 315; one recent analysis notes that in Belgrade alone there are around 2,000 party cadre commissions in sociopolitical organizations, institutions and enterprises (*NIN*, 13 April 1980, p. 9).
28   *Deseti Kongres SKJ: Dokumenti* (Belgrade: Komunist, 1975), p. 394.
29   Bilandžić, op. cit., pp. 313–14.
30   The two directories used in the analysis were *Politicki i Poslovni Imenik SFR Jugoslavije 1972* (Belgrade: Tanjug, 18 February 1972) and *Politicki i Poslovni Imenik* (Belgrade, Tanjug, 15 October 1978, and supplements 1979 and 1980).
31   Cohen, 'Yugoslavia', op. cit.; and R. Lukić, 'Rotation among top government officials in Yugoslavia', in M. Dogan (ed.), *The Mandarins of Western Europe* (New York: Halstead Press, 1975), pp. 293–304.
32   W. Griffith, 'Generational change and political leadership in Eastern Europe and the Soviet Union', in Richard J. Samuels (ed.), *Political Generations and Political Development* (Lexington, Mass. Toronto: Lexington Books, 1977), pp. 125–34.
33   A more detailed analysis of the problem is offered in Lenard Cohen 'Balkan consociationalism: ethnic representation and ethnic interaction in the Yugoslav political elite', paper delivered at the Northwestern

Political Science Association Meeting, Portland, Oregon, USA, March 1979.

34   *Politika* (Belgrade), 16 November 1979, p. 8.

35   The head of the federal government's Personnel Commission recently observed that there are still some functionaries serving in federal organs who manage to remain on the federal level in new jobs after the mandatory termination of their terms of office, although the problem of such so-called 'federal cadre' is decreasing in importance from year to year. He also mentioned that care is taken so that in individual organs there is no concentration of cadre from the same republic or province: *NIN*, 21 September 1980, pp. 26–7. Stane Dolanc, Slovenia's representative in the twenty-three-member Party Central Committee Presidium, recently suggested that persons wishing to serve as functionaries in republic and provincial administrations should complete a 'four-year course in Belgrade' as federal administrators: 'Only if he is acquainted with common Yugoslav interests and problems could someone honestly and correctly behave in his own republic or province', *NIN*, 18 January 1981, p. 11.

36   Ivan Šiber, *Delegatski Sistem i Izborni Processi* (Zagreb: Institut za Političke Nauke Fakulteta Političkih Nauka, 1979); a number of articles have recently appeared advocating the expansion of competition in legislative and party elections (see, for example, *NIN*, 4 May 1980, pp. 26–7).

37   Foreign Broadcast Information Service (hereafter FBIS), Daily Report, Eastern Europe (Springfield, Virginia), 15 December 1975, pp. 17–116, and 20 May 1976, pp. 14–110.

38   See, for example, *Borba*, 29 June 1972, p. 5. A Montenegrin party functionary remarks, 'What does it mean to inquire into the background of a young man who is just starting out? What can a check tell us about a student who has just graduated or a technician who has just reached age 20? Who are we to ask and what are we to check? I agree that we should make certain that he does have professional skills and that he is suitable for the job, but we should not go over looking for any trumped up elements ... There are, I repeat, places in the government and the economy where every society wants people of a certain background. But to take this to the extreme where points are even given in the competition for jobs to those who are members of the party could be dangerous': *NIN*, 29 May 1977, p. 8.

39   *NIN*, 27 July 1980, pp. 10–12; the author did not expand his argument to include the 'Josip Broz Tito Political School' established in Croatia during the mid-1970s, and which has already graduated about 400 professional 'sociopolitical workers'.

40   FBIS, 16 June 1980, p. 130.

41   A Belgrade political scientist observes that 'it isn't rare that the narrow and closed administrative structures on the lower levels of organizations often have greater possibilities for communication with higher personnel and political decision-makers and services, and are the main sources of information about personnel opportunities and the capabilities of people in their area. It isn't impossible that relying on such information specific personnel authorities carry out not only personnel sorting, or the selection of specific people, but also ideological differentiations ... It is perhaps one of the most sensitive and most vulnerable points or weaknesses in our political and party fabric today. Such personnel policy and political involvement broadens the space for "politics as the sleight of

hand", or Machiavellianism and reduces the room for creative activity especially in the sphere of associated labour': *NIN*, 20 April 1980, p. 9.

42   The surveys also indicate that 'moral-political fitness' is a less important recruitment criterion at the lower levels of the delegate structure for example among voters at meetings to select members of delegations, I. Perko-Šeparović, *Analiza Zborova Birača u Izbornim Procesima* (Zagreb: Institut za Političke Nauke FPN, 1979), pp. 111–19, and that whatever criteria are used the League of Communists and other sociopolitical organizations play the dominant role in the recruitment process: I. Grdešić, *Neki aspekti izbora delegata a opcinsku skupštinu* (Zagreb: Institut za Političke Nauke Fakulteta Političkih Nauka, 1980), pp. 45–60.

43   G. Konrad and I. Szelenyi, *The Intellectuals on the Road to Class Power* (New York: Harcourt Brace Jovanovitch, 1979), p. 191.

44   *Borba* (Belgrade), 22 September 1980, p. 6.

45   John Campbell, 'Tito: the achievement and the legacy', *Foreign Affairs*, vol. 58, no. 5 (1980), p. 1058.

    This paper was completed before the outbreak of 'counter-revolutionary' protest among the Albanians in Kosovo (March–April 1981) and the 12th Congress of the League of Yugoslav Communists in June 1982. The composition of the Central Committee elected in 1982 reflected the continued *and even increased* hegemony of professional politicians from the Partisan generation (*FBIS*, 7 July 1982, p. 19). A recent Yugoslav study also revealed that 'no vital breakthrough has yet been made' in decreasing the professionalization of the country's political elite (*Borba*, 7 June 1982, p. 2). A detailed analysis of the Kosovo case can be found in this author's 'Ethno-political conflict in Yugoslavia: elites in Kosovo (1912–1982)', in Bert A. Rockman and Ronald H. Linden (eds), *Elite Studies and Communist Politics: Essays in Memory of Carl Beck* (Pittsburgh, Pa: University of Pittsburgh Press, forthcoming 1983).

PART TWO

Patrons and Clients

4

Political *Seilschaften* in the USSR

GYULA JÓZSA

Explanation of Concepts and Objectives of Study

In mountaineering jargon the term *Seilschaft* stands for a 'roped-party' of climbers whose mutual aid, protection and support enable them to scale heights that would be beyond their individual powers. The metaphor seems an apt one for the phenomena described as 'patronage', 'clientelism' and 'patron–client relationships' (*Seilschaftsbeziehungen*) in contemporary political sociology, not least as we encounter them in Soviet-type societies.

It is interesting, if not really surprising, that Soviet diction-aries and reference works make no mention of these concepts as they are understood in modern Western scholarship. In the *Great Soviet Encyclopedia* 'clientela' is described as a phen-omenon of classical Rome, while 'patronage' is used in the sense of health care and prophylactic medicine.[1] In dictionaries for 'patronage', 'patronize', 'favoritism', 'protection of favor-ites' and 'nepotism', and their German or French equivalents, we do indeed find such inadequate terms as: *pokrovitelstvo, popechatelstvo, sheftsto, zloupotreblenie pravom naznacheniia na dolzhnost* (misuse of the right to appoint), *pokrovitelstvovat, opekat, semeistvennost, kumovstvo, nepotizm, favoritizm*, and so on, but anything closer to our topic we will search for in vain.

As a starting-point Lemarchand's and Legg's definition of the concept of a political *Seilschaft* will be adopted even if its applicability to the Soviet case is contestable and, no doubt, in need of amplification in the course of this study. According to Lemarchand and Legg, a political *Seilschaft* is 'a more or less personalized, affective and reciprocal relationship between actors, or sets of actors, commanding unequal resources and involving mutually beneficial transactions that have political ramifications beyond the immediate sphere of dyadic relation-ships'.

These authors emphasize, in particular, three general criteria of a political *Seilschaft*: '(1) the variable pattern of asymmetry discernible in the patron–client relationship; (2) the locus, extensiveness, and durability of the relationship; and (3) the character of the transactions attendant upon such relationships.'[2]

T. H. Rigby suggested an initial version of this definition when he drew attention to the fact that under Soviet conditions personal affection does not necessarily figure as an essential element in a *Seilschaft*: 'This relationship may or may not involve an affective personal bond; its essential basis is mutual aid. The patron offers protection and preferment, while the client's part is to throw all his energies into achieving his patron's programs ... both "cover up" for each other.'[3] Similarly, the pertinent observations of E. Artzi on the mentality of *Homo Sovieticus* conclude that the bonds in a Soviet *Seilschaft* in general are characterized more by ambivalence than affection.[4]

We know from Khrushchev's memoirs that relations between Stalin's colleagues and the *khoziain* (patron or boss) and also among themselves were characterized rather by a basic fear for their own lives, uncertainty and dissimulation than by affection. Certainly, we are a long way from fully understanding the character and emotional content of relationships in different periods, hierarchical levels and ethnogeographic contexts of the USSR. The scanty career data available will scarcely provide an adequate basis for a psychosociological examination of *Seilschaften*. A further and valuable source of relevant information is to be found in Soviet, and especially émigré, literature, such as the highly interesting milieu descriptions of Zinoviev.

Recent empirically oriented research cannot claim credit for the discovery of political *Seilschaften* in the Soviet system. The 'classics' of Sovietology long ago described in detail the factional struggles for power and alignments within the party as well as the reliance of the protagonists, with greater or lesser success, on the support of their loyal followers. In his unsurpassed monograph Merle Fainsod repeatedly drew attention to the patron–client relationship.[5] However, while we frequently encounter references to the existence and important role of *Seilschaften* in this earlier literature, there have been few attempts to analyze the patron–client relationship as a phenomenon which permeates the system as a whole. What is new in present research on political *Seilschaft* relationships in the USSR, influenced as it is by work in contemporary anthropology, organizational sociology and the sociology of development, is the concern not only to observe the phenomenon and its effects in the dyadic power struggles at the summit of the hierarchy, but to understand the deeper dimensions, politico-sociological roots, genesis, mechanisms, roles and functions of political *Seilschaften* at all levels of the system.

This concern is commendable and justified. Yet difficulties arise from the very beginning of the undertaking. Thus, the basic precondition of any far-reaching analysis of the structure, dynamics, integration, duration, extent, degree of loyalty, interests and priorities within and between *Seilschaften* is precision and reliability in the information on the identity and personal composition of the system of relationships. The scanty available biographical and career data constitute the sole starting-point for a necessarily narrow empirical approach. The shortage of information on political and subjective motives and background factors conditioning career patterns hardly allows a completely reliable assignment of particular persons to particular *Seilschaften*.

Furthermore, the more one proceeds down hierarchical levels, the more inadequate biographical details become. Consequently, for the most part, *Seilschaft* analyses are concentrated on the 'tip of the iceberg'. In order to investigate the 'lower slopes' and 'crevices' all available methods must be utilized. The level of information of basic data on *Seilschaften* in the Soviet context necessitates methodological eclecticism.

If the understanding of *Seilschaften* even in a pluralistic system confronts us with difficulties, this applies many times over in the case of the Soviet system. In so far as an empirical approach requires accurate facts for hypotheses and theory-building or quantifiable data against which to verify the latter,[6] it is applicable as a method for the analysis of only certain aspects of Soviet *Seilschaften*. If the study of the phenomenon is to go deeper and further, then other methods – albeit seemingly 'unscientific' ones – are not only legitimate, but necessary. Thus, much historical knowledge along with the methodology of 'Kremlinology' are indispensable to the task of assigning clients to patrons. More precise understanding of *Seilschaften* can scarcely be expected without close study of the press and eye-witness accounts, that is, without the methodology of political sociography.

The object of the following discussion is to identify the problems and limitations of a precise empirical study of Soviet *Seilschaften*. Proceeding from an endeavor to determine patron–client relationships within the present leadership certain questions will be formulated and then further discussed and elaborated. Unfortunately, given the current state of our knowledge we end up with more questions than answers. The aforementioned sociographic approach will be illustrated by two questions: how do the press and politicians portray *Seilschaft* relationships? Who gets what, when and how by virtue of his membership of a *Seilschaft*? Finally, some considerations will be given to those factors in the system relating to the origin of *Seilschaften*, to their functions or dysfunctions for the system as a whole.

Pilot Studies

Following innumerable references to the role and function of *Seilschaft* relationships in the enormous bulk of literature on elites, mobility and analyses of the system, and so on, at the end of the 1960s, Professor Philip Stewart and his team undertook the first carefully planned attempt to comprehend and interpret, quantitatively and empirically, patron–client relationships and their significance in the career of *obkom* (regional party committee) secretaries. A noteworthy study within the compass of the SEMPRA projects it appeared in 1972, posing the question to what extent patronage connections or 'rational-technical' achievements determined the political careers of 224 *obkom* secretaries in 1955–67.[7]

The computer-based analysis was conceived as a 'partial test of two models' of elite mobility. One model asserts that the critical factor for the advancement of a functionary is his relationship to a primarily power-oriented patron. The other model postulates that it is the practical and efficiency-oriented achievement capacities of cadres which are of decisive importance. These opposing models of elite mobility relate to the ongoing discussion on the priority of politics or efficiency and on the evolutionary tendencies of the system toward either 'stagnation' or 'pluralism'. This empirical study thus arose from basic problems of interpreting the system. To be sure, the authors caution, further juxtaposition of data and theory must be forthcoming in order that no premature conclusions be drawn. In the context of the Brezhnev–Kosygin period (up to 1967) this computer-based study affirmed that as far as the political careers of the *obkom* secretaries under investigation were concerned, technical-rational achievement capacities were more of a determining factor than their *Seilschaft* relationships.[8]

Unfortunately, the study does not report in detail on the techniques and procedures for obtaining the basic data subjected to computation. The starting-point criteria and hypotheses for the confirmation of *Seilschaft* relationships are specified but the study offers no list of patrons and clients from different periods. This unfortunately hinders verification of the basic empirical data and therewith the findings of the study.

Brezhnev's ascent in the 1970s to *primus inter pares*, and with him his followers to key positions in the leadership, illustrates anew the significance of *Seilschaft* relationships in the Soviet Union. The composition of the Brezhnev team shows that within a *Seilschaft* there are roots and branches stemming from various chronological and geographical origins. In the case of the 'Brezhnevites' one can discern five such branches: Dnepropetrovsk (Zaporozhe–Ukraine); the war (18th Army); Moldavia; Kazakhstan; and Moscow, of which the Dnepropetrovsk contingent has evidently proved the most extensive and durable.

In a second interesting study of the *Seilschaft* from a biographical viewpoint Joel Moses was concerned with these regional 'cohorts'. In his valuable and oft-quoted pilot study he shows that (1) the much quicker ascent of twenty-four cadres from Dnepropetrovsk in 1954–73 as compared with other 'climbers' was due to mutual assistance; (2) the 'triumphal procession' of Dnepropetrovsk members has accelerated since Brezhnev assumed the highest party position; (3) the 'climbers' from Dnepropetrovsk have been drawn into different functional apparatuses; (4) since 1954 they have achieved membership in the highest representative organs (Central Committee and Central Auditing Commission) more quickly than functionaries from any other *obkom*; (5) parallel to the ascent of the Dnepropetrovsk group the career mobility of the Kharkov *Seilschaft*, which was promoted by Podgornyi, was slowed down and ultimately halted.[9]

The biographical data of the Dnepropetrovsk group during the Brezhnev–Kosygin period led Moses to conclusions differing from those of Stewart and his colleagues. In the case of the Dnepropetrovsk group *Seilschaft* relationships played a much greater role than is postulated by the technical-rational model. The 'exception' thus becomes the rule. As Moses rightly notes, however, this certainly does not mean that all careers of those in the middle hierarchical levels (and other levels as well) must be traced back exclusively to *Seilschaft* relationships.[10] This study is based not on a quantitative analysis, but on the sociographic interpretation of career data. Its arguments and propositions are clear and readily verifiable. Of particular value in this connection is that the author gives the actual names of those to whom he ascribes specific *Seilschaft* connections.

More recently J. P. Willerton Jr has produced a further valuable pioneering analysis of *Seilschaften*, published along with comments by a number of scholars on the importance, problems and prospects of studying *Seilschaft* relationships in communist states.[11] Willerton investigated 470 Central Committee (CC) members and candidates who were elected in 1966 and 1971, and identified 154 as clients of 18 Politburo members: 26 of Brezhnev, 20 of Podgornyi, 13 each of Mazurov and Shelest, 9 each of Grishin, Kirilenko and Pel'she, 8 of Shcherbitsky, 7 of Kunaev, 6 each of Kosygin, Poliansky and Suslov, 5 of Grechko, Shelepin and Voronov, 3 of Andropov and 2 each of Gromyko and Kulakov. Unfortunately Willerton, unlike Moses, does not provide us with the names of the clients, so the validity of his selection criteria is not subject to verification. His most important conclusions may be summarized as follows:

- *Seilschaft* relationships play a significant role in Soviet political mobility and this applies in all functional areas.
- The party *apparatchiki* in the Politburo have the most clients. Bonds formed or further strengthened within party bodies serve as a particularly favorable basis especially for further assistance or advancement by a patron.
- The greatest number of clients comes from similar functional areas in which the patron had spent most of his working time.
- Of the 30 clients of Politburo members removed in 1966–76 (Poliansky, Shelepin, Shelest and Voronov), 10 lost their CC membership in 1971 and six in 1976. A majority of clients thus follow their patrons into obscurity, with those who had a specialized position in the state or economic apparatus tending to be ousted later than those in the party apparatus. Nevertheless, 47 percent of the clients of ousted patrons were still in office in 1976, a testimony to the official policy of the Brezhnev regime of 'care for cadres'.
- All clients entered the CC later than their sponsors. Most clients are younger than their patron.

- The comparison of the 154 clients with the 316 identified as 'non-clients' also leads to interesting results; 'non-clients' are older than clients, they have been in the party longer, have spent more time in higher posts than clients of ousted patrons or specialists have succeeded in doing. 'Non-clients' form a conglomerate of individuals who are distributed throughout various bureaucracies and represent diverse functional interests.

Willerton's analysis does not touch on such fundamental questions as the demographic structure of *Seilschaften* (nationality, ethnic and local bonds), the hierarchy of patrons and clients, of different 'branches' within a *Seilschaft* and the phenomenon of connections between different *Seilschaften* through linking individuals. Likewise, this first analysis does not deal with the duration and intensity of loyalties, interest priorities, value orientations, patterns of political behavior and conflict resolution within and between *Seilschaften*, or the effect of the accumulation of posts by patrons and clients ('cross-cutting responsibilities') on the integration and disintegration of *Seilschaften*. These questions indicate how far we still have to go in the study of *Seilschaft* relations.

Limits of Quantitative Empirical Study in Identifying *Seilschaften* and their Membership

As already suggested, an indepth study of this phenomenon is only possible if one starts out with the most accurate possible identification of *Seilschaft* membership, the initial critical step being the allocation of individuals to a *Seilschaft*. The question then is: how can we determine who, since when and until when, is to be regarded as a client of a patron? This first step, and all subsequent steps, in a quantitative analysis can be undertaken only on the basis of detailed biographical and career data.

Such data, however, are frequently unavailable, and it seems likely that in the future they may become even more sparse. Since the mid-1970s the number of biographical entries in the yearbooks of the *Great Soviet Encyclopedia* – one of the most important biographical sources – has declined. The 1979 volume of potted biographies of Supreme Soviet members (*Deputaty Verkhovnogo Soveta*), another no less important information source, has not been released to the West. One gets the impression that the Soviet leadership has deliberately restricted these information sources, the availability of which in the early 1970s had stimulated hopes and forecasts that the system was becoming more open.

In view of the imperfect body of information there can be no complete certainty of *Seilschaft* relationships. One can only discover clients and patrons with a relative degree of probability and in limited numbers. The lower one goes in the Soviet hierarchy, the more difficult the analysis becomes. Given the level of information, it is obvious that a quantitiative empirical study of *Seilschaften* is impossible without drawing on the findings of historical, sociographic or 'Kremlinological' methodology. However unpalatable some scholars may find the fact, even the collection of data for research on *Seilschaften* must have recourse to such methods. Otherwise all we will achieve is a pretense at a sociometry of *Seilschaften*, resting on simplified and therefore deceptive criteria or basic data of dubious provenance.

For all the merits of their pioneering works on *Seilschaften* in the Soviet political hierarchy, the above-mentioned authors, with the exception of Moses, have not listed the names of the members of *Seilschaften* identified by them. The scholarly value and integrity of the works is, of course, beyond question, but it does raise serious problems in that there is no way of checking the validity of the criteria employed for linking clients with patrons. In the light of the information available and the imponderabilities of the Soviet (and indeed of any kind of) politically relevant system of personal relationships, such studies can scarcely avoid a measure of oversimplification.

Stewart and Willerton begin with two basic criteria. Those individuals who may be assigned to a *Seilschaft* (1) 'must be in geographic proximity for a given time period', and (2) 'there must be a positive pattern in the promotions and advancements of patrons and clients';[12] that is, as a patron rises in the hierarchy, his clients must be seen to advance with him. These criteria can serve as a starting-point, but only that, for assigning potential members to a *Seilschaft*. For neither 'geographical and chronological proximity', nor 'the positive pattern of precise relationships', constitutes a criterion and the resulting ambiguities will always imbue our suppositions of *Seilschaft* relationships with a measure of uncertainty.

Even in cases where individuals in the course of their careers have served two or more times in positions which bring them into more or less close official contact, we have no justification for *assuming* that the relationship so formed was a 'positive' one. Career data can only indicate the frequency of encounters, not the quality of personal relationships. They show, at the most, the *possibility* of mutual aid.

It is a matter of common experience that in school or workplace not only friendships, but also enmities can develop, and that over time friendships may be transformed into enmities or *vice versa*. From the beginning colleagues can belong to different *Seilschaften* and make careers with support from different patrons, even possibly in the same profession. This elementary fact of life, together with what Michel Crozier terms the 'strategic autonomy of an actor' *vis-à-vis* his social environment, is the central problem for quantitative empirical studies of political *Seilschaften*.[13]

In the same connection we may recall Zygmunt Bauman's very apt reservations about the reliability of the 'temporal-spatial proximity' criterion, namely, the assumption that only the patron can be the *spiritus movens* behind the development of a dyad. He rightly notes that quite independently of temporal-geographic and institutional-functional proximity it is quite possible for career-conscious clients from different lateral functional areas to take the initiative and to attach themselves to a particular patron.[14]

As an example one can cite the case of Katushev. Before 1965, there is no reason to suppose that he crossed paths with Brezhnev in any of the latter's previous areas of service – either in Dnepropetrovsk, Moldavia, or Kazakhstan. Nevertheless, it has generally been assumed since 1965, when Brezhnev personally installed him as first secretary of the Gorky *obkom*, that Katushev was Brezhnev's client. In 1968 he was brought into the CC Secretariat and evidently enjoyed Brezhnev's protection at least until he left that body in 1977. But how can we know with certainty which of them took the initiative to cooperate? It is only known that (like the previous first secretaries of Azerbaidzhan and Georgia) Katushev's predecessor in Gorky, M. Efremov, had also 'compromised himself' before his removal.

'The non-specific character of the patron–client relationship', writes Bauman, 'confounds the map of patronage and makes it exceedingly hazardous to chart its patterns with objective indicators and without access to "inside" information'.[15] We should take this warning seriously and beware of excessive optimism about the prospects for the quantitative empirical study of *Seilschaften* in communist systems. For this to possess any degree of validity it must somehow incorporate 'inside information', and as the nearest approximation to this at least make use of 'qualitative' historical evidence and the hypotheses of 'Kremlinology'. Certainly, the criteria employed by Stewart and Willerton can serve as a valuable *point de départ*, so long as we keep their limitations clearly in mind.

The fact of having worked together in the same functional context should not be taken as sufficient to establish a patron – client relationship. It is only when a repetition of such association occurs that it becomes reasonable to advance the *hypothesis* of mutual assistance in the furtherance of careers. It will scarcely be possible to state with certainty whether the members of a dyad or *Seilschaft* have assisted each other at every point in their career and thereby to discern the pervading 'positive pattern' in their relationship. This positive pattern can be inferred with a relative degree of probability only from the historical and political context.

For such reasons, in our efforts to identify the clients of a particular patron, an important initial step in our view is to distinguish the more or less 'certain' members of the *Seilschaft* from those who are only 'possible'. Nor should we forget that a static picture of *Seilschaften* can be deceptive not only because the makeup of the *Seilschaft* changes over time, but also because the patron was himself at some time a client, and a client at a lower hierarchical level may also perform the function of a patron. And on top of this there is the question of *Seilschaften* through mediating individuals, so that we should be sensitive to the possibility of certain officials figuring simultaneously in more than one *Seilschaft*.

In addition to such ambiguities in the selection criteria and the limitations and difficulties of a fully reliable classification of officials by clientelist groupings, we must also contend with serious problems in the biographies at our disposal. Soviet biographical and career data are rarely free enough of gaps to provide clear indications of the personal relationships of the individuals in question.

Even the most refined computer technology cannot make good these lacunae. Nor can it answer the question of how to identify a positive pattern in the patron–client relationship. To be sure, computer technology following an immense expenditure of work on our databank can refine our selection criteria by such means as factor or regression analysis. It can help us to identify potential *Seilschaften* in a defined political context within a limited timeframe. No computer technology, however, can provide us with an accurate identification of political *Seilschaften*. This state of affairs raises the question whether the anticipated results of a computer-based analysis of *Seilschaften* justifies the enormous expenditure of work involved.

While Willerton's conclusions regarding the attribution of client to patron were formed on the basis of interpreting career data by using traditional methods, the SEMPRA team, it seems, based itself extensively on computer analysis.[16] The present author is currently involved in a project aimed at testing the contribution of computer-based techniques to the study of aspects of Soviet politics, including the identification of clientelist relationships. The results achieved to date offer little ground for rejecting Crozier's emphatic warning, according to which the use of cybernetic models and technology in the study of social systems is no more

> than the regurgitation of a particularly superficial and hollow functionalism which repeats the tricks of an utterly worn-out positive rationalism: *a priori* rationality, normative-deductive logic, a mechanical mode of thinking which ignores the strategic character of human interaction. Perhaps this is the very reason for its success: cybernetics is reassuring, for under the façade of esoteric jargon it permits us yet again to eschew real discussion, and to avoid facing all the consequences of the irreducibly indeterminate, i.e. political, character of social systems.[17]

Given the specific and essentially political character of the Soviet system, the use of computer technology is still more problematical than in the case of systems with greater transparency.

Seilschaften within the Present Leadership: Problems and Hypotheses

The following endeavor to identify *Seilschaften* within the present party and state leadership by use of traditional methods does not claim to complement the pioneering works discussed above with an adequate sociometric account. It is our concern to demonstrate that the analysis of *Seilschaften* must begin with open cataloguing and identification of the persons involved. It should be stated clearly that in the attribution of clients to patrons both the selection criteria discussed earlier and also 'Kremlinological' criteria are drawn upon. The reasoning and grounds for our attribution of connections naturally cannot be set out for each particular individual; however, by recording here the relevant names we seek to facilitate the critical evaluation of our listing. A descriptive and detailed stocktaking would require a separate study which hopefully can be undertaken soon.

The second and more important concern of this endeavor is to formulate some questions and hypotheses relating to political *Seilschaften* in the Soviet Union and draw attention to specific manifestations of the phenomenon. At this still rudimentary stage in the study of this topic the identification of fruitful questions and hypotheses is a necessary step to further enlightenment.

The following analysis is based principally on 214 detailed biographies compiled over recent years under the auspices of the Bundesinstitut für ostwissenschaftliche und internationale Studien in Cologne,[18] augmented by Brezhnev's memoirs,[19] the biographies of Brezhnev by J. Dornberg[20] and M. Morozov,[21] as well as, where necessary, available Soviet biographical compilations.[22]

This investigation will limit itself to the summit of the hierarchy and will not venture into the 'lower depths'. The biographical and career data cover twenty-nine persons serving as Politburo members or candidates or as CC secretaries, fifty-six persons from the central party apparatus (including party press organs and institutes), seventy-four ministers, Council of Ministers chairmen and chairmen of state committees, twenty-eight chairmen and members of the federal and union republic Supreme Soviet presidia, and twenty-six first secretaries of the larger *kraikomy* and *obkomy* of the RSFSR. Those who have died or been removed from office since 1976 will not be considered.

The selection is not representative and does not even include the whole CC. As mentioned, it permits us to investigate *Seilschaft* relationships only at the summit of the party and state leadership. It goes without saying that we can hope for nothing more than greater or lesser levels of probability, and that it is subject to amplification and correction.

As may be apparent from the sources used, attention will be concentrated primarily on the Brezhnev *Seilschaft* or on its various branches. Very important levels and functional areas of the hierarchy such as regional secretaries, the military, social organizations, and so on, must await future research.

We list below the full and candidate members of the Politburo and Secretaries of the Central Committee as of 1981 and set against them those identified as their likely (l) and possible (p) clients. Where there is a family relationship this is specified, as likewise when the client currently serves on the personal staff of the patron. In cases where present clients figured in the past as probable or possible patrons of their present patrons this is also indicated (P):

L. I. Brezhnev:*	V. V. Shcherbitskii (l), K. U. Chernenko (l), A. P. Kirilenko (l), D. A. Kunaev (l), N. A. Tikhonov (l), K. M. Bogoliubov (l), V. E. Dymshits (l), K. F. Katushev (l), I. T. Novikov (l), G. S. Pavlov (l), G. F. Sizov (l), S. P. Trapeznikov (l), A. F. Vatchenko (l), N. A. Shchelokov (l), I. K. Iunak (l), M. S. Tsvigun‡ (brother-in-law, l), Iu. L. Brezhnev (son, l), Iu. M. Churbanov (son-in-law, l), A. M. Aleksandrov-Agentov (assistant, l), A. I. Blatov (assistant, l), V. A. Golikov (assistant, l), G. E. Tsukanov (assistant, l), E. M. Samoteikin (advisor, l), A. A. Epishev (pP), B. A. Ashimov (p), K. A. Mel'nichenko (p), F. I. Mochalin (p), E. M. Tiazhelnikov (p), N. I. Savinkin (p).
Iu. V. Andropov:	K. V. Rusakov (p), O. B. Rakhmanin (p), I. Iu. Andropov (son, l).
M. S. Gorbachev:	V. A. Murakhovskii (l).
V. V. Grishin:	I. V. Kapitonov (l, pP), P. N. Demichev (l), A. V. Grishin (son, l), V. I. Konotop (p).
A. A. Gromyko:	A. A. Gromyko (son, l), I. A. Gromyko (grandson?, l),[23] V. F. Falin (l), A. G. Kovalev (p), I. E. Poliakov (p), M. V. Zimianin (l, pP), P. A. Abrasimov (p).
A. P. Kirilenko:	Ia. P. Riabov (l), A. I. Shibaev (p), V. V. Krotov (p), N. I. Ryzhkov (l), I. I. Pudkov (p), B. N. Eltsin (p), G. V. Kolbin (l), I. K. Iunak (l).
D. A. Kunaev:	B. A. Ashimov (l), S. N. Imashev (p), F. I. Mochalin (p).
A. Ia. Pel'she:**	E. E. Ruben (p), P. E. Strautmanis (p), V. P. Lein (p).
G. V. Romanov:	V. N. Bazovskii (p), V. A. Medvedev (p), V. G. Zubarev (assistant, l).
M. A. Suslov:†	A. Ia. Pel'she** (brother-in-law, l), B. N. Ponomarev (l), G. A. Egorov (p), M. S. Gorbachev (p), V. S. Murakhovskii (p), B. P. Iakovlev (p), M. V. Zimianin (p), P. A. Rodionov (l). Assistants: Iu. A. Krasin (l), V. P. Panov (l), V. P. Stepanov (l), B. G. Vladimirov (l).

* Died, 10 November 1982   ‡ Died 20 January 1982
† Died, 26 January 1982   ** Died, 29 May 1983

D. F. Ustinov:	V. N. Novikov (l), K. N. Rudnev (p), P. V. Finogenov (p), M. P. Georgadze (reportedly friend, l).
K. U. Chernenko:	K. M. Bogoliubov (l), I. I. Bodiul (p), I. P. Kalin (p), P. K. Luchinskii (p), S. P. Trapeznikov (l).
V. V. Shcherbitskii:	I. S. Sokolov (l), A. F. Vatchenko (l), I. I. Sakhniuk (p).
G. A. Aliev:	M. S. Tsvigun‡ (p), A. I. Abrakhimov (p), H. A. Aliev (brother?, l).
P. N. Demichev:	I. V. Kapitonov (l, pP), A. M. Rumiantsev (l), V. V. Grishin (l, pP).
B. N. Ponomarev:	K. N. Brutents (l), S. N. Pankov (p), V. V. Zagladin (p).
Sh. R. Rashidov:	V. A. Karlov (p), N. V. Martynov (p).
E. A. Shevardnadze:	Z. A. Pataridze (p), P. G. Gilashvili (p), T. I. Mosashvili (son-in-law, l).
M. V. Zimianin:	V. F. Shauro (l).
I. V. Kapitonov:	V. V. Grishin (l, pP), P. N. Demichev (l, pP), V. I. Konotop (p), Z. A. Pataridze (p), V. A. Petrovichev (l), P. A. Leonov (p).
V. I. Dolgikh:	P. S. Fedirko (p).

‡ Died, 20 January 1982.

At first glance the high number of identified persons may seem impressive: 106 clients have been associated with patrons. It should be borne in mind that a great amount of work has gone into compiling and evaluating the biographies on which they are based, and this particularly from the point of view of *Seilschaft* connections. In addition, many persons appear in the list more than once depending on whether they are seen as figuring as either a patron, a client, or an earlier sponsor. Friends and relatives as well as assistants and advisors have also been indicated.

The result on the other hand is very poor when one considers that except in the cases of Brezhnev, Suslov, Kirilenko, Gromyko and Chernenko only a few clients or none at all can be associated with most of the party hierarchs. It is also obvious that persons such as Kirilenko or Kapitonov, who must often have had a personal hand in the selection of economic administrators or party cadres, are likely to have a far greater *Seilschaft* than indicated in the above listing.

In itself this necessarily provisional list shows that there are blank spaces even at the top of the party hierarchy: not only have we identified no clients for Tikhonov, Solomentsev, Rusakov, Kuznetsov, or Kiselev, but with the exception of Tikhonov and perhaps Rusakov, one cannot classify them with any degree of certainty in any *Seilschaft*. Before we are in a position to compare one *Seilschaft* with another and not focus solely on the Brezhnevites, there is thus far more work to be done.

A quantitative analysis of the above listing based on the same criteria and questions posed in Willerton's pilot study would certainly confirm the latter's findings: that *Seilschaft* members have helped each other during their careers; patrons place their clients for the most part in those functional areas in which they themselves have assumed leading roles; the higher a patron ascends, the more effectively he can place his clients in various apparatuses and higher representative bodies; should he fall, however, his clients will be likely to fall with him, though in the period of relative stability of cadres under Brezhnev this linkage has not been so direct as in the Stalin and Khrushchev periods. Yet a brief glance at the career data of the individuals concerned suffices to draw the same conclusions. All the less appropriate, therefore, does it appear to resort to a meticulous sociometric analysis in order to verify our *a priori* hypotheses when the same result emerges from the career data of a limited number of individuals such as in the inventory offered above.

To be sure it would be possible, at least in the case of the Brezhnev *Seilschaft*, to add substantially to the number of clients by taking into consideration the findings of Moses and of Dornberg's and Morozov's biographies. But apart from the fact that research on the ramifications of other *Seilschaften* at lower hierarchical levels is still lacking, by extension of the list the uncertainty factor will not be reduced, but will become even greater. For however large the figures we operate with, a one-sidedly quantitative analysis is scarcely capable of taking us further than the confirmation of our initial hypotheses.

It may be that the distinction between the fifty-eight likely and forty-eight possible client–patron associations appears exaggerated. If, however, one disregards the fundamentally political, that is, ambivalent and changeable, character of personal relationships within and between *Seilschaften*, neither a quantitative nor a descriptive empirical approach will lead us to a deeper understanding. How cautious one must be is indicated by the fact that the posited association of Gorbachev and Murakhovskii to Suslov, of Riabov, Ryzhkov and Eltsin to Kirilenko, and Luchinskii and Bodiul to Chernenko, is based solely on the scarcely demonstrable hypothesis that even after decades in Moscow Politburo members continue to determine or influence personnel politics in regions where they previously served.

Brezhnev shows in 1964 how ambivalent such relationships can be. Unexpectedly, the 'crown prince' abrogated his loyalty to his sponsor. Such sudden changes are not characteristic only of political crises, but occur daily. Should one thereby consider those under Brezhnev's patronage also as potential 'renegades' who incidentally have a considerable number of clients behind them?

Our second objective in compiling our listing is to formulate possible questions for the further study of *Seilschaften* in the Soviet context. Naturally we cannot pursue these questions in any detail here, still less undertake to answer them.

At the outset we stated that within the Brezhnev *Seilschaft* there are five discernible branches based on geographical and chronological criteria. Thanks to Moses's study we have detailed knowledge of one of them, namely, the Dnepropetrovtsy.

Our list of Brezhnev's clients contains nine from Dnepropetrovsk (Ukraine), five from Moldavia and four from Kazakhstan. Brezhnev made Epishev's acquaintance during the war and possibly met Savinkin during his military service in the 1930s. Apart from family relations, it is especially difficult to distinguish among the nine mostly younger clients who, being connected with Brezhnev's Moscow period, are necessarily listed as Moscow connections although they come from different regions of the country, for instance, Katushev from Gorky or Tiazhel'nikov who went to Moscow from Cheliabinsk through the mediation of N. N. Rodionov.

There are several reasons why it seems significant to us to distinguish the different branches in a *Seilschaft*. One can conjecture that rivalries and conflicts arise among them, in particular when the supreme integration figure, Stalin, for instance, consciously plays on certain rivalries and favors now one and now another of the *Seilschaft* branches. Should the position of the supreme integration figure (the 'top dog')[24] be weakened or the succession issue begin to make itself felt, a disintegration and restructuring process within a *Seilschaft* or in all the existing *Seilschaften* will set in. The highest-ranking figures at the top of a particular branch ('underdogs' in J. Galtung's formulation), to the extent that they wish to become involved or even claim the role of the new 'top dog', will build up their own *Seilschaft*. To take a current illustration, should it turn out that Bodiul (deputy premier) and Luchinskii (deputy head of the CC Propaganda Department) were brought up to Moscow from Moldavia in 1980 and 1981 respectively not at the instance of Brezhnev or Suslov, but at Chernenko's, then we would have an indication that the latter, evidently a current favorite of Brezhnev, had begun to rectify the weaknesses in his cadre base. One problem here is that while in the case of the Kazakhstan branch it is undoubtedly Kunaev who exercises the role of supreme 'underdog', it is by no means clear who plays this role in the case of the large Dnepropetrovsk (or Ukrainian) branch.

Does communication within a *Seilschaft* or even within *Seilschaft* branches normally follow hierarchical lines, that is, top dog – underdog – underdog 1, 2, 3, etc.? Given the primarily vertical orientation of the system, it is reasonable to assume that relationships in the *Seilschaft* are also orientated for the most part along vertical rather than lateral lines. However, since we are dealing here with an informal group based on personal relationships, the possibility of hierarchical levels being in practice bypassed or ignored cannot be excluded.

Therefore, one should not automatically conclude from the 'strength' of the Dnepropetrovsk group that the new 'crown prince' must come from its ranks. Since 1976 Chernenko, for example, although identified with the relatively smaller Moldavian group, seems to have enjoyed far more intensive advancement than many members of the 'powerful' Dnepropetrovsk group.

Every patron has been or is simultaneously a client and any client has been, is, or can become a patron. These fluid, dynamic and often dual roles demand that the political and social context as well as the time factor be taken into consideration. Any schematic characterization of a *Seilschaft* should thus be seen as an isolated 'action shot' and a quantitative analysis based on it will have only limited value. Such 'action shots' should be taken at different points in time and then compared. Only in this way is anything approaching a realistic picture of the dynamic and changeable character of *Seilschaft* relationships attainable.

To illustrate the dual function of a patron and client one needs only to recall such well-known names from Brezhnev's biography as Khrushchev, Kaganovich, Korotchenko and Mekhlis, with whom Brezhnev could have stood in a client relationship in the 1940s and 1950s. That the roles within a dyad can be changed and a patron be demoted to a client is shown in Brezhnev's case by such figures as Alferov, Grushetskii and possibly Epishev, who had earlier occupied higher posts than their later patron.

Another reason why it seems essential to take account of the time factor is that changes in composition and communication flow within a *Seilschaft*, the exchange of values and conflicts within and between *Seilschaften* can be understood only in the specific historical-political context. At all events the penetration of the apparatuses by particular *Seilschaften* has been a gradual, not abrupt, process in the Brezhnev period; what counted was overcoming the resistance of other *Seilschaften*. One can identify phases of ebb and flow, providing indications of the course of the contest for influence between the *Seilschaften*. Thus, one must ask to what extent the Brezhnev *Seilschaft* benefited from the more than two dozen changes in the central government following the retirement and death of Kosygin (October–December 1980), and at the cost of which other *Seilschaften*.

The distribution of *Seilschaft* members among the different apparatuses (with the major contingent based in the central party apparatus) can be illustrated here only by the example of the Brezhnev *Seilschaft*. We have such little certain knowledge about other *Seilschaften* that we can only formulate questions and suppositions. One thing alone is certain: the lower a patron is placed in a hierarchy, the narrower is his impact and the spread of his clients in lateral functional areas. The picture evidently changes somewhat when one leaves the central machine in Moscow and considers the regional apparatus. There too, however, the capacity to install clients in parallel bureaucracies is dependent on hierarchical standing in the party and the process probably follows a broadly similar pattern to that at the center. We may add that as yet very little is known about political *Seilschaften* in the provinces.

At the end of the 1960s D. T. Cattell presented a study on the Leningrad local government administration which contained very valuable material on what he terms 'family power groups'. His thesis, that the leadership deliberately and with some success engages in rapid, systematic circulation of cadres at regional and local levels in order to hinder the formation of *Seilschaften*, was discussed by T. H. Oliver in his work on career patterns of the Moscow state and party leadership. His work contains very important pointers to the genesis, stability and political implications of the Moscow 'family circles'.[25] Our meager knowledge regarding the non-Brezhnev *Seilschaften* at the center is clear from our listings. The attribution of clients to patrons becomes less certain the longer they have occupied high office in Moscow. Difficult questions arise concerning the duration of loyalty, mutual assistance and changes as between chronologically or geographically different career stages.

Sharp changes in personnel policy in the Stalin and Khrushchev periods enable significant conclusions to be drawn about the geographically derived cohorts of 'Leningraders', 'Muscovites', the Belorussian 'partisans', 'Ukrainians', and so on. The relative political stability of cadres in the Brezhnev period obscures such developments and for the most part permits only vague conjecture. Do these *Seilschaften* and loyalties still survive after years or even decades of separation of the individuals involved? As for Brezhnev's 'Ukrainians' we have a certain degree of clarity: here there is evidence of a remarkable durability of attachments. But with regard to the Leningraders or the Belorussians, whose potential 'top dogs' have been removed from the leadership in recent times (Kosygin, Mazurov and Masherov), we are still groping in the dark. Has Gromyko anything more than Belorussian origins in common with T. Ia. Kiselev, the new party chief in Belorussia? Did Kosygin favor Leningraders and does Ustinov continue to do so?

Up to the beginning of the 1960s the *'komsomol'tsy'* of Shelepin and Semichastnyi formed an influential *Seilschaft*, some of whose members occupy high posts even today. Do they still have connections with the new Komsomol leaders? Do those veterans who held high office under Stalin continue to assist each other with reciprocal favors, for instance, earlier CC secretaries in Moscow and Kiev like Patolichev, Pegov, Puzanov and Epishev? One could ask such questions *ad infinitum*.

Below we list with considerable reservation what should best be described as some *potential* regional cohorts; the lists are of course only partial, and the reader should imagine a question-mark beside each name:

Moscow:	V. V. Grishin, I. V. Kapitonov, P. N. Demichev, V. I. Konotop, P. A. Leonov, V. N. Makeev.
Leningrad:	D. F. Ustinov, G. V. Romanov, V. N. Novikov, K. N. Rudnev, P. V. Finogenov, V. N. Bazovskii, V. M. Falin, A. F. Rumiantsev, V. A. Medvedev, A. K. Antonov.
Belorussia:	A. A. Gromyko, N. V. Zimianin, V. F. Shauro, N. S. Patolichev, I. E. Poliakov, P. A. Abrasimov, T. Ia. Kiselev.
Moldavia:	K. U. Chernenko, I. I. Bodiul, P. K. Luchinskii, S. P. Trapeznikov, N. A. Schchelokov, M. S. Tsvigun.*

* Died, 20 January 1982.

Cheliabinsk:	N. N. Rodionov, V. G. Afanasev, N. S. Pato- lichev, N. S. Solomentsev, E. M. Tiazhel'nikov, M. F. Nenashev, M. G. Voropaev.
Gorky:	I. N. Dmitriev, K. F. Katushev, Ia. N. Khristor- adnov.
Stavropol:	M. A. Suslov,† M. S. Gorbachev, V. S. Mur- akhovskii.
Sverdlovsk:	A. P. Kirilenko, Ia. P. Riabov, B. N. Eltsyn, N. E. Ryzhkov, G. V. Kolbin.

† Died, 26 January 1982.

In addition to the regional factor, there are other demographic features (for instance, age structure) that can assume major significance for a *Seilschaft*. In view of the tendency toward a gerontocracy at the summit of the party and state leadership it is of interest to know which of the top men is endeavoring to promote ambitious young clients and to what extent. On the basis of our provisional listing one gets the impression that those so proceeding in 1981 were Suslov (Gorbachev and Mur- akhovskii), Kirilenko (Riabov and Eltsin) and Chernenko (Luchinskii and Bodiul), while Brezhnev seemed more inclined (or is perhaps obliged?) to rely on old friendships (for instance, Tikhonov). Further study is required to clarify the very interest- ing question of which younger 'top dogs' are displaying a particular dynamism in building up their *Seilschaften*.

In view of the oft-noted demographic developments which will soon reduce the Great Russians to less than half the total Soviet population considerable interest attaches to the national composition of *Seilschaften*. Should it be established that key positions in *Seilschaften* in union republics or other national territorial units are being increasingly occupied by Russians or other East Slavs, then this could be interpreted as a reaction to growing aspirations for national emancipation among the national minorities.

Except for Brezhnev's Ukrainians, Kazakhs and Moldavians, we unfortunately know very little about *Seilschaften* in the union republics. What is known is the 'overseer' function of the second secretary in the union republics and that all regional party leaders strive to have 'their' people in Moscow. The Gosplan chief, Baibakov, is supposed to be especially sensitive to Azer- baidzhan concerns, while Kirilenko, Kapitonov and Tsvigun are said to have or have had good contacts in the Caucasus;[26] the Georgian second secretary, Kolbin, for instance, is one of Kirilenko's men from Sverdlovsk. A special feature of *Seilschaft* formation in the Caucasus seems to be that there are fairly close ties to all forms of corruption, while at the same time they are imbued with a nationalist coloration. So far as the Central Asian republics are concerned, A. Bennigsen's comments are of interest. He notes that in Kazakhstan members of the 'Great Horde' (Oulu Jou) tribe and in Turkmenistan of the 'Tekke' tribe occupy an exceptionally high proportion of key positions.[27]

Whether a connection exists between *Seilschaft* formation in the fringe republics and the traditional 'hawkish' foreign policy role of local party leaders, and what the connection is, deserves investigation. One knows, for example, of the especially hard line taken by the Leningraders in the 1940s and early 1960s *vis-à-vis* Finland, and the Ukrainians of Shelest *vis-à-vis* Czechoslovakia (1968) and the USA (1972). At the last Party Congress (1981) the Ukrainian and Belorussian party chiefs expressed themselves especially forthrightly in relation to Poland while the Central Asian party leaders adopted a similar stance on the Afghanistan question. Is it their patrons in Moscow or their clients in the fringe republics that prompt them to assume this 'hawkish' role?

When we examine the national composition of the officials in our listing we find, not surprisingly, that Russians and other East Slavs predominate in the top leadership. Brezhnev's clients also included two Kazakhs and two Jews. In the absence of studies of other regional cohorts one can only formulate a few hypotheses: the higher a patron is placed in the party hierarchy, the more extensive is not only the lateral but also the national distribution of his clients. Those leaders who, with *inter alia* demographic trends in mind, seek to strengthen their support-base among non-Slav officials, will naturally endeavor to have more clients within the aspiring national elites.

On the other hand, a different reaction to the growing strength of the non-Russian nationalities is also possible. By a self-defense reflex, the 'Russian' and East Slavic *Seilschaften* could retreat into their shells, close their ranks and perhaps diminish their mutual rivalries. In that case, however, certain *Seilschaften* could hive off and under the banner of 'internationalism' enter into political alliances with groups based in the non-Russian republics. However, the increased proportion of Russians in the Central Committee in 1976–81, running contrary as it does to changes over this period in the ethnic composition of the population at large, suggests that the initial reaction will be more of the self-defense reflex variety.

Sociographic Approach: Sources and a Brief Illustration

The uncertainties attached to compiling an inventory of clientelist links and to obtaining the necessary raw data even for those in the top leadership limit the feasibility of quantitative empirical analysis. Questions about duration, intensity of loyalties, interest priorities, value orientations, communication, problems of attitude, behavior and conflict within and between *Seilschaften*, their integration, disintegration and restructuring, can hardly be answered through the techniques of such empirical research.

The 'system of concrete actions' (Crozier) within and between *Seilschaften* in their essential aspects can only be observed, described and evaluated. We suggest, therefore, that what one might call the sociographic approach promises greater knowledge and understanding of political *Seilschaften* in communist systems than does quantitative analysis.

Besides career data, information from the Soviet press, memoirs and political biographies, and statements by witnesses who have lived in the Soviet Union, are available as potential sources for the student of Soviet clientelism. How the latter is reflected in Soviet literature – particularly that relating to party secretaries – would also justify careful examination. In what follows we must confine ourselves to briefly indicating the sorts of things that can be learnt from the sociographic analysis of such sources.

(a) *Evidence of Existence of Seilschaften in Soviet and Other Socialist Countries*

Although the very idea of considering the phenomenon of political *Seilschaften* in socialist systems would certainly be disregarded as bourgeois slander by the Soviets, the existence of political *Seilschaften* is actually conceded in the Soviet media. Furthermore, in the political literature of Poland and Hungary one finds indications that serious study of the phenomenon has begun. When it is referred to in Soviet sources, it is always put in the conventional context of representing such negative phenomena as exceptions rather than as examples of widespread practices. Let us consider a few examples which illustrate how the existence of *Seilschaften* is testified to in the Soviet media, and how it is handled.

Masherov, the Belorussian party chief who died in October 1980 following a car accident, gave an interview in *Pravda* in June 1980, in which he berated the gross overexpansion of the governmental apparatus in the republic. As an example he cited the Ministry for Light and Food Industry, which had increased its personnel strength by 50 percent since 1975. The attitude of civil servants, he complained, often resembled the fundamental principle of private enterprise: *ty mne – ya tebe* ('You scratch my back, and I'll scratch yours').[28]

In July 1980 Aliev, the party first secretary in Azerbaidzhan, censured such negative phenomena in cadre administration as protectionism and corruption (venality).[29] The CC plenum at which he voiced his criticism was also concerned with what in the West became known as the 'caviar affair'. This scandal, involving the illegal sale of caviar abroad, implicated hundreds of economic administrators and ministerial officials and demonstrated the involvement of economic and political elements in *Seilschaft* relationships.[30]

In an interview Ukrainian party chief Shcherbitskii severely criticized those leaders who are 'too close' to many subordinates, while keeping others 'at a distance'. Kosolapov, the chief editor of *Kommunist*, wrote that many comrades shaped their relationships with others not on the basis of party principles (*partiinost'*), but on the basis of relations of friendship, while dressing up partiality as *partiinost'*.[31]

In September 1980 a leading article in *Pravda* sketched the 'ideal' leader, in so doing taking the rare step these days of criticizing an *obkom* – in this case the regional party committee in North Ossetia. Here, it was stated, proper 'business' and 'political' criteria for the selection of cadres in the economic field had been violated. Appointments had been made on the basis of kinship, local ties and servility (*po priznakam rodstva, zemliachestva i ugodnichestva*).[32]

The Rostov regional party secretary, Bondarenko, reported in an interview the dismissal of a certain *raikom* first secretary by the name of Iakovlev, who had 'hauled up' with him (*potianul za soboi*) a friend whom he made chairman of the *raion* executive committee, subsequently concealing many of his misdeeds.[33]

In the last few years – up until the death of Kosygin at the end of 1980 – *Pravda* criticized a number of ministries with increasing intensity. The administrative priority given to departmental and local interests (*mestnichestvo i vedomstvennost'*) in several ministries and other agencies was blamed, among other things, for shortages in meat supplies. And in the course of criticizing these ministries it was revealed that many persons in positions of responsibility had wangled their own supporters (*svoikh liudei*) into high office.[34] Many further such examples could be given, but these should suffice.

In contrast with the kinds of references to *Seilschaft* relationships one finds in Soviet sources, the cadres chief of the Hungarian Central Committee frankly acknowledges that these are something more than a marginal and ephemeral phenomenon: 'We well know that in cadre work the threat of subjectivism and favoritism on the basis of friendship and protectionism is constantly present.'[35] It is astounding, in fact, how candid and cognizant of the problem are references to *Seilschaften* in Hungarian sociological and political literature. To be sure, one would be exaggerating the degree of liberalization in Hungary to expect much more than simply references to such a ticklish theme, although it is worth noting that these are becoming progressively more abundant.[36] The theme is also reported occasionally to be broached in Poland, and this even before the 1980 workers' revolt.[37] An analysis of the Eastern and Central European treatment of *Seilschaft* relationships, as interesting as it may be, would be beyond the scope of this study. The related phenomenon of nepotism in the Soviet Union, Romania and Bulgaria has undergone exhaustive treatment in the Western press.[38]

(*b*)   Who Gets What, When and How in a 'Seilschaft'?

Drawing on Grey Hodnett's description of the interests which are defended by a Soviet politician, Willerton enumerates those interests applicable to a Soviet *Seilschaft* in the following way:

(1)   promotion of their interests as continuing members of the leadership;

(2)   promotion of their factional interests;

(3)   promotion of the functional tasks for which they are responsible;

(4)   promotion of interests associated with their general policy sympathies;

(5)   promotion of sectoral (party governments, and so on) organizational (departmental, ministry, and so on) or geographic (province, republic, region) interests;

(6)   promotion of interests associated with their past career experiences;

(7)   promotion of given interests arising from their membership in various age, ethnic and other background categories.[39]

This is an impressive and probably quite complete list of interests. The only problem with it is that in any particular transaction between actors in a dyad or *Seilschaft*, priorities may change or even come into conflict with each other. In general, it is obvious that all these interests could not be pursued simultaneously or systematically.

The basic problem is that such a list of preferences and interests is so abstract that its link with empirical reality is rather tenuous. It needs to be translated into more concrete terms before it can serve as a lever for the study of Soviet *Seilschaften*. In order to know what the interests of a faction, organization, national group and likewise a *Seilschaft* are, we need to know what are the interests, action patterns and strategies of the *particular actors* composing them. Given our current level of information, the question arises what quantifiable empirical data are available that might be appropriate and sufficient to provide such information. For the present one can scarcely anticipate questionnaire surveys to be conducted among assumed patrons and clients, or that Soviet sociologists would report on anything of the kind.

If we seek to answer the question who gets 'what, when and how' in a *Seilschaft* in a way that relates closely to actual practice, to reality, the vast abstractions of the terminology of political sociology will not take us far. All too easily they become little more than a façade to conceal our ignorance and uncertainties about how things actually work in the Soviet Union. This can reach a point where, as happened on one or two occasions at the 1980 World Congress on Soviet and East European Studies, formerly highly placed Soviet citizens are obliged to state that they are completely unable to recognize themselves and their experiences in the accounts of Western Sovietologists, even when these deal with institutions and events in which they were themselves personally involved.

Brezhnev's memoirs can be considered an important source for sociographic-political research into *Seilschaften*. A few incidents are worth recalling here to illustrate the substantive interests and values which can be presented or exchanged in a dyad. In *Vozrozhdenie (Rebirth)*[40] Brezhnev tells of a clash during the heroic reconstruction in the immediate postwar years when he was *obkom* secretary in Dnepropetrovsk and Tikhonov – today Politburo member and chairman of the Council of Ministers – was director of the local Nikopol pipe plant. Tikhonov had used more funds to improve facilities for workers in his plant than provided for under the plan. During an inspection the Minister for Ferrous Metallurgy, Tevosian, threatened dire consequences, saying that Moscow would be infuriated. Brezhnev defended Tikonov, pointing out that the improvement in working conditions had been undertaken with the agreement of the *obkom*. In order to appease Moscow and fend off the danger which threatened both Tikhonov and himself, Brezhnev promised Tevosian that a *subbotnik* program would be undertaken to complete needed infrastructure work in Nikopol. This positive illustration of the patron's function as protector incidentally brings out two points: support for a client's concerns will cease or at least diminish if the center raises protests; and the price for the (in this case laudable) transaction is likely to be paid not by the parties to it, but by the workers (who in this case were deprived of their day off).

In his *Tselina (Virgin Lands)* Brezhnev relates how, having arrived in Kazakhstan in 1954, he and Ponomarenko had satisfied themselves that 'leaders on various levels in the republic had quite often been appointed so to say not on the basis of their qualifications for the job but of friendship ties', and that 'quite a few leaders lacking in a proper sense of responsibility selected their staff not for their working qualities but on the principle of personal loyalty'.[41] He added that following the record harvest of 1954, comrades had contrived a 'cadre quadrille' in which they mutually assisted each other to gain promotion. Only F. T. Morgun had applied to Brezhnev, which could 'not be considered as usual', not to be appointed to a higher office as he still had much to do in the *sovkhoz* which he directed.[42] Nevertheless, Morgun was in due course to be promoted by Brezhnev, and two decades later, when this Brezhnev follower was conspicuous by his absence at the unveiling of a bronze bust of formal Head of State Podgornyi in Poltava in early 1977, this was the first sign of the latter's imminent downfall.

In Brezhnev's memoirs one finds the names of many persons whose career data show them to have later benefited from 'friendship ties' or 'personal loyalty' in the 'cadre quadrille' undertaken by Brezhnev himself. Kunaev can be taken as an example, Brezhnev's friendship for whom is expressed in the warmest of words, and whom he repeatedly stood by in times of trouble.

Brezhnev's references to Khrushchev's mistakes can serve as a final illustration of the loyalty of a client to his patron; at the same time they illustrate that the costs must basically be paid by those who do not belong to the *Seilschaft*. He relates how a narrow-gauge railroad was built which proved to be a totally inadequate solution to a particular transport problem in Kazakhstan, although its construction and dismantling swallowed up millions of rubles. The author of these memoirs, which are held up in the Soviet Union as standard texts of cadre policy, fails to explain why he did not oppose this obviously wrong investment at the time, and merely comments: 'We pay for our errors, and always to excess, in wartime with men, and in peacetime with material and moral losses.'[43] Such blind loyalty as displayed by Brezhnev for the sake of his career, and the similar hierarchically oriented devotion of many other clients to whoever their patron was at the time, and the concomitant 'mistakes' that were made, certainly cost millions both in money terms and men's lives, and not only in wartime.

Accounts by émigrés contain extremely important material on *Seilschaften* and the interests involved. *Seilschaften* in the Soviet system are usually seen by them as a variety of corruption. The social-psychological genesis of corruption in the Soviet Union, its varieties and extent, its rules of the game have been described in the works of such émigré writers as Zinoviev, Ianov, Voslensky and Zemtsov, based on firsthand knowledge. The last three authors' works may be described as politicosociographic monographs.[44] To be sure, their central theme is not the *Seilschaft* phenomenon; their works, however, contain many inferences of which one must make full use if a better understanding of Soviet clientelism is to be acquired. Proper discussion of this, of course, would require a separate study. Their descriptions, assertions and implications, not to mention their conclusions, may appear to many as exaggerated and imbued with resentment, or simply wrong. The point, however, is that they nevertheless represent testimonies by eye-witnesses which must therefore be taken seriously, be examined and evaluated, if we are to transcend the level of abstract and vague hypotheses on our subject.

Zemtsov's specific assertions relating to Azerbaidzhan are of particular interest. He demonstrates the interaction of political *Seilschaften* and economic corruption at the local and national levels. He illustrates with names and figures the roles and functions of Moscow patrons, the purchase of posts, titles and privileges, and the mutual protection function of clans. Under cover of his purge of 1969–72 Aliev is said to have filled no fewer than 1,983 important posts with his own people from the KGB.[45]

The three authors mentioned clearly take the view that one interest predominates in transactions within the *nomenklatura*, the 'new aristocracy', and notoriously so within and between *Seilschaften*, namely, the material privileges which a power position brings and which are even measured in money terms. They describe in concrete terms what these consist of and what the members of a *Seilschaft* receive. In the West, too, there is a growing literature dealing with the privileges of the leadership stratum in the Soviet Union, of which we should particularly note Mervyn Matthews's recent work.[46]

This proposition of such eye-witnesses is naturally a challenge to those who believe they can detect a fairly marked evolutionary trend toward bureaucratic rationality over the last ten to twenty years. In relation to clientelism this proposition must also be qualified in the light of the bureaucratic orientation of interest priorities in the relationships between patron and client as catalogued by Hodnett and Willerton. The topic of the correlation of rational and functional efficiency on the one hand, and the orientation on power and privilege on the other, in the careers of Soviet functionaries clearly calls for much further discussion. New studies are required to clarify what is involved, for instance, where managers and experts, enjoying support of certain reform-minded patrons in the central party apparatus, begin to form influential *Seilschaften*. In Hungary such *Seilschaften* operating as sponsors of the 1968 economic reforms, like the professorial cohorts of Karl Marx University, today occupy key positions in the administration. If we are to accept the view of such eye-witness accounts as those cited above, *Seilschaften* of this kind no longer exist in the Soviet Union.

The testimonies of eye-witnesses suggest further questions in connection with the *Seilschaft* problem. Ianov's theory of 'aristocratization' and of a growing Slavophile tendency in the USSR is of interest here. Future *Seilschaft* studies should investigate these possibilities more closely. The growing number of children and relations of patrons occupying high positions and the striking shift to 'Russification' in the membership of the latest CC indicate that these postulations may well have some basis.

The System-specific Genesis of *Seilschaften* and its Significance for Soviet Politics

Definitionally, political *Seilschaften* serve above all to promote politically relevant interests of their members as well as to advance their careers. The essential feature of a hierarchically ordered power system in which political *Seilschaften* too stand in hierarchical super- and subordination to each other, is the attempt to politicize all spheres of social activity and control social institutions right down to the basic units. In such a system it is consequently extremely difficult, if not impossible, to distinguish between what is politically relevant and what is not. In the Soviet system it is self-evident that political careers and hierarchical position provide the measure for the level and range of material privilege.

The intention, then, is total political control, but in practice the control of all spheres of social activity is far from complete. Such factors as the elementary aspirations of man for personal autonomy, the obstacles which different parts of the apparatus place in each other's path and the one-sided vertical orientation of official communications play a significant part in this. Under Stalin control was greater than under his successors, but then the basic fear for one's life was a substantial factor in the development of *Seilschaften* (then referred to as 'family circles').

So far as the social basis of the phenomenon in the Soviet Russian context is concerned, Zygmunt Bauman's interesting hypotheses on 'the resilience and inertia of peasant behavioural patterns' and 'the conditions faced by the preindustrial peasant' are most suggestive.[47] Relatedly, Carl Landé notes that the personal followings described in the Soviet Union call to mind the dyadic structure of premodern political systems.[48]

T. H. Rigby cites the following specific characteristics of the Soviet system as factors in *Seilschaft* formation:

> promotion within the bureaucratic hierarchies is the only path to political power;
> the decisive criteria for promotion are not 'neutral' rule-bound achievement norms but the evaluations of superiors;
> rivalries at all levels of the power hierarchies but especially at the summit;
> the builtin pressures on officials to conspire together and employ dubious methods in order to achieve prescribed goals.[49]

Becquart-Leclercq traces the origins of the 'network of connections' (*réseau relationnel*) in France, and the 'redistribution of power' deriving from them, back to the high level of centralization and the *confusion* and *rigidité* of the system. As a defensive reaction to the centralizing structure, and also as a means of overcoming bureaucratic inflexibility and irrationality, personal connections are brought into play.[50] All these conditions also apply under the Soviet system, and indeed to a far higher degree. Here the confusion is manifested not only in the secretiveness of the decisionmaking processes and the overlapping and often concealed lines of responsibility. It is manifested above all in the virtual chaos of competencies as between the various bureaucracies, due largely to the duplication of the leadership responsibilities of the party apparatus on the one hand, and the state and economic apparatus on the other. This chaos of competencies and the concomitant irrationalities are objects of constant complaint (most recently, for instance, in relation to resource development in West Siberia). The Twenty-sixth Party Congress in 1981 demonstrated yet again, however, that despite all such complaints and the leadership's constant measures to improve the economic and administrative mechanism (for example, in a major decree of July 1979 and in decisions of the October 1980 CC plenum) the malady is evidently incurable. In fact, no real improvement can be expected so long as the leadership insists on the universal primacy of politics and centralized direction, and strives to operate according to the contradictory principle 'the party leads and the state manages'.

The inflexibility of the system is, of course, directly related to the high level of centralization. The attempt to get a grip on multifarious local circumstances through the medium of formal and, at the same time, internally contradictory mechanisms of regimentation cannot but fail. Meanwhile the judicial system, limping along as it does at the heels of politics, creates even more confusion rather than relieving it, as witnessed, for example, in the enormous number of amendments to Acts and regulations printed in the official gazettes of the Supreme Soviet and the Council of Ministers. Whether the code of laws (*svod zakonov*) due to be compiled by 1985 will produce more clarity remains to be seen. Contradictory rules are a major obstacle to local initiative and innovation. The constant improvisations they necessitate provoke leading officials into covering themselves through interpersonal understandings. As a consequence of those features of the political and organizational structure that we have indicated above, *Seilschaften* spring up outside the realm of formal legality. To avoid using the legal and institutionalized instruments of decisionmaking, control and communications they resort to other instruments of their own, for example, the *vertushka* (telephone network reserved for the *nomenklatura*) as well as varieties of personal and mutually profitable arrangements. They thereby influence decisions without leaving so much as the slightest trace in the files, and thereby without incurring responsibility in any form.

Seilschaften are by definition the negation of organized and institutionalized relationships, but so long as what is involved here is a purely informal kind of interest representation, they are tacitly tolerated by the central party apparatus – the real sovereign power in the land. Indeed, the latter is no less the scene of shared complicities and secret enmities than other levels of the Soviet system. *Seilschaften* thus even contribute substantially to the functional capacity of the system in so far as they loosen the rigidity of rules and thereby ease the mutual blocking of each other's efforts by the different bureaucracies which results from the aforesaid chaos of competencies and, finally, they are able to patch up conflicts between local and central interests.

In an article indicating the limits of applicability of the bureaucratic politics model to the Soviet system, K. Dawisha has drawn attention *inter alia* to the important role of patron – client relationships. In addition to the priorities of the apparatus, there are also the interests of the *Seilschaften* as well as a number of other interests, for example, groups of specialists.[51] In practice, however, these interests are so little open to scrutiny that we are hardly in a position to identify them and define their respective limits. It is usually only in retrospect, for example, in the wake of major new decisions or power changes, that we may obtain glimpses into the twilight world of the mesh of interests; as, for example, in the case of the decision to invade Czechoslovakia. By contrast, we can do little more than speculate on the interests which came into play *vis-à-vis* the recent occupation of Afghanistan; for example, that Chairman of the Council of Ministers Kosygin and his supposed client and deputy, M. A. Kirillin, might have been against this decision.[52]

W. Odom has argued that *Seilschaften* are not interest groups and that the leadership tolerates them because they obstruct the formation of genuine interest groups.[53] Quite apart from ambiguities in the definitions of interest groups or group interests, and with reservations about the extension of notions based on Western phenomena to the Soviet Union, one can concur with this view only to a limited degree. Certainly, in so far as the notion of interest groups implies formally or informally legalized, organized and regulated representation of interests, one cannot equate these with *Seilschaften*. But in the case of *Seilschaften* the question is one of groups and of the promotion of interests, so it seems appropriate to characterize them as informal interest groups. It is even possible that they will one day serve as the seeds of formal interest groups, though any such development is still a long way off and thus far the leadership has successfully blocked any potential metamorphosis of this kind.

One could also characterize the various dissident groups as *Seilschaften* or 'interest groups' of a kind. In the manner of *Seilschaften* they provide mutual protection albeit along different lines from those of establishment *Seilschaften*, before and after arrest. As 'interest groups' they represent interests which transcend personal well-being and security and relate to conceptions of an alternative order. At the same time they could perhaps better be seen as potential nuclei of future parties.

The general politicization of all areas of life which the ideology serves to justify, weakens or destroys ethical orientations; nevertheless controls over the grassroots have become looser with the abandonment of Stalinist methods. This has fostered the development of the 'second economy' and 'second culture' as well as all kinds of corruption. Analogous to these, *Seilschaft* relationships with their coloration of corruption enable us to speak of a 'second politics'.[54]

In accordance with the ideological self-understanding of the Soviet system the political *Seilschaft* is a form of corruption. Therefore, it is condemned and represented as a phenomenon which only rarely occurs. However, the constant succession of ever-new *Seilschaften* in the top leadership from Lenin down to our own day demonstrates clearly that they are not exceptions to the rule, but permeate all hierarchical and functional levels. As already suggested, this form of 'corruption' possesses at least to a certain degree a system-stabilizing function. The relative stability of cadres in the Brezhnev period has not only favored a certain regularization, but has accelerated the development of *Seilschaften* and local interest networks.

So long as the 'round-dance' of Soviet political *Seilschaften* has only the one outlet, namely, the formation of a power pyramid with a single man at the top, and so long, further, as the orientation on power and hierarchy remains the most important rule of the game (at the expense of bureaucratic rationality, efficiency and the interests of society), thus obstructing the formation of relatively autonomous and equal political *Seilschaften* and other such political and social entities, the political *Seilschaften* will not deserve the eulogy which Alain Besançon accorded to other aspects of corruption of the system in his foreword to Zemtsov's book.[55] In his defence it should be made clear that this eulogy did not apply to corruption as such, but to the striving for individual human autonomy which it embodies. According to Besançon, corruption is 'a manifestation of life, a pathological life to be sure, which for all that is better than death'. It marks 'the rebirth of personal life', 'the triumph of the individual', who is thereby liberated from the shackles of ideology and sets foot on the solid ground of reality. On the basis of personal interests he bargains over what is 'mine' and what is 'yours' and through the medium of the resulting 'negotiated redistribution' manifests a certain autonomy.

In opposition to the 'second culture' (dissidents), from which emanate the most direct challenges to the existing system, and the 'second economy', which tends in the long run to undermine centralized direction, the 'second politics' could become a threat to the one-party regime only if it were to suffer further 'corruption' from its social milieu; in other words, if out of the potential plurality of interests genuine interest groups were to arise.

Notes: Chapter 4

1 *Bol'shaia Sovetskaia Entsiklopediia*, 3rd edn, Vol. 12, p. 304, Vol. 19, p. 284.
2 René Lemarchand and Keith Legg, 'Political clientelism and development', *Comparative Politics*, vol. 4, no. 2 (1972), pp. 151–2.
3 T. H. Rigby, 'The Soviet leadership: towards a self-stabilizing oligarchy?', *Soviet Studies*, vol. XXII, no. 2 (1970), p. 177.
4 E. Arzti, 'Homo Sovieticus', *Crossroads*, no. 2 (Winter 1979), pp. 139 ff.
5 Merle Fainsod, *How Russia Is Ruled*, rev. edn (Cambridge, Mass.: Harvard University Press, 1963), pp. 235–7, 388–9, 213, 240, 412, 475.
6 *Handlexikon zur politischen Wissenschaft* (Munich: A. Görlitz, 1979), pp. 85 ff.
7 Philip D. Stewart, *et al.*, 'Political mobility and the Soviet political process: a partial test of two models', *American Political Science Review*, vol. 66, no. 4 (1972), pp. 1269–90.
8 ibid., pp. 1278–9, 1284.
9 Joel C. Moses, 'Regional cohorts and political mobility in the USSR: the case of Dnepropetrovsk', *Soviet Union*, vol. 3, pt 1 (1976), pp. 63–89.
10 ibid, p. 88.
11 John P. Willerton, 'Clientelism in the Soviet Union: an initial examination', *Studies in Comparative Communism*, vol. VII, no. 2–3 (1979), pp. 159–83.
12 ibid, p. 164.
13 Michel Crozier and E. Friedberg, *L'Acteur et le système* (Paris: Editions du seuil, 1977), p. 25.
14 Zygmunt Bauman, 'Comment on Eastern Europe', *Studies in Comparative Communism*, vol. VII, no. 2–3 (1979), p. 188.
15 ibid, pp. 177–88.

16 Soviet Elite Mobility Project and Research Archive, Ohio State University.

17 Crozier and Friedberg, op. cit., p. 25. The research project referred to, based in the Bundesinstitut für ostwissenschaftliche und internationale Studien, Cologne, has not yet reached the stage where results can be reported here, substantially by reason of the conceptual and technical problems discussed above.

18 An abbreviated selection of these biographies has appeared under the title *A Biographic Directory of 100 Leading Soviet Officials* (Munich: Radio Liberty, 1981).

19 See L. I. Brezhnev, *Malaia Zemlia*, 1978, *Vozrozhdenie*, 1978, and *Tselina*, 1978. (Gospolitiydar, 1978)

20 John Dornberg, *Brezhnev: The Masks of Power* (London: André Deutsch, 1974).

21 Michael Morozov, *Leonid Breschnew* (Stuttgart: Verlag Kohlhammer, 1973). A new biography by Paul Murphy, *Brezhnev: Soviet Politician* (Jefferson, NC: Macfarlane, 1981), was not yet available to the author at the time of completing the present chapter.

22 See Willerton, op. cit., p. 166.

23 See, in this connection, *Novaia i noveishaia istoriia*, no. 3 (1980), p. 224.

24 Interestingly this term of Johan Galtung's was employed in a Hungarian study on the corrupting effects of a hierarchical (political) orientation upon 'genuine' human relationships; see A. Hankiss, 'Közösségek: válság és hiány', *Valóság*, vol. 23, no. 9 (September 1980), p. 16.

25 David T. Cattell, *Leningrad: A Case Study of Soviet Urban Government* (New York: Praeger, 1968), pp. 56, 156; and J. H. Oliver, 'Turnover and "family circles" in Soviet administration', *Slavic Review*, vol. 32, no. 3 (1973), p. 527 ff.

26 Ilya Zemtsov, *La corruption en Union Soviétique* (Paris: Hachette, 1976), pp. 54–5.

27 Alexandre Bennigsen, 'Mussulmans de l'URSS et crise afgane', *Politique étrangère*, vol. 45, no. 1 (1980), p. 19.

28 *Pravda*, 15 June 1980.

29 *Radio Liberty Research Bulletin*, 23 July 1980.

30 *Pravda*, 28 December 1979.

31 *Partiinaia zhizn'*, no. 8 (1980), p. 32.

32 *Pravda*, 22 September 1980.

33 ibid., 14 June 1980.

34 ibid., 6 January 1980.

35 K. Németh, in *Partiinaia zhizn'*, no. 15 (1980), p. 72.

36 L. Bogár, 'Erdekviszonyok, másodlagos gazdaság, korrupció' ('Interests, Economy, Corruption'), *Valóság*, vol. 23, no. 8 (1980), pp. 38 ff.; and E. Hankiss, *Tarsadalmi csapdók* (Budapest: Magvetö, 1978), and 'Közösségek', op. cit., pp. 12–26.

37 Y. Tarkowski, 'Local influence in a centralized system', report presented at Workshop on Local Authorities, Warsaw, 1977, quoted in J. Becquart-Leclercq, 'Réseau relationnel, pouvoir relationnel', *Revue française de science politique*, vol. 29, no. 1 (1979), p. 102.

38 'Vetternwirtschaft im Sozialismus', *Der Spiegel*, 4 August 1980, p. 116; L. Unger, 'Communist rule: all in the family', *International Herald Tribune*, 24 August 1979; and K. Firman, 'Kommunisticheskie dinastii', *Russkaia Mysl'*, 11 October 1979, and 'All in the first family', *Time*, 30 April 1979, p. 23.

39 Willerton, op. cit., p. 162; and Grey Hodnett, 'Succession contingencies in the Soviet union', *Problems of Communism*, vol. XXIV, no. 2 (1975), pp. 13, 11.
40 L. I. Brezhnev, *Vozrozhdenie* 1978, pp. 50–1.
41 L. I. Brezhnev, *Tselina*, 1978, p. 9–10.
42 ibid., p. 52.
43 ibid., pp. 30–1.
44 Alexander Yanov, *Détente after Brezhnev* (Berkeley, Calif.: University of California Press, 1977); Zemtsov, *La corruption*, op. cit., and 'The ruling class in the USSR', *Crossroads*, no. 2–3 (1979); Michael Voslensky, *Nomenklatura: Die Herrschende Klasse der Sowjetunion* (Vienna: Molden, 1980).
45 Zemtsov, *La corruption*, op. cit., p. 149.
46 Mervyn Matthews, *Privilege in the Soviet Union: A Study of Elite Life-Styles under Communism* (London: Allen & Unwin, 1978).
47 Bauman, op. cit., p. 185.
48 Carl H. Landé, 'Networks and groups in Southeast Asia: some observations on the group theory of politics', *American Political Science Review*, vol. 67, no. 1 (1973), p. 120.
49 Rigby, 'The Soviet leadership', op. cit., p. 177.
50 Becquart-Leclercq, op. cit., pp. 120–2, 102.
51 Karen Dawisha, 'The limits of the bureaucratic politics model: observations on the Soviet case', *Studies in Comparative Communism*, vol. XIII, no. 4 (1980), pp. 300 ff., 322.
52 Gyula Józsa, *Kirillins Rucktritt und die Ernennung G. I. Martschuks zu seinem Nachfolger* (Cologne: Berichte des Bundesinstituts, 1980), pp. 10 ff.
53 William E. Odom, 'A dissenting view on the group approach to Soviet politics', *World Politics*, vol. XXVIII, no. 4 (1976), pp. 542 ff., 552–3.
54 cf. T. H. Rigby, 'Early provincial cliques and the rise of Stalin', *Soviet Studies*, vol. XXXIII, no. 1 (1981), p. 5.
55 Zemtsov, *La corruption*, op. cit., pp. 18–19.

5

Political Clientelism in Russia: the Historical Perspective

DANIEL T. ORLOVSKY

> In the Department of General Affairs (Ministry of Internal Affairs) all routine work was done by one of the clerks, Shinkevich, and all important work, such as the working out of legislative projects and the compilation of memoranda on complicated matters, was done by Gurland, a professor of constitutional law at the Demidov Lyceum whom Stürmer had brought from Yaroslavl. Gurland possessed a gifted pen, a sound education, and a talent for understanding the moods of his superiors. His brains and ability supported Stürmer in all the posts he occupied in the capital.[1]

This description of a situation in the imperial Russian central government bureaucracy during the first decade of the twentieth century, written by V. I. Gurko, is duplicated hundreds of times in different permutations in the memoir literature of official Russia during the imperial period (and indeed, as I will argue, before that as well). Although this relationship described by Gurko could be analyzed from a number of viewpoints, it may serve here as an introduction to the question of clientelism in the prerevolutionary bureaucracy. Clientelism as used here is a form of ostensibly 'irrational' political behavior involving mutual support of individuals or dyadic groups in the organizational context of the state bureaucracy. The notion of clientelism within formal bureaucratic structures is used to make sense of an important, persistent and widespread political phenomenon not readily reducible to ideal-typical notions of power relations and to emphasize the historical importance of personal relations in Russian cultural and institutional life. The historian of Russia and many social scientists concerned with Soviet politics now find clientelism and other forms of patronage an inescapable component of the structure of state power with its own impact upon policies and events.

One trend not always avoided in recent studies of clientelism by sovietologists, however, is an overemphasis on clientelism as a product of socialist or the Soviet forms of organization. The underlying assumption here is that revolutions are wholly transformative and that the history of Soviet institutions and political behavior began in 1917. This approach toward clientelism (and indeed other problems in Soviet studies) calls to mind recent debates on the origins of 'Stalinism'. In those debates scholars have moved from linking Stalinism directly to Leninism (as an inevitable or at least wholly logical result) to a more defensible view that considers Stalinism to be more unique and explicable in terms of the social and institutional fabric of the post-1917 party and larger Soviet society. Yet even this approach plays down or ignores altogether carryovers in political culture and more concretely the important weight of institutional life and traditions (patterns of organization and ethos) upon the young Soviet state. In prerevolutionary Russia (and in Muscovy) dyadic relations and larger networks or clienteles had their roots in the clan-based, highly personalized political culture of the Muscovite court and bureaucracy. In Russian history we may find the origin of not simply the domination of the 'personal' over the 'institutional', or the 'legal', but of what might be more aptly seen as the institutionalization of the personal within a variety of political and legal structures.

My view is that clientelism and other patterns of organizational behavior were embedded in the institutional fabric of prerevolutionary Russia as well as in the political culture that legitimized those institutions and politics. As I have argued elsewhere, it is precisely the carryover of such 'survivals' (to use Lenin's term) or addenda, to use the language of modern social scientists, that makes the entire problem of revolution so fascinating and in need of new theoretical departures.[2] One of the key problems of the revolution in Russia that clientelism expresses clearly is the obvious and well-documented appearance of prerevolutionary patterns of organizational and political behavior within institutions that are comprised of new (and old) personnel drawn from very different social groups. The question of such 'addenda' within formal structures is I think one of the more promising areas of research for improving existing theories of revolution and especially the question of revolutionary outcomes. (The existing theoretical literature on revolution is far better at explaining the breakdown of old regimes than in explaining the crucial relationship between the successor regimes and the inheritance of addenda from the past.) As will be shown, Lenin was not the first would-be transformer of Russian institutions to be stymied by those institutions and the social material he inherited. While it can be argued, as Zygmunt Bauman has done, that clientelism is indeed a common and perhaps inescapable feature of Old Regime or absolutist monarchies, and that clientelism cannot therefore be ascribed to 'cultural peculiarities', we can indeed point to the unique character of organizational phenomena within given societies, the degree of their persistence over time, their relative importance *vis-à-vis* other aspects of institutional life and, most importantly, their impact upon politics. The Russian case offers a vivid example of the tensions between personal and institutional authority, and the remarkable tenacity of the informal or irrational within bureaucratic institutions over long time periods. To claim that the phenomenon was ubiquitous, Weberian ideal types aside, is tantamount to reducing the richness of historical experience to the commonplace that all governments consist of officials. The assumption here is not that Russian culture was or is the only source of clientelism, but that it was perhaps a more prominent feature in Russian history and political culture than elsewhere and that the revolution embraced this cultural phenomenon in ways little recognized by students of Soviet politics.

Having established the contours of the historical problem of personalized power relationships within Russian governmental institutions a general statement of the types of clientelism I have found in my research on the nineteenth- and early twentieth-century bureaucracy is appropriate before moving on to more detailed discussion of historical cases. Historically there have been four types of clientelism within government institutions. Although they may exist in combinations, in given examples, it is important to note that the first two types reflect the earliest and most highly personalized or anti-institutional forms of clientelism in Russian history before the major expansion of bureaucratic institutions of the nineteenth century and the movement of Russian government toward the rational-legal order (promised, though not delivered) presaged by the Great Reforms. Again in Russian history the fact that such a rational-legal order in institutional and political life was never attained is in large measure due to the persistence of such earlier manifestations of traditional political culture and institutional life as personal power and large-scale clientelism as they existed within institutions themselves. Just as clientelism survived the expansion of the government bureaucracy to include large numbers of new men – for example, in seventeenth-century Muscovy and during the reign of Peter the Great – so this phenomenon continued into the post-1917 Soviet era within an apparently new institutional context and among officials drawn from the working and peasant classes.

The four types of clientelism are as follows.

(1) *Clientelism of monarchial proximity*: defined by actual physical proximity to the tsar or the preceding tsar (including the period before his or her accession to the throne). Many military men can be included here – men who served with the tsar in regiments, in his suite, and so on. This category also includes military and civilian personnel who through kinship (see category 2, below), and so on, live and work in proximity to the court, or are in close contact with other members of the royal family. In this sense monarchial proximity could also be extended to those individuals close to the tsar, tsarina, grand dukes and duchesses, and so on. As will be shown, in the Imperial State Council on the eve of the Revolution in 1917, a significant portion of the military members of the council has such proximity to the tsar at some point in their careers.

(2) *Clientelism of kinship*: defined by mutually supportive relations based upon blood ties or marriage. This is a vast subject again with roots far into the Muscovite past. In Muscovy and other principalities politics meant clan politics centered around marriages to members of the royal family and alliances among and within high boyar and princely families aimed at solidifying or improving the status and fortunes of kinsmen. In booming Muscovy this was one of the salient features of the developing autocracy as a political system. For long periods in Muscovite history members of elite families acted to protect and perpetuate the mythical and actual power of an unlimited autocrat in order at the same time to further their own individual and clan interests. At the end of the old regime similar patterns were at work. In the State Council and in the high ministerial bureaucracy there was a very high degree of intermarriage among families occupying high rank or status positions as well as numerous examples of the later types of clientelism. Stolypin's marriage into the Neidgart family or

the marriage patterns of State Council members discussed below would be just two examples of how clan politics in more modern times influenced autocratic politics via the medium of the tsar's choice of ministers.

(3) *Clientelism of geographic location*: this form of clientelism corresponds most closely to that noticed by present-day observers of the Soviet Union. Though it undoubtedly existed in Muscovy, it became prominent only later in Russian history because it requires a larger, more highly elaborate bureaucratic system in which there is great possibility of chance encounter of non-related (by blood) officials of different rank in provincial settings. This, more properly speaking, is clientelism of talent and likemindedness, since in the late imperial era it usually took the form of a high provincial official on the way to a St Petersburg career in a central ministry or temporarily holding a provincial post or conducting a central government mission there taking along with him to the capital trusted and highly competent officials to aid his own career at the center. This is a clientelism that proliferates far from the tsar, his court and high social elites as well. Yet it becomes an important source of power at the center and helps to explain the role and fate of institutional life in a revolution.

Another frequently encountered variant in the late imperial period was based on the dyadic links forged by central figures with zemstvo personalities, marshals of the nobility, or others not actually in government, aimed at building a base of support at the center with links to the provinces. Under the old regime there was a massive increase in this form of clientelism as the government and particularly the Ministry of Internal Affairs tried to raise the status and political power of provincial governors who then proceeded to move up the ladder to St Petersburg positions, bringing with them many provincial officials for support.

(4) *Clientelism of institutional position*: this type can be seen throughout the Muscovite and imperial periods and, indeed, under the Provisional and Soviet governments as well. Here the connections and personal relations are formed in an institutional rather than a geographical setting alone. The dyadic relation emerges from prior work *in a specific bureaucratic institution*. For example, the State Chancery under the old regime was a very closely knit breeding-ground for future appointees to high State Coun-

cil departmental and ministerial positions. The young officials serving there, if we are to believe V. I. Gurko and other memoirists, saw it as an elite club (though a club of talented, dedicated professionals) and the personnel records of State Council members for 1916 reveal that a great many of the empire's highest officials served together during the 1880s and 1890s in the State Chancery. The same is true of high officials in the more specialized ministries (Justice and especially Finance, Trade and Industry, and so on) and the even more specialized and highly technical ministries such as Communications and Agriculture. The personal bonds that help propel men up the service ladder are formed in each case in an institutional setting far removed from tsar and entourage or high aristocratic clans. In all cases dyadic relationships arise because superiors' success depends upon getting important tasks accomplished, and in the Russian institutional context this was almost impossible without talented and loyal clients. Though I have not yet sifted through the evidence for such expert ministries as Agriculture and Communications involving agronomists and engineers, it would be interesting to learn just how widespread was clientelism among the technical intelligentsia in the late tsarist bureaucracy. We might assume that in the technical ministries talent played a more important role than in the ministries of general administration, but I suspect that within the technical and professional realm the same types of dyadic relations described above were at work.

Again it must be emphasized that because of the ever-present conflict between institutions and personal power in Russian history, all four types of clientelism could and did exist simultaneously within the Russian court and state bureaucracy. The problem is to gauge accurately the quantitative trends as well as the political impact of the types of clientelism over time. Looked at from this dual perspective we note that in absolute terms – given the sheer size and increased specialization of the state bureaucracy during the last seventy years of the old regime – there was a trend away from monarchical and kinship-based clientelism toward the varieties found within the burgeoning bureaucratic structures of the imperial state administration. The possibilities for new dyadic relations were increasing. Yet, ironically, political power during the reign of Nicholas II accrued even more markedly to those concentrated and numerically smaller sectors of the state apparatus and court in which mon-archical and kinship-based clientelism remained entrenched and indeed flourished.

With this framework in mind let us briefly examine several historical moments that are usually seen as watersheds in Russian political and social history – the transformation of the Muscovite state under Peter the Great (1689–1725), and the era of the Great Reforms during the reign of Alexander II (1855–81). Both of these periods reveal the models of dyadic relations described above, and both also show clearly the tension in Russian history between institutions and personalities and the persistence of 'addenda' (including clientelism), despite ostensible 'transfor-mations' in the formal sphere of institutions.

That the reign of Peter has often been portrayed as one of revolutions from above and massive adoption of Western forms and methods needs no recounting here. What is important to note is the centuries-long history of bureaucracy in Muscovy that antedated Peter and that, in fact, made possible (along with the military service system that it organized and managed) the amalgamation of the empire that Peter inherited. The Muscovite bureaucracy (which coexisted with and around the person of the tsar and the court with their longstanding patterns of kin/ marital relations, and so on) centered in the *prikazy* was devastatingly efficient and organized in a rational manner in many ways far ahead of state administrations in contemporary Western Europe as well as even the Russian administration of the post-Petrine eighteenth century.[3] During the most dynamic century of this bureaucracy's history, the seventeenth, it acted to fill the power vacuum after the Time of Troubles and proved immensely effective in its tasks of statebuilding, leading the resurgence of Muscovite power, and in preparing the way for the Petrine reforms. During the seventeenth century the four clientelism types influenced, for example, the composition of the Boyar Duma with its membership of high aristocrats, and the relation-ship of that older consultative organ to the professional and increasingly powerful bureaucracy of the *prikazy*.[4] Though we would expect clan relations to be a powerful determinant among the aristocrats of the Duma, Plavsic shows that even in the *prikazy* family connections and even something similar to inher-itability of offices were at work – in regard to entrance to service (though not necessarily advancement) – for would-be *prikaznye liudi*.

Thanks to the studies of Robert Crummey on the Boyar Duma and the creation of what he aptly terms 'noble officials' during the seventeenth century, of Brenda Meehan-Waters, who has most carefully traced the fate of the empire's highest 'noble officials' (the *generalitet* or holders of the empire's top four ranks) under Peter the Great, and of S. Troitskii, we can make some generalizations about clientelism in Muscovy and the impact of the Petrine reforms.[5] During the seventeenth century considerable political power had shifted from court circles and the high aristocracy to the *prikazy* – even while unlimited autocratic power was still vested in the tsar with the tacit consent of all concerned elites. The high families and clans recognized the new importance of institutional (bureaucratic) power-bases, and had laid claim to a share of the power that now accrued to the heads of administrative offices. As a result, already before Peter the composition of the Boyar Duma reflected the combination of power and insecurity that provides the classic setting for the rise of clientelism. As Crummey puts it, 'selection into the political elite was determined by genetic accident – and by the social and political experience of the family and clan as much as of the individual'. During the seventeenth century, as the political importance of the Duma diminished, its ranks expanded to include members of less prominent noble families and even obscure provincial ones. This situation peaked during the period 1667–75 after which the old, highly intermarried boyar and high aristocratic families reasserted themselves within the Duma. Whether we speak of the old or new families, however, it appears that kinship and family links were important features in the distribution of political power and status. (See Tables 5.1 and 5.2.)

The important seventeenth-century trends to note are: (1) the movement of high aristocrats into the top offices of the *prikazy* – and the presence of more and more *prikaz* officials in the Duma – a sure sign of the importance of the bureaucracy as a power center in mid- and late seventeenth-century Muscovy; (2) the high percentage of intermarriage among families represented in the Boyar Duma; and (3) the fact that even at this early date in Russian history, *before* Peter the Great, economic weakness among the aristocratic elites and lack of career alternatives made long and continual state service crucial to the retention of status positions and Duma membership for the great clans and their offshoots. State service, clan relations and politics were indeed inseparable, and one is tempted to see personalized relationships as part of the structure of service. Finally, it is important to note in regard to my later discussion of the Imperial State Council on the eve of the 1917 Revolution that seats in the Boyar Duma were

Table 5.1 *Was a Relative within Three Kinship Links already in the Duma when Duma Member Appointed?*

		Yes	No	Unknown	Total (N=)
1613–19	N=	22	26	0	48
	%	46	54		
1620–33	N=	5	12	0	17
	%	29	71		
1634–44	N=	10	16	0	26
	%	38	62		
1645–58	N=	37	48	2	87
	%	44	56		
1659–66	N=	12	15	0	27
	%	44	56		
1667–75	N=	12	17	2	31
	%	41	59		
1676–89	N=	82	104	5	191
	%	44	56		
Total	N=	180	238	9	427
	%	43	57		

Source: R. O. Crummey, 'Origins of the noble official', in W. M. Pintner and D. K. Rowney (eds), *Russian Officialdom*, Chapel Hill, NC, University of North Carolina Press, 1980, pp. 55–6.

Table 5.2 *Was Duma Member a Direct Descendant of a Man Who Was a Boyar or Okol'nichii* at Least Thirty Years Earlier?*

		Yes	No	Total (N=)
1613–19	N=	19	29	48
	%	40	60	
1620–33	N=	5	12	17
	%	29	71	
1634–44	N=	10	16	26
	%	38	62	
1645–58	N=	31	56	87
	%	36	64	
1659–66	N=	4	23	27
	%	15	85	
1667–75	N=	2	29	31
	%	6	94	
1676–89	N=	46	145	191
	%	24	76	
Total	N=	117	310	427
	%	27	73	

* A high aristocratic rank in Muscovy.
Source: As Table 5.1.

distributed among the following types of servitors: (1) military, (2) court/ceremonial, (3) Chancery *prikaz* professionals and (4) the new 'noble officials' or members of the high nobility drawn into Chancery or professional bureaucratic posts because of their growing power. This is exactly the breakdown in the composition of the Imperial State Council, a similarly consultative body, some 250 years later. Furthermore, analysis of the present-day Communist Party Central Committee reveals a comparable pattern of representation of different categories of official.[6] The impact of the structure of state service with its dynamic relations is indicated by the fact that when new men rose to Duma membership, family/clientelist ties were even more important for them in maintaining their positions than such ties had been for the old high aristocracy.

It is now clear that Peter the Great did less to transform the 'deep structures' of Russian institutional and political life than has been commonly thought. Peter, as would be the case with Lenin some 200 years later, was in large measure the prisoner of inherited institutional and social determinants despite the enormous personal and moral authority at his disposal. Brenda Meehan-Waters has shown that Peter's *generalitet* (the top four ranks of the Petrine service class) consisted of a very large percentage of carryovers from the earlier Muscovite period, and this despite Peter's well-documented proclivity for elevating his personal friends, acquaintances and the like (for example, the Menshikovs, Shafirovs, and so on) and the concerted effort of the Petrine state to portray its Table of Rank as based upon merit and social mobility. Also the pattern of kinship-based clientelism at work in the seventeenth-century Boyar Duma persisted. No fewer than 54 percent of the wives of *generalitet* members (130 men) were from other *generalitet* families. Two-thirds of the 1,730 *generalitet* membership were related by blood or marriage and an even higher 76 percent of the native Russians were related. This is not the place to analyze other aspects of Peter's institutional and social reforms, but we should note that in the social sphere – at least relating to the question of state service – what we see is a relabeling, a regrouping and a tightening of older Muscovite service groups and their patterns of service, the state's use of obligatory and enforced state service to force existing and aspiring noblemen to become in large numbers the 'noble bureaucrat' of the seventeenth century. Though Peter clearly wanted talent to count for more in his service state, he could do little given the realities of protracted war, the needs of government and the social material at his disposal. Within his new formal framework the old relationships between clans, personal appointments and favorites, and professional bureaucrats from lower social groups, reasserted themselves. Though Peter desired to build a 'regular' state (*reguliarnoe gosudarstvo*), the results of his massive juggling and renaming of state offices and proclamations of new administrative principles was the continuation of the existing tension between institutions and law on the one hand, and the personal and at times most arbitrary power of the autocrat and the social system that supported his real and mythical unlimited powers on the other. Within the coercive and violent context of the Petrine state clientelism could not fail to flourish, especially within the bureaucratic structures themselves as they began the enormous expansion so well documented by S. Troitskii, Walter Pintner, P. A. Zaionchkovskii and others that along with enlarging the civil service substantially distanced it from the person of the tsar by the mid-nineteenth century.[7]

The persistence of personal commissions to overcome institutional weaknesses, the presence of high consultative bodies to act as repositories for all elites propeled to the top via the various types of dyadic relations, the growth of bureaucracy alongside personal and arbitrary power, the presence of the latter within the bureaucratic institutions themselves and a documentable decrease in competence in the central government machine (as compared to the seventeenth century) that persisted until the 1802 reorganization of the government of Alexander I: these are a large and often ignored part of the Petrine and Muscovite legacy to the later imperial era.

The reform era and reign of Alexander II offer further insight into the clientelism phenomenon at a time when the state administration – particularly the ministerial bureaucracy – had become quite elaborate and powerful (powerful enough to have at least carried out the tsar's ambivalent mandate to issue and implement the reforms of the 1860s, a task beyond the capacity of the ministerial bureaucracy during the first half of the century).

By the mid-nineteenth century the ministerial bureaucracy had grown not only in size, but in political significance. The elaborate departmental hierarchies of the ministries and their individual and collective provincial hierarchies permitted a massive increase in the clientelism of geographical position and the clientelism of institutional position. In fact, my own studies of the Ministry of Internal Affairs during the reign of Alexander II (and during the last half of the reign of Nicholas II) indicate that ministerial operations would have been virtually impossible without the practice of such clientelism on a grand scale. As talented individuals destined for ministerial portfolios moved up the service ladder, they inevitably brought along with them various lower-ranking generalists and experts with whom they had worked in provincial offices, or about whom they learned because of geographical proximity or recommendations of close friends, and so on. By the mid-nineteenth century this was possible on a large scale because of the emergence after about 1840 of an entirely new generation of career civil servants who poured out of the new universities and elite institutions of higher education that had been created during the first half of the century.[8]

The best examples drawn from my own research are the personnel policies of P. A. Valuev, while Minister of Internal Affairs (1861–8) and those of his successors in that office, A. E. Timashev, L. S. Makov and M. T. Loris-Melikov.[9] It would be wrong, however, as I have tried to emphasize earlier, to see as innovative their clever use of subordinates. They continued a long tradition going back to the relations between the *d'iaki* and *pod'iachie* and their aristocratic superiors in the *prikazy*. All of the above-mentioned ministers brought with them to St Petersburg trusted subordinates with whom they had served either in lower organs of the Ministry of Internal Affairs (MVD) in the provinces or in other geographical or institutional contexts. This was simply the accepted and best, if not only, way to get the job done at the center. In fact, it was incumbent on the minister to have an aggressive personnel policy that made full use of all possible clientele relationships within the framework of the rigid and outworn formulae of the imperial service statutes.

Valuev, it must be said, had the most sophisticated personnel policy of the era, and one that clearly made use of all four types of clientelism in our model for the attainment of political ends. Because clientelism in the MVD during the reform era was based on the older forms as well as the newer types supposedly more prevalent in the bureaucratic institutions of the reform era, it foreshadowed what would become the general situation in the upper reaches of that ministry and the tsarist government as a whole on the eve of the 1917 Revolution. Valuev, for example, appointed a number of representatives of the provincial nobility (for instance, P. D. Stremoukhov) in order to build ties to that group. He also appointed several prominent members of high aristocratic families in order to build personal links at court and to the tsar (for instance, Prince A. B. Lobanov-

Rostovsky). With Valuev, we thus have geographical location, institutional position (for instance, D. N. Tolstoi and V. Fuks) and monarchial proximity at work to shore up his powerful, but institutionally and politically unstable office. We also know that he insisted on an enlarged body of officials of special missions (*chinovniki osobykh poruchenii*), trusted troubleshooters to undo ministerial bottlenecks, wherever those might occur. Thus, Valuev and many other tsarist ministers continued the long-standing tradition of clientelism that in earlier times (Muscovy and under Peter the Great, for example) was expressed by the anti-institutional pattern of the tsar's personal commissions to trusted friends.

The best-known clientelist network during the reform era centered around the person of the Grand Duke Konstantin Nikolaevich. In this well-known case, the Grand Duke during the mid-1850s gathered about him in the Naval Ministry a group of the empire's brightest young career officials (the so-called 'enlightened bureaucrats') among them M. Kh. Reutern, A. V. Golovnin and others connected to the Miliutins, the salons of the 1850s and Grand Duchess Elena Pavlovna. They maintained ties with him (providing a base of political support within the ministerial bureaucracy) as most eventually moved up to high ministerial posts throughout the organs of domestic administration.* Variously described as 'party' or interest group the history of the *konstantinovtsy* reveals clearly the great political impact of informal networks and groups based upon clientelism within the formal structures of autocracy. During the late nineteenth century in the Russian government proximity to the tsar or court was no longer enough for sustained political influence. One needed a power-base in the ministerial bureaucracy, and this implied the need for allies within one's own institution as well as within others that had key domestic responsibilities. Finally, we must emphasize again that even the most talented ministers *required* the proximity of personal acquaintances (through service) or close friends in positions as ministerial troubleshooters (officials of special missions). When Valuev argued for more of these officials in the MVD, he claimed that institutional bottlenecks and the unreliability of 'unknown' officials all but made his work as minister impossible. There can be no better example of Landé's model of institutionalized addenda.

---

* The Shuvalov bloc provides another example with a quite different political orientation – as would the group of officials brought in by M. T. Loris-Melikov during his brief attempt to unify and redefine Russian autocracy in 1880–1.

Now we may turn to the end of the imperial era and the state bureaucracy on the eve of the revolutions of 1917. During the last decades of the imperial regime we observe again all four types of clientelism. What is most interesting, however, is that while the bureaucracy itself continued to grow and become more specialized and technically oriented, in the sectors of the bureaucracy that best represented the opposite principles of personal authority (for example, the MVD, the State Council, and Ministry of Justice, and so on), loyalty to the person of the tsar and support of 'addenda' such as clientelism not only continued, but also enjoyed a very significant renaissance that had enormous political implications. Alexander III made a futile attempt to curb the enormous power of his ministers in the realm of personnel that culminated in the reestablishment in 1894 of the Civil Service Inspectorate (closed since 1858) attached to the tsar's own Chancery. The ministers, however, balked largely because they recognized the clear necessity of personal control of their own institutions and the severe constraints imposed upon them by the formal service statutes. The result was a stalemate in the longstanding Peretts Commission set up to work out civil service reform, and a resurgence of clientelism under Nicholas II.[10]

As it became more and more important for officials to have allies to the hostile and arbitrary official world of St Petersburg, and as society itself became more organized and articulate in defense of its various interests, we note an increased tempo of bridgebuilding in the form of personal alliances and relationships within and outside the bureaucracy to key sectors of provincial society (the zemstvos, various mixed-composition provincial directorates and boards, and so on) and other increasingly organized economic and social interests. If we look briefly at the MVD, the process becomes abundantly clear. During the last decades of the nineteenth and on into the twentieth century one of the cardinal tenets of MVD attempts to reform provincial administration was the shoring up and elevation of the office of civil governor in the provinces.[11] Despite many attempts of the representatives of other ministries and members of local and St Petersburg society to curb this clear example of ministerial aggrandizement and anti-institutionalism (the MVD wished to restore the governor to his exalted and somewhat mythical position as master (*khoziain*) of the province in order to reduce competition from the hierarchies of rival ministries and to reassert police and administrative hegemony), the MVD succeeded in maintaining the governors as the dominant official figures in the provinces. Accordingly ministry leadership gave closer scrutiny to the quality of the governors as individuals and their actual knowledge of provincial life and administrative skill. The MVD attempted to professionalize the gubernatorial corps thereby alleviating one of the constant complaints of all bureaucratic reformers and social critics during earlier decades of the nineteenth century. Instead of the mid-nineteenth-century appointments of cashiered generals with no civilian administrative experience, administrative and political mediocrities, or the outright incompetent (especially as compared with the new generations of officials pouring into the regular central departments of the ministries of domestic administration), the MVD began toward the end of the nineteenth century to appoint as governors some men with real ability and experience if not expertise in the affairs of the typical provincial administration – men who might have served earlier in provincial institutions as marshals of the nobility or on the zemstvo executive boards. These men not only had the knowledge and experience, but also the links to provincial society – either through kinship as members of prominent provincial families, friendship, or mutual service in provincial institutions. Thus, at the provincial level the clientelist patterns were on the upswing and all that remained was for these governors to make their way up the service ladder to positions of prominence in the St Petersburg bureaucracy. This distinct deviation from the reform era patterns was a hallmark of the last two decades of the imperial regime. During the reform era provincial administration remained relatively distinct from the central bureaucracy with its burgeoning departments and new generation of officials.* Extended service in the organs of the provincial or district administration represented a kind of service to be avoided by those pursuing a 'career' (their provincial service experience was gained by working in or troubleshooting for central ministry departments). In contrast, at the end of the old regime, many governors themselves were elevated to the highest ministerial positions in St Petersburg, including the posts of Minister of Justice or Minister of Internal Affairs. Indeed, as D. Lieven has found, Alexander III and Nicholas II liked to promote these men to the State Council, feeling that they were familiar with provincial society and rural life. Men such as Sipiagin, Bulygin and Stürmer, with their provincial connections, were elevated in a manner most unlike that observed

---

* This was less true for trained officials of the specialized ministries – Justice, Finance, Communications, Agriculture, etc.

during the reform era and inevitably they brought with them entire hosts of clients from the provinces to fill the highest positions in their respective ministries. Even P. A. Stolypin can be placed in this category as he derived all his relevant service experience from provincial governors' posts – and also brought with him clients to help in his effort to save the autocracy. (The Stolypin case is also instructive because of his marriage into the Neidgart family, an important family of the provincial nobility with representatives in the State Council and close links to the tsar.) In this respect the office of governor represents an early analogue of the later Soviet regional party secretaries who, in fact, more completely emulate the old tsarist notion of *khoziain* of the province with their relative independence, control of appointment power and enormous and highly personalized executive authority.

Another important government organ that illustrates the presence of clientelism of institutional position and kinship in this era is the imperial State Chancellery – the bureaucratic organ attached nominally to the State Council. As already noted this chancery, despite or perhaps because of its high degree of professionalism, was something of a club or training-ground for the sons of many prominent service families, and a good many future high officials all across the imperial bureaucracy during its last years had prior service together in the State Chancellery during the period 1880–1905.[12] V. K. von Plehve, later Minister of Internal Affairs and during the 1880s the head of the Department of Police within that ministry, served in a high State Chancellery post during the 1890s and brought with him to the MVD after 1901 a good many younger men of skill and political suitability for high MVD positions. Clientelism of institutional position as used here, of course, cannot always be substantiated by literary evidence. None the less, it is surely more than a coincidence to see such a high concentration of mutual service in a given place or institution in the official personnel records. We might also mention other early twentieth-century examples of personal ties (the examples are almost grotesquely numerous) such as the appointment of E. Bogolepov as rector of Moscow University followed by his elevation to Head of the Moscow Academic *okrug* and appointment as Minister of Education.[13] According to the memoirs of Lopukhin, this was entirely the result of the protection of a grand prince who was Governor General of Moscow coupled with the fact that Bogolepov was married to a Lieven and thereby had powerful court connections. Lopukhin sees as a prime feature of government under

Nicholas – and a prime cause of government difficulty – the fact that court kinship-influenced appointments of this kind played such a large role during the last years of the old regime. An example of institutional proximity or, better put in this case, ministerial proximity would be the career of one of the most accomplished statesmen of the era, A. Krivoshein (Minister of Agriculture and supporter of many goals of the progressive bloc during World War I). Grandson of a peasant, Krivoshein (regarded by Gurko as a manipulative though talented careerist in the manner that high officials usually describe each other in their memoirs) began his rapid climb upon being introduced to the Minister of Internal Affairs, D. A. Tolstoi (1882–9), who adopted him, keeping him close at his side and giving him important departmental duties and offices in the central MVD. Krivoshein later once again attached himself to the person of a minister by remaining as the only department head not to be removed and replaced by Plehve when he assumed the post of Minister of Internal Affairs in 1902. According to the memoir of Krivoshein's son, Krivoshein made a point of traveling with Plehve on special missions, thus insuring the personal ties so valuable to would-be careermakers in the ministerial bureaucracy. To return for a moment to D. A. Tolstoi – according to Gurko, he made it a practice of elevating provincials from his own Riazan constituency. Thus, Bulygin was raised up into central MVD offices and later became Minister of Internal Affairs during the 1905 revolution.

Let us move away from the ministerial bureaucracy proper, with its more diffused and bureaucratic forms of clientelism based on provincial and departmental officeholding or reputation, to the imperial State Council, the last of the Muscovite and imperial Russian high-status consultative and legislative bodies. (It was the heir of the Boyar Duma, and in its way perhaps a forerunner of the Central Committee of the CPSU.) The composition of the State Council was in large measure determined by unwritten rules of institutional as well as clientelist representation and offers a good paradigm for illustrating the tension between the personal and institutional or legal in Russian political and institutional life. The patterns of representation and careers of State Council members well illustrate the four types of clientelism defined above.

In gathering material for a longer study of the structure of state service in Russia on the eve of the revolution I collected in Soviet archives the personnel records of the State Council membership for 1916–January 1917.[14] Though my primary concern in the larger study is the ministerial bureaucracy and its fate under the Provisional Government after February 1917, I felt that since so many ministers and assistant ministers held State Council membership by virtue of their ministerial office (this was automatic prior to 1906, less certain thereafter), it could be fruitful to trace career patterns and institutional representation of State Council membership to try to generalize about institutional representation as well as clientelist relations. As in any quantitative study, the aim is to uncover patterns that might otherwise remain hidden to the observer of random or isolated service careers or even to the contemporary elite.

The data are drawn from 137 personnel records, virtually the complete State Council membership on the eve of the February revolution. If we return to our earlier discussion of the seventeenth-century Boyar Duma and the composition of its membership, we see immediately that an important institutional pattern has been reproduced. Boyar Duma membership consisted of military servitors, representatives of high aristocratic families who performed ceremonial functions (and therefore held ceremonial rank or office) at the court, 'pure' bureaucrats or those of lower social standing who served professionally in the *prikazy* (*d'iaki*, and so on) and the emerging and very important 'noble bureaucrats' or those members of higher noble families who realized that the locus of power had shifted from the court or even the military to the *prikaz* bureaucracy; and who began to lay claim to bureaucratic office as a means of shoring up family standing in the service status hierarchy or to attain a greater share of political power. In the 1916 imperial State Council the same pattern is visible, since the council membership consists of the same four broad categories of servitors. What is novel in the late imperial example, however, is the degree to which the distinct social and service categories of the seventeenth century had become by 1916 at the highest levels of the imperial service hierarchy remarkably intertwined: in certain sectors of the ministerial bureaucracy (that part of government that we would expect to have become more and more 'professional' during the late nineteenth century) the highest officials who attained State Council membership possessed court and ceremonial qualifications and manifested the types of clientelism based upon proximity to tsar or court, or family ties or provincial ties of office or friendship, and so on, as well as the expected professional qualifications for advancement up the service ladder. At the end of the old regime the phenomenon of protection, for so long a prominent feature of bureaucratic life, was therefore becoming more important and at all levels of government there appears to have been a growing reliance on the clientelism of court and kinship that was closely related to the tsar's personal authority as opposed to institutions or formal law. Put another way, the patterns of service reveal increasing instances of those forms of clientelism (monarchial proximity and kinship) with the deepest roots in Russian history. This provides further evidence that the late imperial bureaucracy was moving away from a commitment to rule of law principles and the kinds of political transformation and institutionalization of Russian political life that might have averted revolution, or might at least have signaled the evolution of the autocracy into some kind of limited monarchy.

The loci of clientelist relations suggested by the State Council personnel records include educational and governmental institutions and geographical areas that produced many State Council members. For example, the St Petersburg University law faculty, the Imperial School of Jurisprudence and the Imperial Lycée at Tsarskoe Selo where many State Council members were classmates during the early or mid-1870s; the State Chancellery and other bureaucratic departments of the State Council; the St Petersburg judicial institutions (the *Okruzhnyi sud* and *Sudebnaia palata* with their attendant judges and prosecutors); provincial offices of many kinds both in the government or in the zemstvos or corporate bodies of the nobility under Nicholas II. This is corroborated by W. Mosse's recent study that shows a large increase in appointments of governors and provincial marshals of the nobility or men chosen from zemstvo ranks under Nicholas II.[15] Perhaps this diffusion of power to the provinces foreshadows the budding regionalism and provincial clientelism in the Bolshevik Party that would appear in Soviet institutions during the Civil War. Mosse has also noted an increase in the numbers of civilian and titled civilian appointees as against military servitors during the second half of the reign of Nicholas II. (See Table 5.3.)

Marriages and kinship were also of far greater importance than has been realized. Time after time in the personnel records one finds that a given State Council member has married either the daughter of a well-known high official or married into a socially prominent family with court connections, or both. It emerges, for example, that I. L. Goremykin was married to the daughter of Senator Kapger, who conducted one of Loris-Melikov's famous senatorial revisions, and that V. K. Sabler, Ober-Procuror of the Holy Synod, was

Table 5.3   *Key Power Centers and Loci of Clientelism in the Imperial State Council, 1916–1 January 1917*

(1)	Provincial governors and vice-governors
(2)	Military governors-general
(3)	Provincial marshals of nobility
(4)	Provincial organs of the judiciary (Ministry of Justice), prosecutors, judges
(5)	St Petersburg judiciary (includes Okruzhnyi sud, Sudebnaia palata, Ministry of Justice central and Senate)
(6)	State Chancellery and all other bureaucratic branches of the State Council
(7)	Tsar's personal institutions or imperial family, including Commission on Receiving Petitions, Ministry of Imperial Court Institutions of the Empress Maria
(8)	Holy Synod
(9)	Key financial policy institutions, Ministry of Finance professionals
(10)	Foreign Affairs
(11)	Military administration staff and other military close to tsar
(12)	Representatives of all other ministries

Note: It is significant that men from the first six categories held many crucial posts throughout the government; that such a high percentage of these men also held titles and/or court positions indicates that the state bureaucracy at the end of the old regime was reinfused with the power of personalities over institutions.

married to the daughter of A. P. Zablotskii-Desiatovskii, the well-known high official and biographer of Kiselev, and that he served long tours of duty in the company of Pobedonostsev during the last decades of the nineteenth century. (See Table 5.4.)

These marriage patterns and the apparently inbred character of the State Council (unsurprising as these may be in an old regime society), together with the patterns of representation within the council, lead me to the following tentative conclusions about clientelism and the nature of the imperial government at the end of the old regime. First, there were three main constituencies in the imperial bureaucracy, all of which exhibited clientelist patterns in personnel policy: (1) the technical and highly specialized career officialdom that resided in the ministries of Finance, Communications, Agriculture, State Control, and Trade and Industry; (2) generalists with a modicum of expertise in chosen administrative areas who sometimes worked in the ministries mentioned above but especially in the most powerful generalist ministry, the Ministry of Internal Affairs (this had been especially true during the 1850s when the 'progressive' officials in the MVD helped spearhead the government's efforts to emancipate the proprietary serfs and issue

Table 5.4 *Some Sample Marriages of Members of the State Council, 1916*

Member	Family of wife
Goremykin	Senator Kapger
Durnovo	Kochubei
Izvol'skii	Golitsyn
Balashev	Shuvalov
Kharitonov	General fon Kaufman
Arsen'ev	Skariatin
Vasil'chikov	Meshcherskii
Bark	Fon Ber (Baroness)
Voevodskii	Shteingel (Baroness)
Velmin	Dolgorukov
Ostrogorskii	Zhomini
Sheremetev	Viazemskii (Princess)
Vorontsov-Dashkov	Shuvalov
Neidgardt	Trubetskoi
Obolenskii	Senator Polovtsov
Medem	Naryshkin
Okhotnikov	Trubetskoi
Korf	Frederiks (Baroness)
Kukol-Iasnopol'skii	Chavchavadze (Princess)
Tol	D. A. Tolstoi
Sazonov	Neidgardt
Sabler	Zablotskii-Desiatovskii
Zinov'ev	Korf
Bulygin	Akimov
Durnovo	Akimov

other reforms); and (3) the large and politically important sector of the bureaucracy very close to the person of the tsar, the court and various institutions and power centers that were usually outside the regular ministerial bureaucracy. Whether outside the latter or within it, these offices fostered opposition to the rule of law and to political change. I have in mind here the State Chancery, the governors and governors-general, the institutions of the Empress Maria, the marshals of the nobility (who were confirmed in office by the state bureaucracy), the judiciary itself and particularly the Ministry of Justice under Shcheglovitov (though there were many dedicated and highly educated men in the ministry). The presence of so many members in the State Council from this last group and the fact that so many of them rose to high ministerial office during the last year of the old regime indicates a resurgence of traditional clientelism on the eve of the revolution in areas of government that had considerable political power. There was something of a tug-of-war between this group beholden to personal power and clientelism and those who favored the rule of law or who had technical or economic expertise. Beginning before World War I, but especially during the war, when economic questions and the war effort became so overwhelmingly prominent, the traditional centers of personalized power in the government began to lose further ground to the more streamlined specialist ministries with their experts as well as to the public and semi-public organs created during the war. The emergence by 1919–20 of the Communist Party as principal arbiter of personnel and control mechanisms over the Soviet regime's technical and managerial bureaucracy in a way represents a reassertion of an institutional relationship that could only promote the older patterns of clientelism associated with personal power in Russian history.

Under the provisional government appointments also tended to be based upon personal knowledge and shared professional or career experience. The main difference was that the newer public organizations, such as the War Industries Committees or Union of Zemstvos, the state Duma, or political parties became sources of high ministerial officials for the new government. For example, Prince L'vov in his capacity as Minister of Internal Affairs brought in several assistant ministers who had held high administrative posts in the Union of Zemstvos. Another source of high officials was the Duma and its chancery. The political parties also produced individuals and networks linked by prior friendship and commitment to the principles of their respective organizations. This is not to say that the nature of the bureaucracy was transformed under the provisional government. My evidence shows that in the technical/specialized ministries – Agriculture, Finance, Trade and Industry, Means of Communications, and so on – the vast majority of old regime professionals, managers and technical personnel continued in place (as indeed would be the case with many of them under the successor Soviet regime).

In the judicial organs known lawyers and personal friends from the St Petersburg and Moscow bar associations were chosen for top Ministry of Justice positions under Kerensky and his successors.[16] The structure of the ministry and judicial institutions as in other areas of the ministerial bureaucracy required the use of clients to circumvent blockages – and facilitate rapid decisions in the midst of the revolutionary situation. Even when the ministers tried to end this dependence on clientage and personal power, they found it virtually impossible to do so. In fact, provincial government ministers were advised by such men as Dem'ianov almost unwittingly (since both the advisors and the ministers were harsh critics of the old regime and its methods and patterns of government) to repeat and reaffirm the older relationships. For example, Dem'ianov comments that the appointment of officials of special missions had to 'always be the personal affair of the minister'. When one of the new department directors tried to appoint such an official without telling the minister *or* the proposed appointee, Kerensky, at that time the Minister of Justice, was outraged. That appointment failed to go through, but we do learn that Kerensky resolved the issue by appointing as official of special missions a 'close friend dating back to days of the school bench' (the *prisiazhnyi poverennyi* Somov). Dem'ianov's memoirs continue with a litany of judicial appointments based upon personal friendship formed at the bar or in the Duma.

Interestingly Kerensky did speak of purging the ministry of the worst elements of the Shcheglovitov era. Yet the dimensions of the problem were not the result of old regime appointment policies alone. Dem'ianov notes that already under the old regime the most talented younger graduates of the law faculties rejected careers in the obviously conservative Ministry of Justice and opted instead for careers as advocates, or in other free professions or government institutions. Despite this desire to purge the Ministry of Justice, it was decided that most of the old *chinovniki* and many judges had to stay – especially as many were young and willing to serve and could not be held responsible for the excesses or ethos of the old regime.

In the technical ministries archival material of the departments concerned with personnel in several ministries indicate little disruption. At most levels of the rank hierarchy there was little or no change in patterns of officeholding, which would indicate that patterns of clientelism were not disrupted. Individuals seen as presenting problems or as having compromised themselves were apparently dealt with on a case-by-case basis, complaints against them usually emanating from the provinces and their mushrooming social organizations.

Though the provincial governors and police officials were by and large removed from office during the first days of the revolution, it would appear that many provincial officeholders from non-MVD branches of the government also remained, if not exactly on duty then certainly not in any formal sense deposed either. From all camps the cry was for organization, the establishment of *vlast'*, of an *apparat*. In the countryside and the cities much in the way of rudimentary organization was generated from below. It was the Bolsheviks who had the clearest sense of this administrative-organizational imperative and who moved quickly and decisively, though haphazardly, to use all possible measures to establish that power and an *apparat* (albeit based on improvisation and not closely directed from the center but at least capable of on-the-spot decisions and action) that greatly furthered the Bolshevik cause. It would be the revolution's task to melt down all the competing centers of power in the provinces (no easy task as the Soviet regime was to learn in its attempt to set up soviets at all provincial levels and control them via a party hierarchy that was almost immediately seen as a necessary control mechanism) – and of course in this meltdown new provincial clienteles (the residue of which went into the new soviets) were created. Though the men and their class origin may have been different, the institutional structure, patterns of organization and above all the nature of clientelism remained strikingly similar to the patterns we have observed during the last years of the old regime – and under the Provisional Government. In this sense it is not a question of numbers of carryovers or bourgeois specialists recruited (or coerced) into serving the young Soviet state. Rather, it is the fact indicated by a considerable body of evidence, that even the new personnel drawn from the lower class faced institutional and cultural pressures that resulted in the reproduction in the new setting of older patterns of organizational behavior. Once the decision had been taken to adopt the ministerial form of government, and to conquer and administer the vast territory of the former tsarist empire, while extending the power of the new state not just to the provinces, districts and cities, but to the *volost'* and village levels, the door was opened to many culturally and institutionally conditioned patterns of organizational behavior present in the long history of bureaucracy in Muscovy and imperial Russia. The task is now to search for the institutional analogues of tsarist structures in the Soviet context and see to what degree patterns of organization and behavior (such as clientelism) are reproduced and what adaptation has taken place. We must try to place the Soviet achievement in statebuilding in historical and cultural perspective. In a revolutionary situation there is an obvious premium on decisive action, a pull toward the use of personal power and the use of extrainstitutional and extralegal means. In this sense the challenge faced by the Bolsheviks to build a state, to construct firm *vlast'* and begin to transform Russian society is similar to the plight of such great tsarist reformers as Loris-Melikov and

Stolypin who had to continually violate institutional and legal norms to accomplish even the modest beginnings of their reform programs. At the same time it raises questions about the limits in a revolutionary situation to the possibilities of change in administrative structures and institutional life. Are the various types of clientelism discussed here features of inherited administrative imperatives that allow less room for deviation than we have previously supposed?

Read in the light of other chapters in this volume it seems obvious that there are fruitful areas for comparison between the politics of officeholding in the Soviet Union and the old regime. Study of the tsarist ministerial government, provincial administration, zemstvos, and so on, may throw light on the evolution and operation of both formal arrangements and informal practices in the Soviet state and Communist Party, both at the center and in the provinces. In particular, tsarist methods of recruitment, personnel allocation, control mechanisms and career patterns should be juxtaposed against the various party personnel and control mechanisms. For example, the role of the tsarist Inspectorate and ministerial-appointment powers and the function of Tables of Organization (*shtaty*) may be fruitfully compared to party personnel mechanisms, patterns of functional and regional specialization, and particularly the *nomenklatura* system.

The challenge is to attain a more accurate measure of the degree of institutional continuity and change. Only then can we begin to formulate more sophisticated theories of revolution that explain the outcomes, and thus the real meaning, of 'transformation', instead of remaining content with generalizations about the breakdown of old regimes.

Notes: Chapter 5

1 V. I. Gurko, *Features and Figures of the Past: Government and Opinion in the Reign of Nicholas II* (Stanford, Calif.: Stanford University Press, 1939), p. 188.
2 The clearest, though still in my view inadequate, recent theoretical discussion of revolution that advocates a structural approach to the breakdowns of the old regime is Theda Skocpol, *States and Social Revolutions* (Cambridge: Cambridge University Press, 1979).
3 On the Muscovite, see Borivoi Plavsic, 'Seventeenth century chanceries and their staffs', in Walter McKenzie Pintner and Don Karl Rowney (eds), *Russian Officialdom: The Bureaucratization of Russian Society*

from the Seventeenth to the Twentieth Century (Chapel Hill, NC: University of North Carolina Press, 1980), pp. 19–45; and Peter Bowman Brown, 'Early modern Russian bureaucracy: the evolution of the chancellery system, from Ivan III to Peter the Great, 1478–1717', PhD dissertation, University of Chicago, 1978. These works provide a complete bibliography on the Muscovite bureaucracy. The Plavsic article should be obligatory reading for all serious students of Russian government institutions.

4   See Robert O. Crummey, 'The origins of the noble official: the Boyar elite, 1613–1689', in Pintner and Rowney (eds), op. cit., pp. 46–75, and the other Crummey studies of the Boyar Duma cited therein.

5   Brenda Meehan-Waters, 'Social and career characteristics of the administrative elite, 1689–1761', in Pintner and Rowney (eds), op. cit., pp. 76–105, and the other Meehan-Waters studies cited therein. Also, S. M. Troitskii, *Russkii absoliutizm i dvorianstvo v XVIII V. Formirovanie biurokratii* (Moscow: Nauka, 1974).

6   John P. Willerton, 'Clientelism in the Soviet Union: an initial examination', *Studies in Comparative Communism*, vol. XII, no. 2–3 (1979), pp. 159–83.

7   An enormous amount of material on the importance of clientelism to the emergence of an 'enlightened' bureaucracy in Russia may be found in W. Bruce Lincoln's forthcoming book, *In the Vanguard of Reform: Russia's Enlightened Bureaucrats, 1825–1881*.

8   Walter M. Pintner, 'The evolution of civil officialdom, 1755–1855', and 'Civil officialdom and the nobility in the 1850s', in Pintner and Rowney (eds), op. cit., pp. 190–226, 227–49, and the other Pintner works cited therein; and P. A. Zaionchkovskii, *Pravitelstvennyi apparat samoderzhavnoi Rossii v XIX v* (Moscow: Mysl', 1978).

9   Daniel T. Orlovsky, *The Limits of Reform: The Ministry of Internal Affairs in Imperial Russia, 1802–1881* (Cambridge, Mass.: Harvard University Press, 1981).

10 See the very important work in progress of D. Lieven of the London School of Economics.

11 Orlovsky, op. cit., pp. 133–45; see also Richard Robbins, 'Choosing the Russian governors: the professionalization of the gubernatorial corps', *Slavonic and East European Review*, vol. 58, no. 4 (1980), pp. 541–60.

12 See Gurko, op. cit., pp. 35–51; and Vergil D. Medlin and Steven L. Parsons, *V. D. Nabokov and the Russian Provisional Government, 1917* (New Haven, Conn.: Yale University Press, 1976).

13 See, for example, V. B. Lopukhin, 'Liudi i politika (konets XIX –nachalo XX v.)', *Voprosy istorii*, vol. 51, no. 9 (1966), pp. 110–12, and no. 10 (1966), pp. 118–36; S. E. Krizhanovskii, *Vospominaniia* (Berlin, n.d.); V. N. Kokovstsov, *Iz moego proshlago: Vospominaniia, 1903–1919*, 2 vols (The Hague: Mouton, 1969); and K. A. Krivoshein, *A. V. Krivoshein (1857–1921), ego znachenie v istorii Rossii nachala XX veka* (Paris: n.p., 1973).

14 All State Council material is taken from TsGIA SSSR (Central State Historical Archive of the USSR) in Leningrad, Fond 1162.

15 W. E. Mosse, 'Aspects of tsarist bureaucracy: recruitment to the imperial State Council, 1855–1914', *Slavonic and East European Review*, vol. 57, no. 2 (1979), pp. 240–54.

16 A. Dem'ianov, 'Moia sluzhba pri Vremennom Pravitel'stve', *Arkhiv russkoi revoliutsii*, vol. IV (1922), p. 120.

6

Political Clientelism in the USSR and Japan: a Tentative Comparison

SHUGO MINAGAWA

One might expect the conduct of bureaucracies of such modern industrial countries as Japan and the Soviet Union to be governed by the norms of rationality, anonymity and universalism. Insecurity, which is believed to be one of the causes of clientelism, should not be greatly felt by officials in these countries who in a material sense enjoy considerable privileges, at least so long as they retain office (though in the case of Soviet officials career security and even personal security have admittedly been low for considerable periods in the past). Yet it has been widely noted that informal alignments based on interpersonal commitments are one of the characteristics of both the Japanese and the Soviet bureaucracies.

This chapter seeks to establish a few common and distinctive features of the 'physiology' of Soviet and Japanese political clientelism. That is to say, it attempts to identify the reasons for the development of clientelism, how it works and what part it plays in the operation of the system as a whole. A comprehensive comparison of political clientelism in these two very different societies would take us far beyond the main focus of interest in this book, and for this reason I propose to limit my consideration of Japanese clientelism mainly to the government bureaucracy, that is, that part of the Japanese system which presents the closest basis of comparison with the Soviet system as a whole.

Since the audience to which this chapter is primarily addressed will generally have some familiarity with case material illustrative of political clientelism in the USSR, but be less familiar with comparable phenomena in Japan, it will be useful to start by looking fairly closely at a particular Japanese case, one which appears to be entirely typical, albeit unusually well documented. The story makes for rather complicated reading, but it is well to remind ourselves that clientelist politics is often very complicated, and it has the merit of illustrating in a concrete way most of the general features of Japanese clientelist behavior to be discussed later.

A Japanese Case

This case concerns Shigeru Sahashi ('S') who served in the Ministry of International Trade and Industry (MITI) in 1937–67. He started his career in the Engineering Bureau, then advanced by moving around a number of bureaux (the so-called 'spiral advancement'): General Affairs Bureau, Textile Bureau, Sendai Local Office, Coal Industry Bureau, Secretariat, Heavy Industry Bureau, Enterprise Bureau and the Patent Agency. He retired as (administrative) Vice-Minister of MITI – the highest civil service post in the ministry – in April 1967.

S's early career suffered many twists and turns because of his uncompromising personality. When he was the chief of the Paper Industry Section in the Textile Bureau, the ministry's employees' union,[1] which he then headed, was suppressed by the director of the Secretariat, Nagayama. S had clashed over union issues with Nagayama several times. S was eventually demoted by Nagayama and transferred to the Sendai local office of the ministry. His clientelist activities really started when he became chief of the Personnel Section in the Secretariat in July 1954. He served in this office for two terms, till July 1957. There are three sections in the Secretariat: the Personnel (literally secretarial activities), General Affairs and Accounting sections. Those heading the Personnel and the General Affairs sections, in particular, enjoyed the highest status of all incumbents of the 200 or so posts at section-chief level in MITI (including its extraministerial offices), and so had better chances of becoming bureau chiefs. (There are seven bureaux and three extra-ministerial bureaux, and the director of the Secretariat also has bureau chief rank. Again, as in the case of section chiefs, not all bureau chiefs have equal status. The chief of the Enterprise Bureau, for example, had better chances to become vice-minister for the ministry.) The main area of responsibility of the General Affairs Section is to work out programs for the general management and policy coordination of the ministry. The Personnel Section is responsible for such matters as recruitment, dismissal, advancement, marriage arrangements, postretirement jobs, and so on. The three sections in the Secretariat operate under the direction of a director. As the Secretariat deals with confidential matters of the ministry, such as policy adjustments, personnel matters and the ministry's budget, the vice-minister chooses his right-hand man as its director. Likewise the latter usually appoints his trusted followers as its section chiefs. The vice-minister was at that time Ishihara, and the director of the Secretariat was Matsuo. The chief of the General Affairs Section in the Secretariat was Zenei Imai ('I'), who had been S's chief rival right through his career in the ministry, although they shared the same patron.

The chief of the Personnel Section can by no means act solely on his own initiative, although he is assigned to implement the ministry's day-to-day personnel policy. He evidently enjoys greater latitude to act on personnel changes below the section-chief level. Above that level, however, he is more likely to receive instructions from the director of the Secretariat, the latter having sought the opinion of the vice-minister or the Tuesday Club (formed by retired high-level officials of MITI). But if the section chief happens to have an uncompromising personality and a vision of future personnel policy such as S had, and provided the director gives him his blessing, the section chief can occupy a pivotal position in personnel management.

It should be noted that about the year 1954 the Japanese economy passed from the period of postwar recovery to that of expansion. The first postwar prosperity period started in 1955. Ever since Japan was admitted into the IMF and the World Bank in 1952, the Japanese government had been under constant pressure to become an IMF Article Eight country, that is, to establish an open economic system like those of other developed countries. S appears to have been seriously concerned about the competitiveness of Japanese industries in an open economic system, and therefore worked out a personnel policy to cope with this contingency. He succeeded in recruiting nineteen very able graduates out of 200 successful candidates whom he interviewed personally. S also took note of the intellectual ability of Yoshihiko Morozumi ('Z' – recruited in 1943), who then held the position of research counsellor in the Secretariat. Z had a high reputation in the ministry for his outstanding logical mind. In order to facilitate Z's objective of studying the French mixed economy system S sent him to Paris, where he was attached to the Japanese Embassy as a trade attaché. S had also established very close personal bonds with Chihaya Kawade ('C' – recruited in 1939), Hideyuki Kawahara ('H' – recruited in 1941) and Yukio Miyake ('Y' – recruited in 1943). C was at that time the chief of the First Section of the Enterprise Bureau, and

Y the chief of its Second Section. The post of First Section Chief, whose future career prospects are usually bright, is normally given to one of those promising officials whose creative minds are tested and in constant demand in the ministry. H was then the minister's secretary in the Secretariat. C, H and Y, if not Z, shared the same temperament and aspirations as their patron, S.

When S was promoted to be deputy chief and later chief of the Heavy Industry Bureau, C succeeded to S's previous post, as chief of the Personnel Section in the Secretariat, and a little later C became S's deputy in the Heavy Industry Bureau, while Y became the minister's secretary in the Secretariat.

When S became the chief of the Enterprise Bureau, he succeeded in placing his key followers in strategic positions so as to mobilize them to his own ends. H became the counsellor of the planning section in the Secretariat, and Kenzo Ototake ('O' – recruited in 1941, another of S's loyal followers) became chief of the General Affairs Section in the Secretariat. Z was hastily recalled from Paris to head the First Section of the Enterprise Bureau, which position had been kept vacant by S for two months – a very unusual occurrence in Japanese governmental personnel management. Y was also chosen to head the Industrial Funds Section in the Enterprise Bureau. S's clientelist machine, which became known as the 'nationalists', moved in full swing to realize their patron's main policy objective: to reinforce domestic industries in anticipation of the impending change in Japan's economic situation.

S's clientelist machine made such determined efforts in the ministry that a countermove by the so-called 'internationalists' was made. The internationalist group was gradually formed around I (the Chief of the International Trade Bureau), who made his career largely in the field of international trade. It is said that their countermove was prompted not so much by the policy issue, as by S's uncompromising personality and his obvious clientelist activities. The 'internationalists' moved carefully, however, to counterbalance S's weight in the ministry. S had to concede an important post to one of I's followers, Yoshihisa Ojimi ('J' – recruited in 1941), whose career had largely been made in the field of domestic industry and thus differed from I's, but who nevertheless shared the latter's temperament. J was to head the newly created Research Section on the restructuring of industry in the Secretariat. This section had to inquire into which of the country's industries would be reinforced by law. Such an inquiry could be expected to contribute significantly in the process of drafting and realizing any related legislation.

The ministry duly drafted a Bill on 'Temporary measures for the promotion of specified industries'. It was originally drafted by two junior officials (Konaga and Uchida – both of them S's followers) in the Heavy Industry Bureau. This initial draft was designed to support certain weak industries (those designated as 'classified industries'). When Z came back from Paris, however, he revised it by introducing a more systematic approach, that is, by linking weak industries laterally so that all weak industries could be reinforced in a harmonious and synchronized way. The Bill went before the Diet for approval three times, and although certain amendments were made each time, it was never passed. Needless to say, S and his followers in the ministry mobilized all available forces including their social networks in order to influence interested parties, such as the Fair Trade Commission and in particular financial and industrial circles. But to no avail –they turned it down. Moreover, the ruling party had shown very little enthusiasm. It was a Bill without political sponsors.

S, aggrieved at the failure of his efforts, placed the responsibility partly on the minister's (then Hajimi Fukuda – Ohno faction, Liberal Democratic Party) lukewarm support for the Bill. Unfortunately for him, this was just the time when the new vice-minister was to be named as successor to the retiring vice-minister, Matsuo. In MITI it was almost taken for granted that the chief of the Enterprise Bureau (now S) would succeed the retiring vice-minister. Despite repeated warnings from Matsuo, however, the minister ignored all precedents, and named S's chief rival I as successor to the retiring Matsuo. We do not know whether the 'internationalists' engaged in any campaign behind the scenes against the Bill and against S personally. S was now demoted to the post of director of the Patent Agency, an extraministerial office of MITI. Presumably the minister decided on his demotion for two reasons: S's open criticism of himself and his unconventional behavior in not reciprocating favors.[2] Although S himself was removed from the center of power in the ministry, some of his followers managed to gain control of the nerve system of the ministry. For instance, C became the director of the Secretariat, H became the chief of the Personnel Section and Y became the chief of the General Affairs Section in the Secretariat.

In the meantime the former vice-ministers, Ishihara (retired in 1957, then became inspector of the Tokyo Electric Power Co.) and Tokunago (retired in 1961, and became deputy president of the Japan Steel Corporation), in particular, paved the way to reinstate S as vice-minister, by apologizing to the Ohno faction for S's past misbehavior. When a Cabinet reshuffle took place in October 1964, he was finally made vice-minister of the ministry. S promptly appointed one of his trusted followers, H, as director of the Secretariat. C also became the chief of the Heavy Industry Bureau, but not of the Enterprise Bureau which was the first-runner position for becoming the vice-minister and which was then occupied by Shimada, who would have become the vice-minister if S had not made a comeback. A year and a half later, however, S dramatically decided to abruptly terminate his tenure, out of deep grief at the sudden death of H.

The minister, Miki, then had to appoint a successor to S from among three contenders, namely, Shimada (chief of the Enterprise Bureau – recruited in 1939), C (S's follower) and Kurahashi (director of the Patent Agency – recruited in 1938; most inopportunely his secret political maneuvering with the Ohno faction was now revealed). In the end, with a view to restoring harmonious human relations in the ministry, Miki decided to appoint a neutral, non-contested man, Yamamoto ('M' – recruited in 1939) as S's successor. This outcome would scarcely have been anticipated by S who probably had in mind the following line of succession by his trusted followers: he would be succeeded first by C and then by H and eventually by Y. Now that C was out of the competition and H had passed away, such a scenario became irrelevant.

The new vice-minister, M, who succeeded S, was however not altogether neutral. Much of his career in the ministry had been associated with the field of international trade. Indeed, at one time he was the deputy to the then chief of the International Trade Bureau, I, S's chief rival. M chose I's follower J as his right-hand man, the director of the Secretariat. It seems that the reigning vice-minister usually has a right to name the director of the Secretariat. The relations between the vice-minister and the director, however, are usually delicate, complex and sometimes tenuous. If the vice-minister does not have a domineering personality, the director can fully realize his very large formal responsibilities. It is thus a combination of the personality of both, and the degree of trust and affective ties between the two, that determine their relations. In J's case, he seems to have acted on personnel matters a great deal on his own. He mobilized able officials with long overseas trade experience, offering them important non-international trade posts. For instance, Komatsu who returned from West Germany was promoted to be chief of the General Affairs Section in the Secretariat, Wada who returned from Canada became chief of the Industrial Machine Section in the Heavy Industry Bureau and Masuda who returned from Belgium became chief of the Iron and Steel Affairs Section in the Heavy Industry Bureau. By and large it has been the practice of the Japanese government bureaucracy to produce competent generalists, that is, officials with experience in varied types of work and in various fields. In MITI, however, there had been a strong tendency for officials who had undergone international trade apprenticeship abroad to be reassigned to comparable policy positions in the central office. Until then the 'internationalists' had been regarded as not fit to hold the vice-ministership, which should be occupied by a man commanding a profound knowledge in the administration of domestic industries. Indeed, it was J who firmly established the present routinization of the line of succession to the vice-ministership: director of the Secretariat – chief of the International Trade Policy Bureau (formerly the International Trade Bureau) – chief of the Industrial Policy Bureau (formerly the Enterprise Bureau) – vice-minister. The routinization not only blurred the distinction between the 'nationalists' and 'internationalists', but also minimized political interference in the personnel affairs of the ministry. Previously there had been a loosely routinized path from the Enterprise Bureau chief to the vice-minister. But this line of succession was too short, inviting occasional political interference as in the case of S.

It is not certain, however, if the routinization of the line of succession has lessened clientelist activities. The fate of routinization is always susceptible to unforeseen contingencies such as sudden death or ill-health or early retirement of the heir apparent, thus leaving room for clientelist maneuvering. Whether this routinization was devised with intent to suppress the advancement of S's followers, we do not know. The fact is that none of S's followers ever found a place in the vice-ministership, which has been taken over by the old 'internationalists'. The possible exception to this is Z, who eventually reached the vice-ministership. Earlier Z had been the director of the Secretariat and he was not particularly keen on promoting S's followers. He may, in fact, have acted in that way out of a realization that the nature of the contemporary national economic system, which was affected by the international economic environment and Japan's increasingly important place in international trade, required structural changes including personnel changes in the government industrial administration. Although Z's pro-

fessional competence was highly regarded by S, he had repor-
tedly never established close personal bonds with him. Indeed,
S was said to have made the ironical remark some time after his
retirement: 'When I happen to meet Z occasionally, he says
ostensibly I am the one who brought him in to a sunny place'
(emphasis added).[3]

The detailed account of the case given here has been possible
because it is unusually well documented, with complementary
accounts by a number of observers.[4] The fact that the Ministry
of International Trade and Industry was somewhat more
dynamic than other ministries, that the policy issue came to the
fore at a time of uncertainty in Japan's economic situation,
together with the personality of S, a man who did not mince
matters, combined to bring the case to the surface, to the good
fortune of outside observers. However, it should be stressed
that there is ample evidence that the structural and behavioral
patterns revealed by this case are also operative in other
ministries. For this reason, we feel justified in drawing on it to
illustrate the comparative remarks on Soviet and Japanese
clientelism that follow.

Causes of Clientelist Behavior

Despite the fact that there exist, mostly on a journalistic level,
numerous descriptions of Japanese clientelist activities, little
attempt has been made to examine such questions as the causation of clientelist behavior, its system of membership, the
durability of clientelist links and the effects of clientelism on the
Japanese political system. By contrast, several students of
Soviet politics have carried out serious studies aiming to clarify
such questions. With reference to the 'physiology' of both
Soviet and Japanese political clientelism, however, very few
empirical examinations have yet been undertaken. Comparative examination of these aspects must, therefore, remain a
tentative exercise at the present time. More substantial efforts
of comparison will only be possible after more extensive empirical findings are available.

A patron–client relationship is, according to Carl H. Landé's
definition, 'a vertical dyadic alliance', an alliance between two
persons of unequal status, power, or resources, each of whom
finds it useful to have as an ally someone superior or inferior to
himself.[5] It may be almost impossible to pinpoint the exact
reasons as to why two individuals form a patron–client relation-

ship; yet with the limited available material on the subject, we may nevertheless roughly divide the individual's motivations into two categories, which may be termed functional and non-functional. Examples of functional motivation may be observed in those aspects of the politicoadministrative process most obviously subject to clientelist activities, namely, recruitment, advancement and postretirement security, but may also manifest themselves in the policy process. It would be a mistake, however, to explain the norms and incentives for clientage relationships solely in functional terms. To appreciate the full range of an individual's motivations one may need to examine the contexts of clientelism, which include also non-functional components of a structural, cultural and environmental kind.

Recruitment and Advancement

Speaking of clientelist activity Keith Legg says that 'nowhere is this clearer than in the area of recruitment and advancement'.[6] Japan and the Soviet Union are no exception to this. In Japanese government bureaucracy we saw this in the case history from MITI where the chief of the Personnel Section is responsible for recruiting twenty or thirty trainees for higher-level positions every year.[7] The criteria for the recruitment of trainees in Japan are on the whole conservative and formal. The energetic recruiting efforts shown by S when he was chief of the Personnel Section is somewhat exceptional, although one can certainly point to other cases where persons who have passed the special higher examination decide to enter a ministry as a result of much persuasion or personal connections. None the less, it is not likely that the trainees establish affective relationships with particular seniors right from the beginning. The recruits often undergo a training period of about six years, learning the work of a particular ministry. Take the Ministry of Finance, for instance, where the trainees in their first year will be dispersed through the planning and research groups of the General Affairs Section in each bureau or in the Personnel Section or Archives and Documents Section in the Secretariat in order to obtain some basic familiarity with the ministry. In their second year the trainees will usually be sent to local revenue offices to learn the actual taxation system on the spot. In their third year they may take an academic course in economic theory given either at the ministry or at an academic institution abroad. In their fourth and fifth year they will be trained under some assistant section chief or full section chief. In the sixth – as a final training-ground – they will be posted to various local revenue offices again, but this time as superintendent. The above-mentioned training period is usually given to all recruits. It helps to cultivate in the recruits a sense of identity with the ministry. After this training period, they will ordinarily be shifted from one section to another every two or three years. The main purpose of this spiral career mobility is said to be the ideal of producing generalists rather than specialists, and also to ward off sectionalism.[8]

Almost all recruits reach the position of section chief. By the time a junior becomes a section chief he will probably have established particularly good relationships with certain senior officials. As we have noted earlier, not all section chiefs enjoy equal status in the ministry. Hierarchy exists in the ministry not only vertically, but also laterally. Career mobility above assistant section chief is in most cases a matter of moving sideways. The important question is, therefore, to *which* post one is assigned both at the level of section chief and of bureau chief, given the fact also that the line of succession has been routinized in almost all the ministries. Moreover, senior posts above section chief level are so scarce that their attainment becomes uncertain. As a rule of seniority is strictly applied in career mobility, it follows that if an official remains, without being able to advance himself further, in one position, during a normal rotating period, he then becomes a bottleneck for the juniors who wish to advance their careers. In such a case he will usually be advised by his senior to retire earlier than the customary retiring age of 55. To avoid such a contingency, an official at section-chief level may search for a patron powerful enough to guard his tenure. On the other hand, when an official becomes Bureau Chief, he is so concerned with policy issues that he is in a position to recommend those juniors who are close to him for key positions. We have already observed that when S moved from chief of one bureau to chief of another, he took with him some of his men or posted them in strategic positions. It is the director of the Secretariat, and to a lesser extent the chief of the Personnel Section (although his main function is to maintain harmony and solidarity within the ministry), who are structurally located to establish clientelist relationships with juniors whom they have earmarked during or after the training period.

The practice of recruiting able juniors as faction members is not a recent phenomenon. In the imperial Japanese army during the Meiji era, for instance, there were the Satsuma and Choshu domain cliques. As the army machine began to be concerned with complex policy issues under a rapidly changing inter-national environment, each clique had to recruit men of ability, searching beyond the traditional clique boundaries.[9]

Postretirement jobs do not in all cases constitute advance-ment for senior officials, but it is one of their major concerns, probably as great as advancement within the ministry itself. When a senior official retires from the ministry, its Secretariat will usually provide him with an appropriate postretirement job. If he were asked to retire under pressure from above, and declined to do so, then the Secretariat would be very reluctant to provide him the best available job upon his eventual retirement. In 1976, for instance, when Hayashi (at that time chief of the Industrial Environment Bureau of MITI, recruited in 1947) refused to retire, the Secretariat asked instead another Bureau Chief, Moriguchi (chief of the Industrial Information Bureau of MITI, recruited in 1947) to retire, and Moriguchi complied. Hayashi stayed on in the ministry, attached to its Secretariat, but was given no specific post and his wages were reduced by half. Eventually Moriguchi assumed the post of deputy presi-dent of Daiei (ranking no. 1 in the service industry), whereas Hayashi took up the post of deputy president of Jasco (ranking no. 4 in the service industry). The above case indicates, none the less, the psychic insecurity: the high-ranking officials who reach a position such as that of vice-minister or Bureau Chief while still in their early fifties have to search for postretirement jobs outside the bureaucracy.[10]

If one compares the employment situation of the retired 'nationalists' and 'internationalists' of MITI, the latter clearly have done better. In the case of S, probably by reason of his right-hand man's sudden death and his own uncompromising personality, he could not secure an appropriate postretirement job, and therefore he set up the Sahashi Economic Research Institute by himself. He then took up the directorship of an obscure organization called the Japan Leisure Center. Since some of the senior 'nationalists' occupy posts in certain steel firms – such as Tokunaga (deputy president of Japan Steel Corporation) and Matsuo (chairman of Nippon Kokan K.K.) – C found a position in Kawasaki Steel Corporation as its deputy president, and Y in Nippon Kokan K.K. as its managing director. The rest of the 'nationalists' were resigned to taking up secondary posts, although in quite good companies. The retired vice-ministers of the 'internationalists' are dispersed into a number of industries. For instance, S's chief rival I occupies the post of president of the Nippon Oil Chemical Co. To follow the rest in succession: M is deputy president of the Toyota Motor Co.; Z, who changed his loyalty later to the 'internationalists', is president of the Electricity Development Corporation (this is one of the two public corporations attached to MITI); J is president of the Arabian Oil Co.; Yamashita is managing director of the Mitui Co.; Komatsu is managing director of the Kobe Steel Co.; and Wada is advisor to the Industrial Bank of Japan. (Being advisor to one of the leading Japanese banks is one of the stopgap posts, since higher-level officials are not permitted to assume postretirement jobs in private companies within two years after retirement. Wada took up the position of his predecessor, Komatsu, who was until recently advisor to this bank.)

The pattern of recruitment, advancement and postretirement jobs described above thus provides abundant evidence of clientelist behavior. Exploiting such institutional resources as the formal functions of the Secretariat the clientelist group can chart out a pattern to the advantage of its members. Such a pattern is not, however, immune to the danger of destruction by unexpected factors as is shown in S's case.

In the Soviet party–state bureaucracy patterns of recruitment and advancement have been far less routinized than in the Japanese case. None the less, certain tendencies of routinization have been observable at all periods, albeit changing with changes in the top leadership regime. As to recruitment, to take an example on a regional (*obkom*) level, two types of criteria seem to operate in the recruitment of its first secretary. First, recruitment of a regional first secretary may be influenced by the candidate's practical-administrative background, according to the requirements of a particular region. The reassignment of a regional secretary to a comparable policy position may operate not only on a lateral level, that is, from region to region, but also vertically, that is, from region to center.[11] In the case of lateral reassignment the transfers sometimes seem to be for purposes of troubleshooting, that is, a more experienced secretary is sent from a more developed region to strengthen the leadership of a less developed region that may be in serious trouble economically.[12] A would-be first secretary might also be required to have experience in various types of work. According to some observers, the possession of both specialist and managerial experience, making for economically competent generalists, became, under the Brezhnev leadership, a more important consideration in promotions than either patronage or recent economic performance.[13] Secondly, there is the criterion of a formal succession of posts, for example, under the Brezhnev regime the majority of new first secretaries have been recruited from the second secretaries of the *obkom* or the chairmen of the soviet executive committees of the same region,[14] whereas under the Khrushchev regime many first secretaries were recruited from outside the region. By routinizing recruitment in this way the Brezhnev regime may have, indeed, intended to maintain a delicate balance among contending groups. The application of such objective criteria may be intended to reduce the political element in such appointments, although it is by no means certain that it has succeeded in doing so.

As for patterns of advancement from the *obkom* first secretary position, again partial regularities are observable: a republic (except RSFSR) regional first secretary may be advanced to a republic party or government post. A Ukrainian regional first secretary may, however, be advanced to a Ukrainian party or government post, or, if he is fortunate, advanced directly to be an RSFSR regional first secretary (although rare at present, this happened with several Khrushchev protégés in the 1950s). The first secretary of the Ukrainian or Belorussian Central Committee may be advanced directly to a higher party or government post at the center. An RSFSR regional first secretary may advance directly to a higher party or government post at the center. It should be noted that there exists a hierarchy among the republics and among the regions,[15] and of course a senior party post usually carries superior status to a senior government post on the same administrative level. Most advancements are those of sideslips like those in the Japanese government bureaucracy.

Nevertheless, promotion in the Soviet Union is determined not only by such objective criteria as performance, career background, or seniority, but also by political considerations. One kind of political consideration is evident in the efforts shown by the post-Khrushchev oligarchs to establish legitimate rules for career advancement. To maintain a delicate balance of power the Brezhnev regime needs to distribute rewards, such as promotions, in some relationship to the strength of groups within the ruling coalition.[16] Moreover, the Brezhnev regime may have been careful not to unnecessarily antagonize those who had lost in the intergroup struggles. We learn from Willerton's analysis that about 47 percent of the clients of demoted patrons have retained their Central Committee membership,[17] having thus been compensated with appropriate appointments and opportunities. In the early Brezhnev–Kosygin period

Brezhnev may have wanted to establish what Carl Landé terms a 'personal alliance system'. Landé distinguishes between 'traditional' dyadic relationships with vertical links and 'modern' relationships with horizontal links. In the latter relationships the central individual has status, resources, or power roughly equal to those of his several partners.[18] The Brezhnev regime evidently combines both 'vertical' and 'horizontal' links, and may be best characterized as a coalition of several complex vertical dyadic alliances. The findings presented by Joel Moses indicate that Brezhnev in particular had, indeed, cultivated relationships of the former kind as well, that is, fostered political advancement by patronage. He claims that about 75 percent of Dnepropetrovsk 'cohorts' (Brezhnev's) as against only about 18 percent of the Lvov and Kharkov 'cohorts' (Podgornyi's) were able to advance beyond Ukraine to receive career assignments in other republics or at the federal level.[19] John Willerton also observed a positive pattern between the advancements of Brezhnev and his clients.[20] In other words, the advancement of Brezhnev's clients, particularly since 1964, was not constrained so much by the aforementioned objective criteria.

The crucial question here is obviously who is to determine and recommend the advancement of officials. A key to the building of a power-base in the Soviet Union may still be to have control over personnel selection. At one time Podgornyi was able to place his Kharkov subordinate, V. N. Titov, as the junior Central Committee Secretary in charge of organizational-party work (equivalent to the director of the Secretariat in the Japanese government bureaucracy) and also another Kharkov subordinate, N. A. Sobol, as Second Secretary of the Ukrainian Central Committee (the secretary in charge of personnel selection in that republic). They were, however, removed from control over personnel selection before Podgornyi could materialize his own power-base through that channel. In the early post-Khrushchev period (1966) Brezhnev made a major advance by transferring his old second secretary in Zaporozhe (and his successor in Dnepropetrovsk), A. P. Kirilenko, to the responsibilities of general supervision over personnel selection and also of the urban economy that Podgornyi had relinquished. Within the framework of routinized advancement, Brezhnev gradually succeeded in moving his protégés from Dnepropetrovsk, Zaporozhe and Moldavia into key political posts.[21] Indeed, the growing influence of Brezhnev by 1973 which is reflected in the doubling of Dnepropetrovsk 'cohorts' in senior positions can be explained either, as noted above, by their common career association with a single major political patron (Brezhnev), or as Joel Moses suggests,[22] with a plurality of patrons (assuming a cooperative arrangement in the Politburo between Brezhnev, Kirilenko and the present Ukrainian First Secretary, Shcherbitskii).[23] Such a cooperative arrangement, like that of the vice-minister and the director of the Secretariat in the Japanese ministries, would be a key to establishing such a group's power-base.

In the Soviet Union, whether it is due to a temporary or a permanent 'personal alliance system' in Brezhnev style, other Politburo members than the General Secretary and Central Committee secretaries appear to bring pressure for the selection of personnel from their territorial or policy domains. Jerry Hough points out, for instance, that officials from Belorussia (Mazurov's region), from Leningrad (Kosygin's region) and from Kharkov (Podgornyi's region) have been much more successful than the average. The same is true of top foreign-policy officials (an area with which Suslov was involved) and of top industrial and construction officials (the area of responsibility both of Kosygin as first deputy chairman of the Council of Ministers and of Brezhnev as the Central Committee Secretary for industry under Khrushchev from 1956 to the summer of 1960).[24]

Even under Stalin's reign a second line of patrons seems to have enjoyed a certain latitude in the selection of lower political posts. N. S. Patolichev's recent memoirs reveal that his success and failure in career advancement was due in large part to the relative political power of his patron, Politburo member A. A. Andreev. If Patolichev is to be believed, he owed his primary allegiance to Andreev, rather than to Stalin, although the latter exercised ultimate authority over his career advancement. Even at Patolichev's level, he was allowed to recruit his own adherents as his subordinates.[25] In the Soviet Union the promotion of an official appears to be basically determined or recommended by his immediate superior, which would obviously invite the flourishing of vertical relationships.

Clientelism and Policy

We have observed earlier that clientelism in the Japanese government bureaucracy is linked with every aspect of the policy process. For instance, we saw that at a critical point S brought his most able clients into the key positions in his office (chief of the Enterprise Bureau). In the Japanese government bureaucracy it is the vice-minister or more frequently one of his bureau chiefs who usually launches policy initiatives leading to a new law or regulation with political ramifications and implications for the work of other ministries. The Japanese government bureaucracy, which is by and large a line organization, is characterized by work-group solidarity within the 'frame', to use Chie Nakane's term. This office solidarity often renders cooperation difficult not only between ministries, but also between bureaux and sections within a ministry. To overcome such difficulties there exist at least two institutional tools for arriving at a consensus. *Ringi-sei*, which is the process of obtaining consensus by circulating a draft plan within the ministry concerned, is a formal internal consensus formation process.[26] Another institutional tool is that of the advisory committee drawn from business circles, academics, parliamentarians and retired bureaucrats. Such a committee provides the ministry with a forum well suited for preliminary consultation prior to formal ministerial or interministerial meetings. There is a high probability of obtaining a preliminary consensus among the interested parties in this carefully manipulated setting.[27] Policymakers can also use this forum to legitimize their draft of a bill.[28] The advisory committee system is a formal process for obtaining an external consensus. In addition, however, at some point the draft must be cleared with the appropriate division of the ruling Liberal Democratic Party's Policy Affairs Research Council, and also at a meeting of the vice-minister and bureau chiefs of the ministry concerned, or a meeting of the vice-ministers of all the ministries. To avoid open confrontation the policymakers in the bureaucracy usually engage in extensive informal consultations, mobilizing for this purpose their personal cliques and social networks, a process which overlaps with the aforementioned two formal consultation processes. Nevertheless, there are occasions in which an open confrontation does surface, providing a way, at least for one party, to gather together backing for a measure or a countermeasure. A recent example occurred with the plan by former Prime Minister Fukuda to set up a new Ministry of Energy Resources; the validity of this was openly challenged by the then Vice-Minister of MITI, Wada, who was in fear of losing administrative control over energy resource matters. Twenty days after this premeditated challenge, Prime Minister Fukuda admitted that it was still premature to carry out his plan. During these twenty days the whole resources of the ministry had been mobilized to deal with the danger.[29] First of all, the bureau chiefs met to discuss a strategy for countering Fukuda's plan. Then Wada personally approached the then Vice-Minister of the Ministry of Finance, Kichise, for assistance; in view of the large financial implications of setting up a new ministry, Ministry of Finance approval would obviously be required. Kichise had been a contemporary of Wada in the accounting section of the old Japanese imperial navy, and the two may well have kept alive ever since a loose horizontal dyadic alliance, in which one could count on the other's help in time of need.[30] The director and the section chiefs of the Secretariat, all trusted clients of Wada, played an active part in influencing the interested parties. At first, they appealed to other ministries which were affected by Fukuda's other administrative reform plans, to concert their efforts to counter these plans. Secondly, they approached former ministers of MITI, in particular, Miki and Nakasone, now leaders of countermainstream factions in the Liberal Democratic Party. And, finally, they appealed to industrial and commercial circles either directly or through social networks such as school ties and family relations not to support Fukuda's plan. The final outcome was a victory for Wada, who stayed on as vice-minister of MITI until his natural retirement from office.

Students of Soviet politics are divided on the question whether clientelism in the Soviet Union is closely related to the politics of the policy process. Jerry Hough, for example, appears to believe that Soviet factional activity is concerned almost entirely with the acquisition of position and has relatively little policy content.[31] First of all, he asserts, an anti-faction rule makes the formation of any substantial network of alliances along philosophical lines among regional and other middle-level officials difficult. Secondly, these middle-level political officials refrain, in order to avoid damaging their political chances, from policy controversy or even a policy stance. And thirdly, the nature of censorship strengthens the tendency for policy-relevant alliances to remain compartmentalized within specialized 'whirlpools' with selective censorship making it difficult to appeal through the press for outside allies.[32] Jerry Hough's negative estimate of the factional element in the policy process thus appears to be based on a view of middle-level officials as structurally and ideologically restricted in their behavior. Joel Moses, on the other hand, points to the fact that Dnepropetrovsk 'cohorts' have assumed a very wide range of policy responsibility and authority in such diverse institutions as the Ukrainian, Russian and All-Union Councils of Ministers, the Komsomol, economic planning organs, political publishing houses, trade union councils, heavy-industry and consumer-sector ministries, the foreign ministry including the diplomatic corps and the secret police.[33] Moses appears to assume, therefore, that the influence of a major political patron probably depends in some measure on his ability to mobilize as wide a base of political support as possible for his policy initiatives in the Soviet bureaucracies. If the Soviet Union has moved toward the model of 'institutional pluralism' as Jerry Hough claims it has,[34] it is imperative, on the part of a major patron, to protect his policy initiatives and his own political position by placing as many loyal subordinates as possible in a wide range of functional and political key positions.

Although we do not have direct evidence of a faction-dominated policy process, it seems reasonable to assume that factional activity connected with efforts to establish a dominant position within the ruling oligarchy inevitably takes on policy content. Khrushchev's party bifurcation plan in 1962, for example, was ostensibly designed to promote cadres with skills in technical and economic works. Armstrong considers, however, that the party bifurcation was directed against the agricultural regional first secretaries.[35] Another example mentioned by Carl Linden was Khrushchev's anti-Stalinist campaign.[36] This was used more than once to regain the offensive whenever he lost ground – as a means of keeping critics off-balance and to define the terms of political battle in his favor.[37] In the process of the anti-Stalinist campaign, moreover, Khrushchev needed the support of the Leningrad party organization against the 'group', but in return the Leningraders exacted a price for their aid in terms of expanded influence in the leadership.[38]

In the process of policy implementation, clientage 'networks' may give play to the initiating power of the patron. Robert Miller points out that the Brezhnev regime has tried a number of territorially and functionally limited agricultural integration experiments, allowing local party officials considerable latitude in devising models tailored to local circumstances.[39] His analysis of agricultural integration in the USSR shows that the most radical and comprehensive experiments have been carried on in Moldavia by Brezhnev's protégé, I. I. Bodiul. It appears, in this case, that as one of Brezhnev's active clients, Bodiul displayed his strong commitment in the search for strategies of policy implementation, while his patron Brezhnev protected Bodiul and his own position by silencing criticisms of the radical Moldavian approach to agricultural reorganization.[40]

Such evidence, albeit fragmentary, shows that power politics among contending leaders certainly may take on policy content. The clientelist activity involved, however, may take varying forms depending on the political circumstances at the time, the nature of the particular regime and/or the nature of the policy under consideration.

Non-functional Motivation

As mentioned above, N. S. Patolichev is said to have had affective personal ties with A. A. Andreev, Central Committee secretary under Stalin.[41] As yet, however, there appear to be no serious studies of cultural factors which may impart an affective aspect to Soviet clientelist relations. A few scholars who have studied Soviet clientelism are inclined to link clientelism exclusively or predominantly to institutional, social and situational causation.[42]

In Japan it is almost taken for granted that subordinates are tied personally, emotively and particularistically to the leader.[43] Chie Nakane asserts that a group in which members are positioned hierarchically in a rigid pyramid operate within a common 'frame', which may be a locality, an institution, or a particular relationship that binds a set of individuals into one group. The institutional frame fulfills the important function of keeping the members together, whatever factions are found within it, and since members are classified primarily by the institution, whatever internal rivalries they may feel, they realize that they are all in one boat racing with another boat.[44] Takeshi Ishida also asserts that a strong sense of identity with the organization and conformity to its goals is accompanied by a sense of competition both externally with other organizations and internally in loyalty to their own organization. The orientation of the members is not toward individual achievement but toward merit acquired by individual contribution to the goal of the organization. In this case 'conformity' and 'competition' are not mutually opposed, but rather mutually reinforcing.[45] If we take such assertions (which still need to be tested empirically) at face-value, there seem to exist two kinds of loyalty: one to the organization, and the other to the patron. However, the two kinds of loyalty appear to overlap one another, since clientelist activities are tied in with policy content within the organization. There may well be an occasion, none the less, when a client values the integrity of the organization more than his status and gains within a clientelist group. He will thus limit informal group participation, or modify it so that it does not interfere with his formal position, or even go over to another clientelist group whose objects appear to him closer to the goals of the organization, as we saw in Z's case. Such behavior is, however, extremely difficult to carry through. The relationship between the patron and the client involves a mutual psychological or emotional dependence. The relationship binds not only the client; it also binds the leader who, though he may often appear to be able to exercise a great deal of power, finds his authority checked and controlled at a great many points.[46] The members of the clientelist group may share egalitarian sentiments, despite the fact that there exists official ranking and informal status within the group. Without such sentiments, there would not exist a feeling of shame or sense of guilt for not returning favors to one's patron or one's clients. A noted Japanese psychologist, Takeo Doi, has conceptualized this notion as 'active dependency'.[47]

The Japanese, generally speaking, appear to be attached very strongly to abstract *mores* regarding the exchange of favors.[48] The importance of reciprocating gratifications is internalized in the course of the socialization process of the individual, so that he feels morally obliged to give benefits to those from whom he has received them. The important point is 'the norm of reciprocity', as Alvin Gouldner terms it,[49] which is internalized not only by those in weaker positions, but also by those who have the power to take, without giving anything in return. The relationship between the patron and the client is, indeed, emotionally and psychologically one of mutual dependence. Such a relationship is reinforced structurally in Japanese organizations. The actual role of an individual in the organization does not always or necessarily correspond to his rank or status assigned formally by the organization.[50] When the group is in action the roles of individual members are readily adjustable to changing situations, such as we saw in the relationship between the vice-minister and the director of the Secretariat, or between the director and the section chiefs of the Secretariat. The lack of clear role differentiation in the organization makes it easier for subordinates to reciprocate favors on an equal footing, given the fact that a subordinate often *de facto* carries out the work of his immediate superior, and so nurtures the clientelist formation. On the other hand, this offers the subordinate an opportunity to maneuver against his competing colleagues.

Membership of the Clientelist Group

Chie Nakane notes also that the *oyabun–kobun* (patron–client) relationship comes into being through one's occupational training and activities, and carries social and personal implications, appearing symbolically at the critical moments in a man's life.[51] She goes on to say, however, that the informal hierarchy and the factions which develop among a group's members (the invisible organization) overlap and supersede an institution's formal administrative (visible) organization,[52] although this latter vertically organized structure could well serve as a 'starting-mechanism',[53] through which individuals can initiate social interaction giving rise to vertical dyadic alliances. As already observed, the informal hierarchy does not fully correspond with the formal organizational hierarchy.

There exist two kinds of informal group members: one consists of 'inner-frame' members who are still in active service in the ministry, and the other of 'outer-frame' members who are either retired officials taking up positions in a cluster of 'colonies' or 'satellites' such as public corporations, or official clients of the ministry such as private enterprises. Clientelism in the Japanese government bureaucracy by and large is formed gradually, as officials search for reliable and able (as the groups' activities are strongly oriented to policy issues) subordinates in the process of the spiral promotion of the patron himself. Its members are, thus, made up of persons from a number of bureaux and sections. The reciprocating process in the Japanese system is a lifelong one, even though, upon the retirement of the patron from office, the roles of patron and client are reversed. The new patron who can command better resources and have access to the political processes is now in a position to return the favors he received from his original patron. If, for example, the latter now heads a public corporation, larger subsidies from the ministry may mean an increase in his corporation's sphere of influence, or at least in its prestige. Although dyadic relationships are a lifelong process, the structure of power relations in the informal group headed by the new patron may not be quite the same as that of the group headed by the original patron. With the demise of the latter, no matter which member of the group succeeds, the group cannot maintain the same structure of membership with the new leader who has his own clients tied particularistically to himself. The duration of the clientelist relationship is, strictly speaking, of only one generation: the working life of the patron. Stability of clientelist groups will also be affected by external factors such as changes in the structure of political leadership.

In the Soviet Union factors such as insecurity and unpredictability in attaining and retaining power and, to a lesser extent, the policy process, appear to have contributed to clientelism. Clientelist bonds in the Soviet political system are largely formed during the patron's mid-career period, most commonly around regional and republic party secretaries. Joel Moses has presented evidence of a direct linkage between the political influence of a central patron and local 'cohorts'.[54] As the avenues for career advancement at regional level have become more institutionalized (a development which admittedly could prove shortlived) it is certainly arguable whether the regional first secretaries (especially those in the RSFSR) who link the higher levels with the lower ones are still motivated to form clientage networks in their regions. The motivation may naturally vary depending on personal attitudes and ambitions of the individual regional first secretaries. Apart from the political advantages such an official enjoys as a regional boss, one should also note the effects of the peculiar institutional setting in which he operates: the lack of clear role differentiation between various organizations in each level, and in particular, the overlapping system of party and government officials, together with the system of other controlling agencies. This bears some resemblance to the unclear role differentiation we have discussed in the Japanese government bureaucracy, although the latter relates to vertical role differentiation, whereas the Soviet case relates to lateral role differentiation. Such an institutional setting may encourage a regional first secretary to assume the role of patron. The regional first secretaries, furthermore, may establish horizontal alliances with other regional secretaries, most likely in the form of alliances with others sharing the same major patron (for instance, a senior Politburo member). Here they are likely to alternate in roles of patron and client depending upon the situation in which the exchanges take place, despite the fact that there exists a hierarchy among the regions.[55] The aggregate of clientage links, therefore, can provide the regional first secretary with valuable resources, as does his access to a senior Politburo member.

However, it should be noted, first, that the above descriptions are static views of the clientage networks formed around regional party secretaries. The patron–client relationship would develop and grow over time, as both individuals rise in the hierarchy.[56] This time factor would greatly contribute, unless the patron himself were demoted in the meantime, to the formation of complex vertical dyadic alliances and even coali tions of alliances. Secondly, although the groupings arise out of regional variations, their members, as the patrons advance up the hierarchical ladder, will be dispersed into diverse institutions cutting across regional and organizational boundaries. As we noted earlier, the more widely its members are dispersed, the better the clientelist group may work as a policy support system.

The fate of the vertical dyadic alliances will largely be determined by the rise and fall of the major patron. The way the patronage network is to maintain or to expand its membership varies according to the character of the regime, as we observed earlier in comparing the Brezhnev and Khrushchev regimes. Nevertheless, if the major patron were the General Secretary, he would be in a far better position to initiate broad political programs directly or indirectly for the well-being of his protégés than his associates in the Politburo, who are largely limited to counteractions. If the other associates in the Politburo perceived a threat both to their own careers and to the stability of oligarchic rule, they might attempt to topple the General Secretary, as happened to Khrushchev twice during his reign (once unsuccessfully and once successfully). Power relations of the vertical dyadic alliances under a new major patron will in most cases differ from those of the former alliances, as do those in the Japanese government bureaucracy. Moreover, if the current policy of 'stability of cadres' continues, a new major patron might find it even more difficult to break up other rival patrons' regional 'networks'.

Some Similarities and Differences

In Japan personal cliques are generally regarded as a social evil. Likewise, in the Soviet Union factionalism is much discussed as running counter to ideological principles and the party's interest. Albert Craig, however, recognizes the positive functions of bureaucratic cliques in Japanese government bureaucracy, of which

> One is to bypass an occasional blockage up-and-down the organization by forming a conduit for communications outside of channels. Another important function is lateral communication with a high level of trust. The coordination of work on a horizontal axis is often difficult within Japanese bureaucracy since vertical ties are so important that they always take precedence. But if

the chief of one bureau was formerly the section chief in another bureau, he may well know its present section chief and will certainly know some of its permanent lower officials. This may enable him to reach them directly without going through the other bureau chief, especially if he is close to the present chief. His effectiveness as a bureaucrat depends in some measure on the cultivation of such personal ties . . . Personal cliques are limited to the confines of a single ministry since officials are not transferred from one ministry to another. Consequently personal cliques are of no use in coordinating work between ministries . . . If an acquaintance from the same class at Tokyo University is in another ministry, a short telephone call may accomplish what would take days or weeks . . . In a variety of ways, the informal system within the bureaucracy complements and is necessary to the formal system.[57]

Thus, Craig attaches particular importance to the communication function of clientelism within the ministry and with other ministries in the course of policymaking and implementation. We have also observed that its career mobility function goes beyond the boundaries of the government bureaucracy. Through clientage networks, interests may be aggregated and articulated at different levels. One of the singularities of Japanese clientage is that its activities are so closely related to every aspect of the policy process. If one focuses on each aspect of clientage separately, one misses its dynamic element, that is, that patron–client networks expand the bureaucracy's capacity for policy innovation, hence enhance the bureaucracy's adaptability to its changing environment. Rapid turnover of officeholders and routinization of recruitment and advancement are very much in gear with the positive functions of political clientelism. By imparting to the Secretariat (in charge of personnel and organizational matters) such a crucial role in each ministry political clientage in the government bureaucracy is not only tolerated, but also structurally maintained to perform its positive functions which are hidden under the formal institutional setup.

In the Soviet Union, as indicated in the preceding sections, the participants in the chain of clientelist relationships appear to treat political clientage as one of several possible alternatives to furthering their career perspectives and to acquiring political power. Clientage networks may also be mobilized for support of the patron at a critical moment such as a succession crisis. It is not clear, however, whether the clientelist activities are closely related, as those of Japanese clientage constantly are, to the policy process.[58] We have noted earlier, however, that vertical dyadic alliances are operating in every level of the entire Soviet political system. It would not be altogether impossible to assume that Brezhnev's 'cohorts', for instance, might have lent their support to their patron's policy initiatives. In the course of policy implementation, they might have been more likely to cooperate with one another for the fulfillment of individual targets, as suggested in relation to the regional first secretaries and as observed in the agricultural integration experiment in Moldavia.

Trends have been observed in the past similar to those found in the Japanese government bureaucracy, namely, to recruit competent generalists rather than specialists, to routinize advancement, to keep policy-relevant alliances compartmentalized within specialized 'whirlpools', to use Jerry Hough's apt metaphor (though, in the Japanese government bureaucracy, this occurs in the offices of lower-level officials more than in those of higher-level officials), and also to maintain unclear role differentiation. Despite such similar trends, the main areas of Soviet clientelist activities judging by the available evidence, are centered on the pursuit of group members' career prospects and the acquisition of power. We have observed that the causation of clientelism operating within the Japanese government bureaucracy and within the Soviet political system at large appears to be closely linked with political and functional motivations along with cultural factors. Yet historically one of the strongest factors in the Soviet system contributing to clientelist formation was evidently insecurity and unpredictability of tenure, whereas in Japan this factor appears to be lacking; clientelism appears grounded in the culturally deep-rooted particularistic behavior of individuals. This difference in the origins of political clientelism might be expected to have consequences for its functions in the two countries. In the Soviet Union, moreover, as long as certain elements such as the length of service required for advancement in each level and the timing of retirement from office remains less formalized, the clientage networks may not be able to express their functions fully in the area of the policy process. Such a state of political clientage in the Soviet Union may, indeed, become an element of destabilization in the power structure of leadership, offsetting its positive functions. From this analysis, we can conclude that political clientage, while manifesting substantial differences in Japan and the USSR, nevertheless operates as a systemic adjusting mechanism in both countries.

Notes: Chapter 6

1 The ministry's employees' union is a part of the Public Service Employees' Union, and is composed of only lower-level officials. Although S, as a union leader, was opposed to the then government's policy of curtailment of administrative manpower, he formed the Committee for the Dismissal of Inefficient Officials. Through this committee the union selected inefficient officials who were to resign voluntarily, and in turn the union provided them with alternative jobs within or outside the ministry. He also succeeded in setting up criteria of incompetency for higher-level officials, who as a rule did not become members of the union. Some higher officials were quite annoyed at him, yet could not disregard him because he was backed by the union. In order to minimize S's pressure, the ministry created a new section of labor in the General Affairs Bureau which was headed by S. The latter was then placed in a position to mediate the interests of the ministry and the union.

2 When S was chief of the Heavy Industry Bureau, he received favors from the Ohno faction – the minister, Fukuda, being a member of this faction – in connection with budget appropriations; S did not, however, return these favors by having his Bureau take action in the interests of the faction; see K. Hayashihara, *Uchimaku – Tsusansho* (Tokyo: Yell Books, 1976), pp. 97–8.

3 See Y. Honda, *Nihon Neo-Kanryoron* (Tokyo: Kodansha, 1974), p. 28.

4 The main sources for this case are as follows: S. Shiroyama, *Kanryo-Tachi no Natsu* (Tokyo: Shinchosha, 1975); Hayashihara, op. cit.; T. Kusayanagi, 'Tsusansho', *Bungei Shun Jyu*, vol. 52, no. 9 (1974), pp. 110–26; Honda, *Nihon Neo-Kanryoron*, op. cit., and 'Tsusan Kanryo no Seitai', *Zaikai Tenbo*, vol. 22, no. 8 (1978), pp. 62–138.

5 See Carl H. Landé, 'The dyadic basis of clientelism', in Steffen W. Schmidt, Laura Guasti, Carl H. Landé and James C. Scott (eds), *Friends, Followers, and Factions* (Berkeley, Calif.: University of California Press, 1977), p. xx.

6 Keith R. Legg, 'Clientelism and advanced industrial societies', *Studies in Comparative Communism*, vol. 12, no. 2–3 (1979), p. 197.

7 By 'career officials' I mean those higher-level officials who have passed a special higher examination. The characteristics of the career officials and lower-level officials can be distinguished roughly on the basis of whether they are generalists or specialists, technicians, or clerks, and whether they have relative freedom for creative work or solely perform mechanical and routine tasks, and whether they have the satisfaction of having power or the frustrations accompanying routine tasks. Craig asserts that the office in which the lower-level officials work together and the degree to which their career mobilities are limited is below the level of cliques. See Albert T. Craig, 'Functional and dysfunctional aspects of government bureaucracy', in Ezra F. Vogel (ed.), *Modern Japanese Organization and Decision-Making* (Berkeley, Calif.: University of California Press, 1975), p. 17. In seeking to explore the comparability of Japanese bureaucrats with their Soviet counterparts this chapter examines only the higher-level officials whose bureaucratic behavior is governed by laws, customs and politics.

8 See H. Sakakibara, *Nihon o enshutsusuru Shinkanryozo* (Tokyo: Yamato Shobo, 1977), pp. 56–8.

9   See H. Nishimura, *Showa Rikugun Habatsu Kososhi* (Tokyo: Dento to Gendaisha, 1975), pp. 44–5.
10 See B. Kanayama, 'Kanryodo no Kenkyo', *Chuo-Koron*, no. 7 (1978), p. 243.
11 See Joel C. Moses, 'Regional cohorts and political mobility in the USSR: the case of Dnepropetrovsk', *Soviet Union*, vol. 3, pt 1 (1976), p. 79.
12 Philip D. Stewart, *et al.*, 'Political mobility and the Soviet political process: a partial test of two models', *American Political Science Review*, vol. 66, no. 4 (1972), p. 1280.
13 ibid., p. 1279.
14 See T. H. Rigby, 'The Soviet regional leadership: the Brezhnev generation', *Slavic Review*, vol. 37, no. 1 (1978), pp. 1–24.
15 See Peter Frank, 'Constructing a classified ranking of CPSU provincial committees', *British Journal of Political Science*, vol. 4, pt 2 (1974), pp. 217–30; and Mary McAuley, 'The hunting of the hierarchy: RSFSR *obkom* first secretaries and the Central Committee', *Soviet Studies*, vol. 26, no. 4 (1974), pp. 473–501.
16 See Stewart, *et al.*, op. cit., p. 1279.
17 See John P. Willerton, 'Clientelism in the Soviet Union', *Studies in Comparative Communism*, vol. 12, no. 2–3 (1979), p. 80.
18 Carl H. Landé, 'Networks and groups in southeast Asia: some observations on the group theory of politics', *American Political Science Review*, vol. 67, no. 1 (1973), p. 105.
19 See Moses, op. cit., p. 82.
20 See Willerton, op. cit., pp. 166–7. Jerry Hough has also stated that the officials from Belorussia (Mazurov's region), from Leningrad (Kosygin's region), from Kharkov (Podgorny's region) and, of course, from Dnepropetrovsk were much more successful than the average, especially if we correct for the higher age of the Kharkov officials. See Jerry F. Hough and Merle Fainsod, *How the Soviet Union Is Governed* (Cambridge, Mass.: Harvard University Press, 1979), p. 540.
21 Hough and Fainsod, op. cit., pp. 258–9.
22 Moses, op. cit., p. 85.
23 ibid., p. 78.
24 Hough and Fainsod, op. cit., p. 540.
25 See N. S. Patolichev, *Ispytanie na zrelost* (Moscow: Izdatelstvo Politicheskoi Literatury, 1977), reviewed in T. H. Rigby, 'How the *obkom* secretary was tempered', *Problems of Communism*, vol. XXIX, no. 2 (1980), pp. 57–63.
26 Albert Craig claims that the *Ringi* process is highly visible and peculiarly Japanese. A draft may be circulated for unimportant matters, but for significant matters, the primary function of the *Ringi* system is to circulate information about decisions already taken. See Craig, op. cit., p. 24.
27 See T. J. Pempel, 'The bureaucratization of policy-making in postwar Japan', *American Journal of Political Science*, vol. XVIII, no. 4 (1974), pp. 656–62.
28 Ehud Harrari, 'Japanese politics of advice in comparative perspective: a framework for analysis and a case study', *Public Policy*, vol. XXII, no. 4 (1974), pp. 575–7.
29 See Hayashihara, op. cit., pp. 10–25.
30 See Landé, op. cit., pp. xiv–xv.
31 See Hough and Fainsod, op. cit., p. 541.
32 ibid., pp. 540–3.

33 See Moses, op. cit., p. 78.
34 See Hough and Fainsod, op. cit., p. 526.
35 John A. Armstrong, 'Party bifurcation and elite interest', *Soviet Studies*, vol. 17, no. 2 (1966), pp. 417–30.
36 Carl Linden, 'Khrushchev and party rules', *Problems of Communism*, vol. 12, no. 5 (1963), p. 32.
37 ibid., p. 35.
38 Carl Linden, 'How strong is Khrushchev? – II', *Problems of Communism*, vol. 12, no. 6 (1963), p. 58.
39 See Robert F. Miller, 'The politics of policy implementation in the USSR: Soviet politics on agricultural integration under Brezhnev', *Soviet Studies*, vol. 32, no. 2 (1980), p. 191.
40 See also the case of the demoted Estonian leader, Johannes I. Kebin, in ibid., pp. 183–4.
41 See Rigby, 'How the *obkom* secretary was tempered', op. cit., p. 60.
42 See Stewart, *et al.*, op. cit., p. 1270; T. H. Rigby, 'The need for comparative research', *Studies in Comparative Communism*, vol. XII, no. 2–3 (1979), pp. 161–2; and Zygmunt Bauman, 'Eastern Europe', in ibid., pp. 184–9.
43 H. Fukui, 'Factionalism in a dominant party system', paper delivered at 1974 Annual Meeting of the American Political Science Association, Chicago, USA, 28 August to 2 September 1974, p. 3.
44 Chie Nakane, *Japanese Society* (London: Weidenfeld & Nicolson, 1971), pp. 57–8.
45 Takeshi Ishida, *Japanese Society* (London: Random House, 1974), pp. 37–40.
46 Nakane, op. cit., p. 66.
47 L. T. Doi, 'Amae – a key concept for understanding Japanese personality structure', in R. J. Smith and R. K. Beardsley (eds), *Japanese Culture: Its Development and Characteristics* (Chicago: Aldine, 1962); and L. T. Doi, 'Giri-Ninjo: an interpretation', in R. P. Dore (ed.), *Aspects of Social Change in Modern Japan* (Princeton, NJ: Princeton University Press, 1967).
48 See NHK survey data, 1973 and 1978, *Gendai Nihonjin no Ishikozo* (Tokyo: NHK Books, 1979), pp. 206–8.
49 See Alvin W. Gouldner, 'The norm of reciprocity: a preliminary statement', in Schmidt, *et al.*, op. cit., pp. 28–43.
50 See Nakane, op. cit., p. 81.
51 ibid., p. 43.
52 ibid., pp. 57–8.
53 See Gouldner, op. cit., p. 39.
54 This linkage is substantiated by the post-1964 decline of Kharkov (Podgornyi) cohorts relative to the increasing career advantage collectively enjoyed by former Dnepropetrovsk (Brezhnev) cohorts; see Moses, op. cit., p. 87.
55 Such interchangeable roles of patron and client are said to be practiced at the societal level in communist countries; see Bauman, op. cit., p. 186. Some scholars would prefer to analyze them in terms of 'networks' rather than patron–client dyads.
56 See Willerton, op. cit., p. 163.
57 See Craig, op. cit., pp. 14–15.
58 Uri Ra'anan argues that Soviet factions display little long-term commitment to issues. They are inclined to advocate certain policies only as long

as they are competing with rival groups that propagate a different approach. Once such competitors are defeated finally and unmistakably, manipulation of the issue in question loses political significance; see Uri Ra'anan, 'Soviet decision-making and international relations', *Problems of Communism*, vol. XXIX, no. 6 (1980), pp. 41–7.

Conclusion: Some Theoretical Considerations on Advancement within the Political Elite in Soviet-Type Systems

BOHDAN HARASYMIW

Having read the foregoing contributions to this volume one may be pardoned for calling to mind the story about the blind men describing an elephant. Each description encompasses only part of the whole subject. But this is a common handicap in the social sciences: our focus is often limited, our studies often unwittingly complementary yet apparently disparate, if not contradictory. In this concluding chapter I should like to suggest how our contributors' studies might be seen as fitting together, and some directions for further research.

Our knowledge of political recruitment in Soviet-type systems is steadily improving. Increasing availability of biographical data makes possible the reconstruction of the career paths of central and middle-level party and government leaders. Yet this abundance of information requires some theoretical organization if it is to contribute to a further refinement, as opposed to the mere accumulation, of our knowledge of elite recruitment and advancement. Although they do so implicitly, the studies in the volume indicate the outlines of a larger theoretical framework into which such work may be shaped. The task of this concluding chapter is simply to make those implicit indications explicit.

Within the broader field of political elite recruitment, the studies in this book deal, more specifically, with the process of advancement within the political elite from lower to higher positions. This process, it is further suggested, may be regarded as either a dependent or independent variable. That is, advancement within the elite may be considered as on the one hand being determined by a number of factors. On the other the overall character of the system of advancement (classifiable presumably in some meaningful way or other) itself has an effect on the political system (in terms, presumably, of processes, policies and development). Some elaboration of these two aspects is in order.

Advancement as a Dependent Variable

Assuming the unit of analysis to be the individual the first and most general question one should ask is: what determines that person's chances of advancement in the elite hierarchy? The answer seems to be threefold. Advancement is determined by: (1) the existence of patron–client links, that is, of clientelistic links between the subject and a patron or patrons; (2) the operation of the rules of selection, the 'opportunity structure' which exists independently of its subjects and which prescribes the sequence of offices leading to the top; and (3) the suitability of the candidate in terms of qualifications for the role associated with the post to which advancement is contemplated. If the strength of each of these determinants could be measured for a given universe or sample of politicians, then it might be possible to classify political systems according to the predominance of a particular set of determinants – clientelism, structure, or role – over the others. This in turn, as proposed in the succeeding section, could be the basis for hypotheses concerning advancement within the political elite as being an independent factor determining certain features of the wider system of politics. One might also observe and record temporal variations which could be explained as the result of socioeconomic changes. The evolution of the political system could thus be periodized in some manner relevant to the pattern of elite recruitment and advancement.

If these three sets of factors – clientelism, structure and role – may indeed be considered the determinants of advancement, we are nevertheless a long way from being able to combine them into an overall theory of the process. What is the relationship between them? Do they operate in tandem, or in opposition to one another? Does a candidate require positive scores on all three in order to advance, on just two, or is one adequate? Presumably, where patron–client links are strong, there structure and role requirements are weak, and *vice versa*. Candidates for promotion would have to present clientelistic ties or other characteristics appropriate to the advancement system in order to be successful. The subject's probability of advancement, in other words, would be calculated from a comparison of his characteristics and the strengths of the three sets of factors in the given system as determined historically.

Yet this would be not altogether satisfactory as a theory of advancement or promotion, assuming theory to be our ultimate goal. The procedure would merely be one of matching the case at hand with the historical pattern up to that point. It would entail no significant or genuine part to play for the three factors, from a strictly theoretical viewpoint. Such meaningful parts would only come into being if, as implied earlier, the relationship among the three sets of factors were made clear. This has not yet been done by students of elite recruitment. Intuition suggests, for example, that structure must affect the operation of clientelism. But which structural arrangements in the political career system facilitate, and which obstruct, clientelism? That there is some connection is actually the main thesis of Daniel Orlovsky's chapter. Yet is this a general phenomenon or peculiar only to Russia (and the Soviet Union as its successor)? A tantalizing question for further research. All the more tantalizing in view of Shugo Minagawa's emphasis on motivation as a cause of clientelism, which suggests that the structural peculiarities of bureaucracy in Japan and the Soviet Union respectively contribute little if anything to differentiating the forms of clientelism operating in these two countries. Is it that clientelism is endemic to bureaucracy, and that variations in bureaucratic forms have no independent effect on forms of clientelism? Perhaps hierarchy, the common element of all bureaucracies, facilitates the establishment of dyadic relationships. Does the commonality between Japan and the Soviet Union extend further than this? Surely, the element of insecurity is a more important feature in the USSR and should stimulate a greater degree of clientelism there than exists in Japan. Further identification of the interrelationships among the three sets of causal factors will obviously be needed for a fuller understanding of the advancement process, in particular the connection between the structure of opportunities and clientelism, will have to be explored.

In regard to the relationship between opportunity structure and clientelism it seems fair to make the following tentative statements. A non-bureaucratic structure of opportunities will likely encourage clientelism to the extent that formal and impersonal rules of advancement are liable to be absent. A bureaucratic structure may on the other hand, for this same reason, discourage clientelism. But at the very same time it may also facilitate it by reason of its hierarchical principle of organization as well as by the inevitable informal features which are endemic to bureaucracies. The more that opportunity in a particular case conforms to Weber's ideal type of bureaucracy, should we say that the less room is afforded to clientelism? Yet one should not underestimate the ability of individual persons to make even a highly structured system work for themselves; in general, though, a tendency for clientelism to be influenced by opportunity structure should be a useful assumption.

In the Soviet Union itself it may seem paradoxical that clientelism coexists with a very bureaucratic opportunity structure. This resolves itself when it is recalled that, although bureaucratic in form, the Soviet governmental and party structure is not really like a civil service. The recruitment and promotion system, the *nomenklatura*, does not operate on the basis of impersonal rules, although party, government and mass organizations are hierarchically structured. Thus, bureaucracy coexists with insecurity, unpredictability; this encourages clientelism. In Soviet-type systems which have retained the *nomenklatura* the connection between opportunity structures and clientelism is likely to persist; where it has been discarded, as in Yugoslavia, the two factors are probably more independent.

Is some general relationship likewise conceivable between role – including performance in the given position – and clientelism? This will probably have to wait on a proper elaboration and classification of types of political roles. For the time being it may not be inappropriate to suggest that if in a given system clientelism outlives the particular individuals involved at any one point in time, if it is established as a feature of the system independent of individuals, then it may be part of the role in each half of the dyad. Thus, the more extensive or persistent clientelism is, the more important the role of patron or client is liable to be among the politician's other roles; it may, in fact, come into conflict with them and overwhelm or succumb to them. A multiplicity of other political roles characteristic of members of the political elite, however, might be expected to reduce the salience of clientelism in advancement. The relationship, therefore, between clientelism and role may be thought of as involving reciprocal influence rather than one shaping the other.

As to the association between opportunity structure and role, the only plausible (albeit tentative) statement which can be made is that the latter must be influenced by the former. That is, roles in the political elite have to correspond in some degree with the structure of the career ladder; the more specific it is, the more are they, and the more diffuse it happens to be, so will they. Opportunity structure influences roles; roles are keyed to opportunity structure. Or at least it seems reasonable to assume so.

If the discussion thus far has to some extent disentangled the three supposed elements of what might be a model of advancement within the political elite, the next problem is that of comparability. Are intersystemic comparisons possible, and can reasonable equivalents for the three sets of determinants of advancement be identified for differing political systems? This is most likely a long-term objective, given the present relatively undeveloped state of research. For the time being we shall perhaps have to be satisfied with intrasystemic comparisons. In these it will be possible to hold at least one of the three factors constant so as to ascertain the strength of the others – structure, role and clientelism. For example, one might examine the advancement of persons to or from the position of *obkom* secretary in the USSR. These party officials may be assumed to share both a common role as well as a similar opportunity structure. With those two factors effectively controled for, one could then ascertain the part played by patron–client links in the advancement of such personnel. Something of this sort has already been done by Philip Stewart and his associates, who found that patronage ties acounted for very little of the variance in the political mobility of 224 persons who advanced from *oblast* first secretary in the RSFSR in 1955–67.[1] But the relationship requires a good deal more testing because of the very problematical nature of evidence relating to clientelism in the Soviet context. Those problems in turn present a serious obstacle to the further task of controling for clientelism in order to study variation in structure and role. Comparisons of the advancement process within, let alone between, political systems, therefore, face substantial challenges. But that is inevitable in relatively new fields.

It is conceivable that we may not be satisfied with explanations (or classifications) of the advancement process in terms of the three sets of factors, that we may wish to push the analysis further back to find the determinants of the determinants, so to speak. One of these, given most explicit attention in John Miller's chapter, is the selectors' preferences. Indeed, Miller's objective is to explain Soviet staffing procedures as directly attributable to the preferences of those in charge of such personnel links. It would be unrealistic, of course, to expect a direct and total correspondence between policymakers' intentions and policy outcomes. Although selectors' preferences undoubtedly do play a role in the process of advancement, it is probably better to conceive of their playing that role indirectly. That is, such preferences may be thought of as contributing to, but not solely determining, each of the three sets of factors responsible for advancement. The complexion or character of each factor is, in other words, the resultant of influences which include the appropriate preferences of the selectors as well as other features of the socioeconomic environment. What might these be? From the references made by our contributors, as well as the literature on political recruitment, the following generalizations seem to emerge. Clientelism, as it affects advancement, appears to be influenced by: political culture (look for the persistence of historical patterns, as Daniel Orlovsky suggests, as well as for such elements as trust, norms of reciprocity and familism) and policy issues in addition to, as already mentioned, selectors' preferences and the opportunity structure.[2] The structure of opportunities, in its turn, is shaped by: formal or legal opportunity; existing political institutions (bureaucracies, political parties and elections); social structure (especially mobility and social status – higher-status persons are more likely than those of lower status to be advanced in industrial societies, for example); ambition; and, as before, the preferences of the selectors.[3] Roles are formed by a combination of influences from the opportunity structure, selectors' preferences and social structure (in terms of occupational roles rather than status or mobility).[4] Still more indirectly, it seems plausible that the selectors' own backgrounds probably influence their preferences, and that economic development (in terms both of level and rate) has some impact on political culture (movement presumably toward more rational-legal norms), policy issues and social structure (embracing the status, mobility and role aspects). In the most general sense, then, there is in political systems probably some connection, however tenuous, between the character of economic development and the sort of persons promoted within the elite, but this is mediated more directly by a whole series of intricately related normative, personal, structural and social factors.

Advancement as an Independent Variable

If the foregoing presents the rudiments of a model of advancement or promotion in the political elite with advancement appearing as the variable to be explained, a much less elaborate framework is possible using advancement as the independent or determining variable. This relative theoretical underdevelopment can probably be attributed to the lack of attention in the elite-recruitment literature devoted to what effects advancement has on political systems generally.[5] Our contributors' suggestions, therefore, in this regard blaze no new trails, nor do they stray much from the recognized path.

How does advancement within the elite affect politics, then, and how can the 'system of advancement' be conceptualized? Is any obvious connection conceivable between kinds of advancement systems and their influence on the operation of other aspects of political life? In answer to the first question the authors of this volume indicate that advancement generally can be expected to have a threefold effect: on public policy, conflict at the elite level and change in the political system. Joel Moses, for example, postulates that conflict may develop within the political elite owing to differences of attitudes which in turn would have their origin in the functionally specialized career patterns of middle-level Soviet officials. What is specifically likely to happen when these personnel eventually rise to the top leadership, and how these specialized career experiences are liable to come into play, remain intriguing but as yet unanswered questions. It is perhaps premature, given the state of theory in elite studies, even to ask them.

In his study of Yugoslavia Lenard Cohen similarly draws from the differentiation among elites implications for conflict and for future instability. But is he, like Joel Moses, not generalizing about the composition of the elite rather than about the advancement system itself? Which is legitimate enough and certainly a well-established undertaking in elite studies. But if so, then neither of them is treating the advancement system as an independent variable which somehow affects the political system quite apart from the impact its personnel have on it. Perhaps there is good reason to focus on people instead of on systems of recruitment or promotion, since there is a common expectation that individual leaders do make a difference to public policy.[6] Another good reason for avoiding them (systems) is that these are theoretically uncharted waters.

What is required is a classification of advancement systems and an elaboration of the theoretical links between them on the one hand, and such features of the political system as public policy, elite conflict and change on the other. A hint of this is contained in Daniel Orlovsky's examination of the continuity between Russian and Soviet clientelistic patterns in the state bureaucracy. The predominance of clientelism, he says, must have had an 'impact upon policies and events'. He is speaking of clientelism generally, not only as an instrument of advancement. Yet without undue licence one may extract from this the notion that the Russian-Soviet advancement system is predominantly of the clientelistic type with unspecified public-policy consequences. Shugo Minagawa, in his comparison of Soviet and Japanese clientelism, sets out to discover, as he puts it, 'what part it plays in the operation of the system as a whole'. This is a more ambitious objective than Orlovsky's valuable yet tentative and intuitive projection of a direction for future research. It probably goes unrealized, but suggests likewise that: (1) advancement systems may be classifiable as predominantly clientelistic (the category into which Soviet-type systems apparently fit, according to some of our contributors, although such a contention is difficult to square with the findings of Moses and Miller that advancement seems very strongly to depend on specialization, whether occupational or regional), organizational (advancement occurs primarily through some institution), or socioeconomic (advancement results chiefly from the matching of aptitudes, of social with political roles); (2) each type has some corresponding effect on the political system or consequences for it; and (3) there is a need for theoretical elaboration of the linkages between these two sets of concepts. So far, we have hints that advancement systems may be classifiable in this way, and that Soviet-type systems are predominantly clientelistic, but no real treatment of these as a kind of independent variable which determines the character of the political system.

Plotting a New Course from our Present Position

The fruitfullness of further research in the subject of advancement within the political elite will require stricter definitions of concepts, more explicit theoretical frameworks and greater attention to problems of operationalization than many of us engaged in the study of Soviet-type systems have been used to. Some good definitions of concepts are already available; others have to be developed. Theoretical frameworks are not readily available, but they are indispensable for systematic study and must be evaluated critically as well as tested empirically. This includes the model outlined in the preceding pages. Operationalization is the most troublesome step, in view of the known limitations of existing data and on the practicable techniques of gathering fresh information. Some of the hazards and opportunities of creating new knowledge may be illustrated from the contributions to the present volume. We have before us a challenging, and I should hope inspiring, agenda.

The foregoing chapters have focused on two aspects of elite advancement – structures and clientelism. Whether these two elements have been or can be successfully disentangled is a moot-point which deserves to be taken up and resolved in any further work on this subject. For example, the Soviet *nomenklatura* system, so apparently ideal as a concrete object of study, is obviously in need of reconceptualization. Is it merely an element of, or equivalent to, the entire 'structure of opportunities'? Does it embrace the clientelistic element of elite advancement (note T. H. Rigby's assertion that the *nomenklatura* and patronage are inevitably linked) as well, or is it indeed synonymous with the whole advancement and promotion system, really a type of system altogether? My own preference would be to use the party *nomenklatura* as the operational definition for the Soviet political elite in terms of the personnel included within it, and as equivalent to the opportunity structure of Soviet politics from the structural point of view. In so far as certain positions within it give the incumbents the power of appointment and promotion, the *nomenklatura* can be regarded as defining in a structural sense the potentialities for clientelism. The clientelistic networks that do develop around it I should treat as 'addenda' to the institution of *nomenklatura*, but these can be expected to develop only at certain very specific nodes.[7] It will be up to later studies to identify these nodes, to make the necessary distinctions (between the 'structure of opportunities' and the *nomenklatura* as a patronage system) and to formulate explicitly the necessary conceptualizations.

One distinction not made in the present volume is between clientelism and patronage. Presumably patronage is the career component of clientelism.[8] Another area where greater conceptual precision is desirable has to do with the 'functional' nature of patronage. Gyula Józsa, for instance, states that patronage facilitates the functions of interest articulation and of advancement. A fuller sense of the significance of this would require presumably the elaboration of a structural-functional framework, and the situation of patronage within it. Future studies, therefore, of patronage and its 'functions' will need to take less for granted, to be more explicit on this score.

On political clientelism there is a growing literature as exemplified by the collection of articles entitled *Friends, Followers, and Factions*, edited by Steffen Schmidt and associates. There Carl Landé provides an excellent definition of the term:

> *A patron–client relationship is a vertical dyadic alliance, i.e., an alliance between two persons of unequal status, power or resources each of whom finds it useful to have as an ally someone superior or inferior to himself . . .*
> Patron–client relationships . . . [1] involve the direct personal attachment of two individuals to each other . . . [2] exist for the purpose of exchanging favors and providing mutual assurances of aid . . . [3] are easy to create, but . . . [4] have some distinctive features which set them off from alliances between persons of equal socioeconomic status.[9]

The obstacles to operationalizing this concept in Soviet-type societies, even one as open as Yugoslavia, are daunting to say the least. How can we tell when an alliance exists? When the attachment is direct and personal? When favors have been exchanged? For the Soviet Union especially, the requirements of the definition can probably never be met. To use mere geographical proximity of two individuals as an indicator of patronage ties, as done by Stewart and his coworkers among others, seems of questionable validity when placed beside the concept as here defined.[10] There is, unfortunately, no escape from the latter's stringent demands. In the event we should perhaps speak only of 'quasi-clientelism' in contexts like the Soviet one, since we are unable to observe the players themselves, merely their shadows. For the play of Soviet politics, we Westerners have very poor seats.

More daunting still are the problems of pursuing inquiry along lines suggested by our authors. Imagine the task of verifying Daniel Orlovsky's statement that 'clientelism . . . was perhaps a more prominent feature in Russian history and political culture than elsewhere'. Even if it could be measured and compared, an obvious subsequent question would be how to assess the significance of its magnitude. What, in other words, does more or less clientelism mean? And how much of a part does clientelism play in the advancement of individuals to elite positions? These are especially pertinent questions in light of John Willerton's finding that in 1976 47 percent of 'identified clients' retained their CPSU Central Committee membership, despite having lost their presumed patrons.[11] If clientelism helps one get to the Central Committee, is it as helpful in allowing one to stay there? Is it, furthermore, as prevalent beyond the Central Committee and the Communist Party? Obviously, we cannot generalize about clientelism in any of the Soviet-type systems until, as Rigby says, we have conducted in a systematic and comparative way a good many more case studies.[12]

Further research should proceed along two parallel tracks – cases and theory. Since interest and resources are limited, no one will care to do both types, so that some division of labor will have to be effected. But each pursuit must be aware of the other. We need more work on modelbuilding, such as that presented here by Minagawa. His chapter includes mention of two models. In the first the formation of clientelistic links generally is ascribed to two sets of motivations, functional and non-functional. Although there are definitional difficulties with this model, it has the virtue of emphasizing motivation, an element admittedly absent in the model put forward in the present chapter (because of misgivings about the possibility of ascertaining individual motivations in many political systems, especially those of the Soviet type). An important question which has to be decided, therefore, is whether individual motivation can, given the circumstances, be safely ignored as a factor in clientelism or else controled for, or if it can indeed feasibly be studied using perhaps a refinement of Minagawa's model.

The second model put forward by our Japanese colleague states that the determinants of Soviet party recruitment (so far as the *obkom* secretary at least is concerned) are: (1) 'the candidate's practical-administrative background, according to the requirements of a particular region'; (2) the existence of 'a formal succession of posts'; and (3) two kinds of 'political consideration' (Khrushchev's attempt to establish legal-formal rules of promotion vs Brezhnev's appeasement of coalition groups). These resemble the elements of the model in the present chapter, except that the latter attempts to be more universal and more explicit about relationships among its elements. It is interesting that in both the basic notion of role makes its appearance, yet except for brief mentions by Moses and by Minagawa, that concept is not utilized in any of the analyses in this volume. Nor, with the exception of Lenard Cohen's study, and to some extent John Miller's, is the role of nationality or ethnicity explored. Similarly, how the qualifications of political leaders match up with the roles of the party and of the government as institutions within society also require study. Besides institutional and individual roles, research is also needed, as John Miller pointed out in the conference version of his paper, on the structural element of advancement. He offered two suggestions for the Soviet specialist that are worth repeating. First, 'fitting the RSFSR more clearly into the picture we have of medium-level *nomenklatura* lists, and clarifying the boundary between All-Union and republic lists are both tasks still to be undertaken'. Related to this 'would be [information] concerning personnel who are *candidates* for central appointment, that is, who are on the *uchetnaia nomenklatura* of the center and on the *osnovnaia nomenklatura* of an *obkom*'. Whichever of the three emphases is chosen for empirical study in further research – structure, role, or clientelism – it will be necessary to do so with an eye on the other two, so to speak, in order for such case studies to be more easily subsumed under the common model thus making possible a cumulation rather than further fragmentation of our knowledge. It seems to me, however, that focusing on structure and (aptitude for) role will yield more satisfactory explanations of advancement within the political elite than will clientelism, particularly for systems of the Soviet type.

As noted earlier, our own curiosity will likely demand that causal or other explanations be provided for the component factors of a model, that structure, role and clientelism themselves be explained in addition to being used to explain elite advancement. Thus far, attention has been focused on clientelism; none has been given the other two. Daniel Orlovsky, for example, mentions in regard to Russia and the Soviet Union 'institutional and cultural pressures that resulted in the reproduction in the new setting of older patterns of organizational behavior', the latter referring to clientelism. Here, incidentally, is implied a link between organizational structure and clientelism, but the nature of these 'pressures' presumably arising therefrom is not clearly identified. Still, this gives us a lead in further work. Shugo Minagawa concludes that in the Soviet Union, in terms of his model of clientelism (that is, determined by functional and non-functional motivations), 'factors such as insecurity and unpredictability in attaining and retaining power and . . . the policy process appear to have contributed to clientelism'. In Japan, by contrast, the chief impulse for clientelism is presumably provided by the cultural norm of reciprocity. While it is interesting to know the genesis of clientelism in these two cases, it is possibly of even greater importance, having uncovered the essential difference in that respect, to explain what effect the difference itself then has on the apparently dissimilar patterns of elite advancement. In this and other respects research will have to go beyond what has been accomplished in the present volume.

T. H. Rigby may have been overly optimistic when he said at the outset: 'we trust that this volume will bring us a step closer to properly understanding the sense in which "cadres decide everything" in Soviet-type societies.' While the preceding chapters have not greatly illuminated the way in which 'cadres decide everything', they have made two indirect contributions toward that end. They have conveyed how important and complex is the process of 'who decides who the cadres are', so to speak, and how a 'proper understanding' requires theory as well as data to bring it to fruition. It seemed to me that the theoretical elements in our contributors' work were often fragmentary and implicit; they needed to be identified, made explicit and connected together. In doing this, the present chapter has sought to help both the reader and the researcher. For the reader, it may have given a wider context within which to interpret the various contributions and to draw them together. For the researcher, it may provide guidelines for further study as well as a gentle reminder to avoid in doing so the once-immense gap between theory and fact, between history and political science, so well summed up in the old definition of the historian as a political scientist without concepts, the political scientist a historian without facts.

Notes: Conclusion

1   Philip D. Stewart, *et al.*, 'Political mobility and the Soviet political process: a partial test of two models', *American Political Science Review*, vol. 66, no. 4 (1972), pp. 1269–90.
2   See Steffen W. Schmidt, Laura Guasti, Carl H. Landé and James C. Scott (eds), *Friends, Followers, and Factions: A Reader in Political Clientelism* (Berkeley, Calif.: University of California Press, 1977), Pt I, especially the essay by Alvin W. Gouldner, 'The norm of reciprocity: a preliminary statement', pp. 28–43.
3   For an exposition of some of these elements, see: Morris Janowitz, 'Social stratification and the comparative study of elites', *Social Forces*, vol. 35, no. 1 (1956), pp. 81–5; Kenneth Prewitt, *The Recruitment of Political Leaders: A Study of Citizen-Politicians* (Indianapolis, Ind. and New York: Bobbs-Merrill, 1970); Robert D. Putnam, *The Comparative Study of Political Elites* (Englewood Cliffs, NJ: Prentice-Hall, 1976); Joseph A. Schlesinger, *Ambition and Politics: Political Careers in the United States*

(Chicago: Rand McNally, 1966); David C. Schwartz, 'Toward a theory of political recruitment', *Western Political Quarterly*, vol. 22, no. 3 (1969), pp. 552–71; and Lester G. Seligman, *Recruiting Political Elites* (New York: General Learning Press, 1971).

4 On roles and elite recruitment, see: Moshe M. Czudnowski, 'Political recruitment', in Fred I. Greenstein and Nelson W. Polsby (eds), *Handbook of Political Science*, Vol. 2 (Reading, Mass.: Addison-Wesley, 1975), pp. 155–242; Herbert Jacob, 'Initial recruitment of elected officials in the US – a model', *Journal of Politics*, vol. 24, no. 4 (1962), pp. 703–16; and I. William Zartman, 'The study of elite circulation: who's on first and what's he doing there', review article, *Comparative Politics*, vol. 6, no. 3 (1974), pp. 470–6.

5 How recruitment into and advancement within the political elite might affect politics is given passing mention by several leading authors, including: Gabriel Almond and G. Bingham Powell, *Comparative Politics: System, Process, and Policy*, 2nd edn (Boston, Mass. and Toronto: Little, Brown, 1978), p. 109; Lester, G. Seligman, *Leadership in a New Nation: Political Development in Israel* (New York: Atherton Press; London: Prentice-Hall International, 1964), p. 7, and *Recruiting Political Elites*, op. cit., pp. 15–17; Prewitt, op. cit., p. 22; Dwaine Marvick, 'Continuities in recruitment theory and research: toward a new model', in Heinz Elau and Moshe M. Czudnowski (eds), *Elite Recruitment in Democratic Polities: Comparative Studies across Nations* (New York: Wiley, 1976), pp. 29, 36–7; and Zartman, op. cit., pp. 477–81.

6 Valerie Bunce, *Do New Leaders Make a Difference?* (Princeton, NJ: Princeton University Press, 1981).

7 On clientelistic relationships as addenda, see Carl H. Landé, 'The dyadic basis of clientelism', in Schmidt *et al.* (eds), op. cit., pp. xxi–xxiii. The 'structure of political opportunities' as it appears at the national level in the United States is elaborated in Schlesinger, op. cit.

8 But cf. also Daniel Orlovsky's contrary usage in the phrase 'clientelism and other forms of patronage', which has the latter subsuming the former.

9 Landé, op. cit., p. xxi; emphasis in original.

10 Stewart *et al.*, op. cit., pp. 1273–4, 1285. The geographical proximity approach to the study of patronage receives incisive critique in Zygmunt Bauman's, 'Comment on Eastern Europe', *Studies in Comparative Communism*, vol. 12, no. 2–3 (1979), pp. 188–9, in the symposium on clientelism in ibid., pp. 159–211.

11 John P. Willerton, 'Clientelism in the Soviet Union: an initial examination,' *Studies in Comparative Communism*, vol. 12, no. 2–3 (1979), p. 180.

12 T. H. Rigby, 'The need for comparative research on clientelism: concluding remarks', in ibid., pp. 210–11.

Index